Response to Intervention

Curricular Implications and Interventions

 **John J. Hoover**

University of Colorado, Boulder

PEARSON

Boston   Columbus   Indianapolis   New York   San Francisco   Upper Saddle River
Amsterdam   Cape Town   Dubai   London   Madrid   Milan   Munich   Paris   Montreal   Toronto
Delhi   Mexico City   Sao Paulo   Sydney   Hong Kong   Seoul   Singapore   Taipei   Tokyo

Vice President and Editor in Chief: Jeffery W. Johnston
Senior Acquisitions Editor: Ann C. Davis
Editorial Assistant: Penny Burleson
Vice President, Director of Marketing: Quinn Perkson
Marketing Manager: Erica DeLuca
Senior Managing Editor: Pamela Bennett
Senior Project Manager: Mary M. Irvin
Senior Operations Supervisor: Matt Ottenweller
Senior Art Director: Diane Lorenzo
Cover Designer: Candace Rowley
Cover Art: Jupiter Images
Full-Service Project Management: Aptara®, Inc.
Composition: Aptara®, Inc.
Printer/Binder: LSC Communications
Cover Printer: LSC Communications
Text Font: Minion

Every effort has been made to provide accurate and current Internet information in this book. However, the Internet and information posted on it are constantly changing, so it is inevitable that some of the Internet addresses listed in this textbook will change.

Library of Congress Cataloging-in-Publication Data

www.pearsonhighered.com

ISBN 13: 978-013-703483-3
ISBN 10:   013-703483-0

Preface

THE INSTRUCTIONAL DEMANDS PLACED ON TODAY'S STUDENTS ARE MORE complex, comprehensive, and demanding than ever. Response to intervention (RTI) is the decision-making cornerstone as we transition away from the decades'-old prereferral model to a more contemporary way of thinking about the best ways to instruct our K–12 students. *Response to Intervention: Curricular Implications and Interventions* will empower you to select, implement, differentiate, and evaluate the curricula and interventions necessary to meet the needs of all learners in your classroom and school through RTI.

Purpose of This Book

Response to Intervention: Curricular Implications and Interventions is designed as a blueprint for improving your ability to provide research-based curriculum and evidence-based interventions to all K–12 learners. A critical aspect of RTI is the increased significance of curriculum and its implementation, differentiation, and evaluation for all learners. This book provides educators, who already have some understanding of the basics of RTI, with value-added content and tools to deliver a highly productive and results-driven curriculum for all learners.

Why Is This Book Needed?

What does RTI really mean to the classroom teacher and other educators most directly involved in its implementation? Because a fundamental component in an RTI model is the delivery of high-quality core instruction in the general classroom, knowledge about and expertise in using curriculum within RTI is essential. Recently, many excellent books have been published on RTI, providing the "nuts and bolts" of the framework, such as the three-tiered triangle model, universal screening, and data-based decision making. Although these books provide some discussion about the numerous facets of curriculum, classroom teachers require a more in-depth understanding of curriculum to implement RTI successfully. *Response to Intervention: Curricular Implications and Interventions* is a much needed resource providing teachers with information demonstrating how curriculum and its implementation are integral to the success of any multi-tiered RTI model.

With the tremendous increase in the number of students placed in special education over the past decade, a new way of thinking about students' needs has evolved. Specifically, the quality of instruction that students receive is central to reversing the trend of increased referrals and associated placement in special education. The foundation of quality of instruction is the curriculum implemented in the classroom, which, in turn, provides the basis for making sound response to intervention decisions. This practical book targets this area in detail, clarifying the role of the classroom teacher within RTI models by delivering research-based curriculum and evidence-based interventions to meet the needs of all learners in grades K–12.

For Whom Is This Book Written?

The primary audience for this book includes those who are directly responsible for teaching the curriculum within an RTI model (e.g., general and special education classroom teachers, bilingual/ESL teachers, speech-language specialists, school-based interventionists). In addition, various support personnel (e.g., the school psychologist, assessment specialist, social worker) will find this book of value as they adjust their roles to best meet RTI learners' needs. This book is written as a guide for educators representing classroom instruction and RTI school-based decision-making teams who are charged with the critical task of making informed curricular adjustments based on screening and progress monitoring data.

Intended Outcomes

The nine chapters in this book are designed to produce the following six primary outcomes:

1. Describe the critical role of curriculum implementation in RTI models
2. Deliver research-based curriculum and evidence-based interventions with fidelity
3. Lead or contribute to RTI curriculum implementation decision-making teams
4. Interpret learners' progress data to make necessary curriculum adjustments
5. Apply five key components of curriculum in teaching and learning
6. Describe connections between RTI and special education decisions

Key Features of This Book

This book is written for educators most directly involved in classroom instruction and, as such, has several highly practical features:

- Learner outcomes listed at the beginning of each chapter
- Application suggestions provided at the end of each chapter
- Numerous tables and figures to illustrate important concepts
- Over 30 reproducible forms and guides for application of the book's content in the classroom and school environments
- Presentation of numerous evidence-based interventions, screening and assessment practices, study skills, and learning strategies
- Models for structuring RTI teams, making informed curricular decisions, achieving cultural competence, and differentiating instruction
- *RTI Curriculum in Practice*, brief vignettes written by practitioners that illustrate the practical application of key concepts presented in each chapter

This book is divided into three interrelated parts:

- Part I: Curriculum and Response to Intervention Models
- Part II: Response to Intervention Curricular Supports and Decision Making
- Part III: Meeting Differentiated Response to Intervention Curricular Needs of All Learners

Part I discusses the foundation for implementing a multi-tiered RTI curriculum in today's classrooms. Part II provides models for making effective RTI team decisions through collaboration among educators to best initiate curricular adjustments and differentiations and to select the most appropriate tier of instruction. Part III emphasizes the critical role of differentiated instruction in multi-tiered instruction, along with the significance of study skills, learning strategies, and culturally responsive teaching to meet the RTI curricular needs of all learners. The application of RTI at the secondary level is also included due to its significance in the education of middle and high school learners. Readers are encouraged to reproduce all forms provided in the book, as these tools are for direct use in the classroom and school environment.

Acknowledgments

I wish to begin by acknowledging the support and guidance of my editor, Ann Davis, whose insight contributed significantly to the development, revision, and final version of this book. I also wish to thank the field reviewers of my book for their thoughtful comments and meaningful suggested revisions: Michelle Alvarez, Minnesota State University, Mankato; Trent Atkins, The University of Montana; Jennifer Diliberto-Fender, Greensboro College; Michele Kelk, Webster University; and Paul Lancaster, Grand Valley State University.

This book is about the practical application of curriculum in the classroom and would not have been possible without the contributions of many practitioners whom I have had the privilege of working with, teaching, and supporting over the years as they strive tirelessly to improve the education of all learners. I wish to especially thank the following practitioners—Subini Annamma, Amy Boele, Nancy Harrelson, Susan Hopewell, and Robin Hoover—who contributed to the book by providing chapter vignettes describing their successes in the implementation of curriculum within RTI models in their schools or classrooms. In addition, special thanks are extended to Susan Hopewell and Amy Boele for their contributions to Chapters 7 and 6, respectively. An important feature of the book is the various tools included for use in classroom and school settings to apply curricular implementation and differentiation of knowledge and skills. Many practical guides are provided for easy transfer of knowledge and skills to the educational setting. Adapted versions of these forms and guides have been used by numerous elementary and secondary educators over the past several years; their feedback assisted in ensuring the inclusion of highly useful and practical tools to apply key curricular aspects within RTI models. In particular, I wish to acknowledge Amy Boele for her field reviews of the tools included in this book.

Contents

List of Tools

▶ PART I

Curriculum and Response to Intervention Models

THE FOUNDATION OF A comprehensive response to intervention (RTI) model is the implementation of a research-based curriculum and evidence-based interventions along with monitoring of students' progress to determine academic and behavioral proficiency levels, rates of progress, and necessary curricular adjustments. Part I of this book provides content, examples, and numerous practical ideas for understanding curriculum fundamentals within RTI. This includes discussion of five interrelated curricular components that operate simultaneously within the classroom (Chapter 1); an overview of RTI, including research-based curricula and selected evidence-based interventions (Chapter 2); and detailed coverage of processes and practices for determining RTI curricular needs (Chapter 3).

Part I includes the following three chapters:

1. Components of Curriculum Implementation
2. Response to Intervention Framework: Research-Based Curricula and Evidence-Based Interventions
3. Response to Intervention Assessment to Meet Curricular Needs

CHAPTER 1

Components of Curriculum Implementation

▶ Overview

KNOWLEDGE OF KEY CURRICULAR factors is essential to meet the curriculum implementation demands of multi-tiered response to intervention (RTI). This includes an understanding of five key curricular components of teaching and learning found in every classroom, three key types of curriculum operating simultaneously in every classroom, and the significance of these topics in the implementation of multi-tiered RTI.

► Key Topics

- ► Curriculum defined
- ► Explicit, hidden, and absent curricula
- ► Curricular components of instructional content, interventions, arrangement, management, and monitoring
- ► Interrelationship among curricular types, curricular components, and multi-tiered instruction
- ► RTI and the implementation of five curricular components

► Learner Outcomes

After reading this chapter, you should:

1. Be knowledgeable about an integrated definition of curriculum implementation
2. Be able to assess the extent to which explicit, hidden, and absent curricula function in everyday classrooms
3. Be able to describe the interrelationship among the five curricular components of effective teaching and learning
4. Understand how a variety of curriculum factors, in addition to content, contribute significantly to the implementation of multi-tiered RTI
5. Be familiar with the historical progression of curriculum implementation for struggling learners, including those with disabilities, over the past five decades

SIGNIFICANCE TO CONTEMPORARY CLASSROOM INSTRUCTION

A fundamental aspect of RTI is the effective and proper implementation of curriculum to meet the needs of all learners. Educators in today's classrooms must ensure that the curriculum has been implemented with integrity for all students prior to making general assumptions about suspected learning or behavior problems as intrinsic to the student. As a result, we are faced with the challenge of implementing the curriculum in the manner in which it is intended to be implemented, as well as providing corroboration that effective implementation has actually occurred. This is significant in the process of multi-tiered RTI due to the increased emphasis on providing sufficient opportunities to learn within a curriculum that has been implemented with integrity. To best meet this challenge, we must understand the critical factors that provide the basis for making effective curriculum implementation decisions if we are to meet the needs of all learners. A complex issue for teachers is to understand the curriculum they are required to implement, along with the outcomes reflecting student learning. Many educators view the curriculum primarily as the content they must teach, with little or no consideration of other critical curricular elements that are essential to effective teaching. This chapter begins by presenting an integrated and practical discussion of curriculum and its implementation that serves as a foundation for implementing RTI. First, however, several key terms used throughout the book are defined. These terms are categorized within several broad headings to simplify their use.

Response to Intervention

Multi-tiered instruction—Levels or layers of instruction that increase in duration and intensity based on the learner's response to that instruction

Response to intervention (RTI)—Process within multi-tiered instruction that determines the extent to which a learner responds to instruction (i.e., what is taught) and uses the RTI results as a basis for subsequent multi-tiered curricular decisions

Fidelity—Implementation of the curriculum and assessment in the manner in which they were designed and researched to be used (i.e., consistently and accurately)

Universal screening—Process by which all students are screened (usually three times per year) for progress toward curriculum benchmarks

Progress monitoring—More frequent monitoring (e.g., monthly, biweekly) of students' progress toward benchmarks or objectives

Diagnostic assessment—Process by which specific learners' needs are pinpointed, which may include evaluation for a possible disability

Cut score—Assessment proficiency level or score (e.g., the 25th percentile) that learners are expected to achieve to be considered as making adequate progress toward benchmarks

Curriculum and Instruction

Curriculum implementation—The integration of instructional content, arrangement, interventions, management, and monitoring in the classroom

Curriculum differentiation—Modifications or adaptations of curriculum implementation to meet a variety of students' needs

Curricular types—Three types of curriculum found in every classroom (explicit, hidden, absent)

Differentiated classroom—A classroom that contains structures and procedures designed to deal simultaneously with the variety of factors that students bring to the learning environment (e.g., varied preferences for learning, varied experiential backgrounds, cultural/linguistic diversity, range of reading levels, self-management abilities, time-on-task levels)

Differentiated instruction—Use of evidence-based interventions in the implementation of research-based curricula to meet the varied educational needs/preferences of students in differentiated classrooms

Collaboration in curriculum—The process of cooperatively implementing the curriculum and performing assessment to meet the needs of all students

Culturally responsive curriculum—A curriculum that is contextually relevant to all students, including culturally and linguistically diverse learners

Evidence-based curricular interventions—Specific teaching and learning techniques with demonstrated effectiveness for their intended purposes in research and validation studies

Research-based curriculum—Comprehensive curricular programs that have been developed, researched, and validated to be effective in teaching and learning (e.g., a reading curriculum)

Interventionist—An educator with specialized skills who provides targeted curricular supports to struggling learners using either push-in or pull-out methods

Benchmarks—Grade- or age-level academic and behavioral standards

Learner and the Curriculum

Struggling learner—A student who fails to exhibit adequate proficiency or rate of progress toward academic and/or behavioral benchmarks

Study skills—Educational tools used by students to promote more efficient and effective task completion (e.g., various reading rates, time management skills, library usage abilities)

Learning strategies—Strategies used by students to increase access to and retention of curricular content and skills (e.g., active processing, rehearsal abilities, coping skills)

Essential Curriculum Factors

Viewing curriculum and its essential components in an integrated manner provides educators with a comprehensive perspective that allows them to understand more clearly what they teach, as well as allowing them to make more informed curricular decisions for all learners. In addition, the demands of multi-tiered RTI require today's teachers to have greater knowledge about curriculum, as illustrated in Figure 1.1.

As Figure 1.1 shows, three critical factors must be addressed in implementing the curriculum for all learners in multi-tiered RTI:

Factor 1: Curriculum *implementation* must be done the way it was designed to be done (i.e., with fidelity); in a consistent manner; and with challenges to students to facilitate the development and use of higher level thinking abilities.

Factor 2: Opportunities to learn must include curricular *differentiations* designed to achieve desired needs or outcomes; relevant to the learner; and implemented during classroom instruction.

FIGURE 1.1   Three Critical Curricular Factors

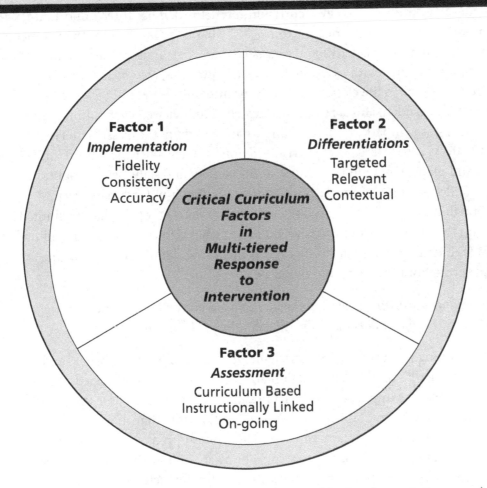

Factor 1
Implementation
Fidelity
Consistency
Accuracy

Factor 2
Differentiations
Targeted
Relevant
Contextual

Critical Curriculum Factors in Multi-tiered Response to Intervention

Factor 3
Assessment
Curriculum Based
Instructionally Linked
On-going

Factor 3: Effectiveness of the curriculum and its implementation requires *assessment* that is based on the curriculum taught in the classroom; is linked directly to what has been taught; and is conducted on a regular basis to closely monitor students' progress toward curricular benchmarks.

Curriculum implementation, differentiation, and assessment are discussed in detail throughout this book, beginning with an exploration of important factors that educators should be aware of to meet the needs of all learners in multi-tiered RTI (i.e., those who achieve above, at, and below benchmark levels). This includes the definition of curriculum, five curricular components, and three types of curriculum, each discussed relative to multi-tiered RTI. We begin with the definition of curriculum referred to throughout this book.

How Is Curriculum Defined?

How one defines curriculum depends on how one implements, differentiates, and assesses curriculum. For some educators, curriculum is simply all planned occurrences in the classroom (Wiles & Bondi, 2007). For others, curriculum is narrowly defined as the content they teach every day. Still others view curriculum in a manner that is more refined than all classroom occurrences and broader than content. However curriculum is defined, it has three important components: (1) the intended outcomes, (2) what is taught, and (3) the manner of implementation. Eisner (2002) suggested that curriculum pertains to instruction that is planned with associated intended outcomes, recognizing that much more may occur in the classroom that is meaningful and relevant, even though it may be unintended. Hosp, Hosp, and Howell (2007) viewed curriculum as the course or path embarked on, reflecting what is taught in the classroom. Hoover and Patton (2005) stated that curriculum must also consider the setting, strategies, and management in the context of the content and skills being taught.

Reflecting on various definitions of curriculum put forth over the past several decades, McKernan (2008) wrote, "we have on [the] one hand a limited, and on the other a more expansive, notion of what is to count as a curriculum" (p. 11). Blending these important aspects of various definitions, *curriculum* as used throughout this book is defined as:

> *Planned learning experiences with intended outcomes while recognizing the importance of possible unintended outcomes.*

Working from this definition, elements related to both the "what" and the "how" of curriculum implementation and assessment are emphasized; these elements become important when RTI results are discussed. These interrelated aspects are important; Hoover and Patton (2005) wrote that "how one defines this term (curriculum) relates directly to how one approaches it (curriculum implementation)" (p. 7). Educators must be aware of how they define or view curriculum because their perspectives are directly connected to how they implement, differentiate, and assess curriculum effectiveness.

Significance to Multi-tiered RTI

The curriculum must be implemented with fidelity, contain reasonable and needed differentiations, and include ongoing monitoring of student progress. In implementing any curriculum, teachers must make daily decisions about implementation based on students' needs (e.g., the need to restate instructions, provide additional practice to learn content, or reinforce a concept in a culturally relevant way). The way curriculum is defined or viewed will directly affect the instructional decisions necessary to implement curriculum in multi-tiered RTI models.

Three Types of Curriculum

Researchers and curriculum specialists have explored the fact that different *types* of curriculum operate simultaneously in the classroom (Eisner, 2002; Hoover, 1987; Joseph, Bravmann, Windschitl, Mikel, & Green, 2000; Schubert,

TABLE 1.1 Types of Curriculum

Type	Description	Example(s)
Explicit	Formal/stated mandated curricula that contain explicit steps and procedures to follow for proper implementation; stated and intended outcomes	Any grade-level curriculum, such as Basal Reading series, Investigations (Mathematics), and Wilson Reading
Hidden	Practices and procedures resulting from decisions made when implementing the explicit curriculum; unintended outcomes that occur as the explicit curriculum is implemented	Use of cooperative learning groups; deviations from the explicit curriculum to take advantage of a teachable moment; actual learning that occurs as the explicit curriculum is implemented
Absent	Curricular aspects excluded (either intentionally or unintentionally) from classroom instruction that are appropriate to the explicit curriculum	Evidence-based interventions not used in the classroom; groups or peer work not used in teaching and learning; supplemental materials not used to support explicit curriculum learning

1993). In his classic and innovative textbook on curriculum (*The Educational Imagination*), Eisner (2002) identified three types of curriculum: (1) explicit (stated curriculum), (2) hidden (unofficial curriculum), and (3) null (excluded curriculum). Because the null represents that which does not exist, the term *absent curriculum* is used to clarify the intent of the null curriculum. The three types of curriculum are summarized in Table 1.1.

As Table 1.1 shows, the *explicit curriculum* includes everything in the curriculum that is stated, such as:

- Steps for implementation
- Suggested supplemental activities or tasks
- A proper sequence for presenting material
- The amount of time to spend on particular topics
- Procedures for evaluation
- Suggested groupings (e.g., pairs, cooperative groups)

These and similar types of instruction and guidance give teachers important and necessary scope and sequence parameters for implementing the explicit curriculum in a manner consistent with its research base and associated recommendations for its use. However, each teacher brings a unique background and perspective to the teaching and learning situations, and every learner has a unique experiential background. As a result, implementation of the explicit curriculum will vary as teachers (1) make important on-the-spot decisions reflecting their perceptions of the curriculum (i.e., curriculum defined), (2) draw on their prior experiences in implementing the curriculum, or (3) accommodate the unique and diverse characteristics that students bring to the learning situation.

The concept of a *hidden curriculum* is fundamental to understanding the effectiveness of curriculum implementation. If the influences of the hidden curriculum on learners' outcomes, achievement progress, or social-emotional development are not recognized, the teacher's ability to understand learners' progress is greatly limited. Often the hidden curriculum provides a more realistic context for interpreting screening, monitoring, or diagnostic curriculum assessment results. It is essential to consider factors such as management procedures, tone of voice, proximity, class groupings, time of day, and other similar classroom conditions that complement the explicit curriculum, based on the teacher's decisions, rather than only explicitly stated instructions or steps in the curriculum materials or teacher guides.

The need to pay attention to what is not included in curriculum implementation is especially important for students who require increased opportunities to learn. The *absent curriculum* may explain the lack of adequate progress toward benchmarks or objectives more accurately than the explicit and/or hidden curriculum alone. As Eisner (2002) points out, what we exclude from daily teaching and learning may be just as important as what we include. Examples of absent curriculum include:

- Evidence-based interventions excluded from teaching and learning (e.g., direct instruction techniques)
- Extra time to complete assigned tasks or activities (e.g., increased wait time for a response)
- Additional time to prepare for a task before completing it
- Cultural examples (that are excluded) that, if used, may put mandated content into a relevant context for diverse learners (e.g., exclusion of research on cultural events)
- Self-management procedures that learners are not allowed to employ (e.g., self-monitoring)

It should be obvious that what we elect to teach as well as what we choose to exclude impact student progress, as well as academic and behavioral growth.

Significance to Multi-tiered RTI

All three types of curriculum—explicit, hidden, and absent—must be considered to make informed decisions in multi-tiered RTI models. Multi-tiered instructional decisions begin by implementing the explicit curriculum with fidelity. However, as different student needs emerge based on universal screening and progress monitoring, other curricular factors must be considered to make informed decisions. Multi-tiered RTI teams that interpret curriculum-based assessment results should consider both hidden and absent curricula to ensure a complete understanding of the documented progress. Chapter 6 provides detailed coverage of the topic of determining curricular needs, which includes considering the interrelationship of the three types of curriculum operating in all classrooms. Form 1.1 provides a guide to help educators identify and determine the extent to which each type of curriculum is implemented in classroom instruction. This form should be completed periodically by classroom teachers to determine the influences of explicit, hidden, and absent curricula on learners' progress toward benchmarks.

Essential Curricular Components

In addition to clarifying the teacher's perception of how curriculum is defined and the ways in which the different types of curriculum operate in the classroom, the key elements of comprehensive curriculum implementation must be understood. Researchers and educators view the composition of curriculum in various ways. For example, as discussed, some see the curriculum as the content taught (Hosp et al., 2007); others view it as content, process, and products (Bender, 2008); and still others, such as Eisner (2002), see curriculum as a broader set of occurrences in the classroom. When considering the broader set of occurrences as well as others' views of curriculum, Hoover and Patton (2005) identified and discussed selected elements that reflect most aspects of curriculum and its effective implementation.

Drawing on the discussions in these and other related sources, five essential components have been identified for effective curriculum implementation in multi-tiered RTI models. These are illustrated in Figure 1.2. The five components include:

- Content and skills to be taught and assessed through research-based curricula
- Evidence-based interventions used to teach content/skills, manage behavior, and support differentiated instructional needs
- Instructional arrangements or settings in the classroom used to implement the research-based curriculum and evidence-based interventions in order to teach and assess content/skills
- Overall classroom and instructional management, which includes addressing both academic and behavioral aspects of teaching and learning
- Evaluation of progress to assess learners' growth toward achieving benchmarks and/or meeting supplemental needs

As typical classroom occurrences, events, practices, mandates, and procedures are studied, nearly all of the major instructional aspects of curriculum are found to fall within one or more of these curricular components. The premise emphasized throughout this book is that:

Effective curriculum implementation can only occur in the context of all five components, viewed and implemented in integrated ways in the classroom.

FIGURE 1.2   Five Essential Curricular Components

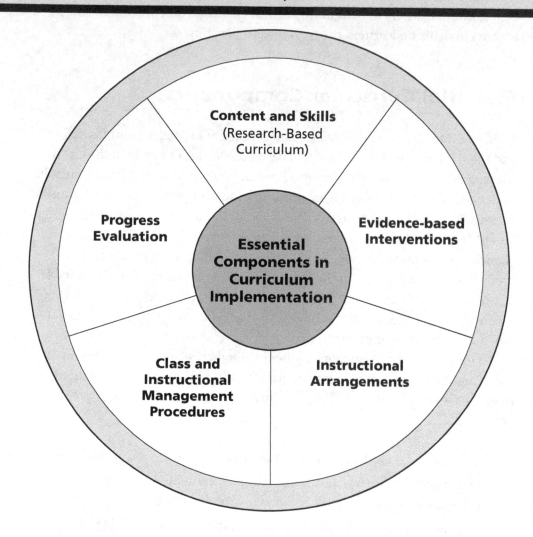

Understanding and applying these five components is necessary given the dynamic nature of classroom instruction, assessment, and management, as shown in Table 1.2.

Significance to Multi-tiered RTI

As multi-tiered RTI models continue to grow in stature and importance, concern for the five components of curriculum implementation will also increase. These components are important because teachers need to understand and interpret more comprehensively students' response or lack of response to instruction. Being knowledgeable about and attending to only some of these components leads to an incomplete picture of the multi-tiered instruction used in today's schools. Therefore, as we employ multi-tiered RTI models, educator teams must be aware of the content/skills, evidence-based interventions,

TABLE 1.2 Components within Effective Implementation of Curriculum

Component	Description	Examples
Content/Skills (Research-Based Curriculum)	Subject area knowledge, skills, ways of thinking, and outcomes connected with the mandated state or district curriculum, which is research based	District reading curriculum outcomes National Reading Panel Report (2000) Math reasoning skills
Evidence-Based Interventions	Research-tested and validated teaching interventions	Direct instruction Classwide peer tutoring Scaffolding Teacher-scripted lessons
Instructional Arrangements	Use of various groupings, pairs, or independent work to facilitate acquisition of content and skills	Cooperative learning groups Paired learning Independent practice
Class/Instructional Management Procedures	Classroom structures established to manage learning, manage behavior, and facilitate opportunities to learn	Self-monitoring Positive behavior supports Proximity control Shaping
Progress Evaluation	Regular assessment of learners' progress toward curricular benchmarks/objectives (may occur through universal screening or ongoing progress monitoring)	Curriculum-based measurement Performance-based assessment Running records

instructional arrangements, management procedures, and progress evaluation applied to all learners in order to provide the proper tier of instruction and duration of interventions. Chapter 2 provides more detailed coverage of these curriculum issues relative to multi-tiered instruction. Form 1.2 is a guide for documenting aspects of instruction associated with the five curricular components that must be considered to ensure effective teaching for all learners in a multi-tiered RTI model. The form should be completed by classroom teachers periodically to clarify the delivery of each component within the curriculum implementation process.

As Form 1.2 shows, although each of the five curricular components is distinct, collectively they represent much of what goes into effective curriculum implementation. In addition, although educators must be familiar with the specifics of these components, their integration in instruction is most important when educating students using multi-tiered RTI models.

Integrating Curricular Components in Classroom Instruction

The above discussions illustrate the many complexities of curriculum implementation to meet all learners' needs. Focusing on only one or two curricular components greatly limits educators in several ways. The following *RTI*

Curriculum in Practice illustrates a typical classroom situation reflecting the needs of a struggling learner and RTI curriculum implementation.

RTI CURRICULUM IN PRACTICE

Addressing the Interrelationship Among Curricular Elements

Description

A learner is struggling to make adequate progress in a content or skill area (e.g., reading fluency, math computation, higher level thinking). The learner is taught using a research-based curriculum and an evidence-based intervention. Each of these is considered appropriate for the content/skill area being taught. The learner is taught in a large-group setting and is given some independent work time to practice the skills. The teaching intervention used requires the learner to respond quickly to the teacher's instructions and to complete tasks rapidly. The learner prefers to work with others rather than independently. The procedure used to evaluate the learner's progress is appropriate for assessing the targeted content. The learner does not have a learning disability or a behavior problem. However, after several weeks of instruction, the learner is not making adequate progress toward the targeted benchmarks. The multi-tiered RTI problem-solving team meets to evaluate the learner's progress and decides how best to proceed with the learner's education. Based on the progress monitoring results, the team decides to recommend a change in the evidence-based intervention and break the content down into smaller, more manageable steps to deal with what they believe to be the learner's underlying issues.

Analysis of the Response to Intervention Team's Decision

In many situations similar to this one, the education team might initially conclude that there is some problem in using the evidence-based intervention and the curriculum content as it is currently structured. However, further examination of the situation shows that the student is perfectly capable of learning the content with no changes, using the original evidence-based intervention, *provided that these are implemented within a different instructional arrangement or setting.* Rather than doing large-group work, this learner succeeds well in small-group settings in the general classroom and accomplishes assigned tasks more easily when working in pairs rather than independently. In this situation, the instructional arrangement (i.e., the instructional setting) directly affected the acquisition (or lack of it) of content. Failure to consider the instructional arrangement caused the education team to make two incorrect recommendations:, (1) that the evidence-based intervention should be changed when that was not the issue and (2) that the content should be broken down into smaller steps when the learner was capable of learning it as currently structured. In this situation, the instructional arrangement should be adjusted as a first attempt to help the learner succeed while leaving the content and evidence-based intervention the same. If the intervention and/or the content structure is altered while the instructional arrangement remains as is, the progress monitoring results will likely be the same because the suspected problem has little or nothing to do with the intervention or the content.

Significance to Multi-tiered Response to Intervention

The interrelatedness of the five components is critical in multi-tiered RTI to help educator teams make informed, accurate decisions once universal screening or progress monitoring suggests that a learner may be struggling. As will be discussed in Chapter 3, progress-monitoring results indicate the level and rate of progress; however, educators must interpret these results to provide effective tiered instruction. All five curricular components must be considered before deciding how to adjust instruction if necessary.

Historical Perspective: Meeting the Needs of Struggling Learners and Response to Intervention

One aspect of multi-tiered RTI that should be considered early in this book is its use in meeting the needs of struggling learners, particularly those with learning disabilities. RTI is about the education of all learners, and its emphasis on quality of instruction has changed the way we view the process of teaching in addressing academic and behavioral needs. Implementation of the curriculum to meet the needs of struggling learners has changed systematically. For several decades, these needs were addressed within the prereferral model. In this model, learning or behavior problems were handled initially in the general education classroom and later in special education settings once more serious problems emerged. The prereferral process was often highly informal, with no consistent documentation of progress, little use of data to make decisions, and sporadic use of evidence-based interventions. This facilitated a "wait to fail" process whereby students who struggled in school needed to demonstrate significant gaps in their learning before they could receive more concentrated and intensive supports (Hoover & Klingner, in press).

Since the late 1960s, efforts to meet the needs of struggling learners, especially those with disabilities, have included a move away from self-contained instruction toward full inclusion in the general education curriculum (i.e., the Tier 1 core curriculum). An understanding of this shift is essential to fully grasp the current curricular emphases in RTI models. Table 1.3, developed from information in Hallahan and Kauffman (2003) and Hoover and Patton (2005), summarizes the curricular perspectives that have evolved over the past five decades to serve students with special needs.

As Table 1.3 shows, the emphasis in teaching learners with special needs evolved from separate and different to significant inclusion in the general classroom curriculum. Today, implementation of the curriculum for struggling learners and those at risk involves providing layers, or tiers, of instruction that increase in duration and intensity based on the learner's needs (Fuchs & Fuchs, 2006; Vaughn, 2003). As will be discussed, in meeting the needs of these learners, who previously were often placed in special education, the emphasis is on ensuring effective teaching in the general classroom (i.e., Tier 1). Therefore, as Table 1.3 shows, curriculum implementation for struggling learners has systematically evolved to its form today: the high quality general class core curriculum found in the multi-tiered RTI model. This model is described in Chapter 2, focusing on its unique contributions to the implementation of curriculum.

TABLE 1.3 Historical Perspective of Curricular Implications for Struggling Learners in Elementary and Secondary Schools

	Time Period	Prevailing Theme(s) About Special Needs	Educational Setting(s) for Meeting Special Needs	Key Considerations Concerning Education	Key View(s) of Curriculum Implementation
I	Early 1960s	Separate special settings were needed to address disabilities	Self-contained classes	Struggling learners with disabilities would be best served in special, separate classrooms	Specialized curricula were needed to educate individuals with disabilities
II	Late 1960s	Instruction in separate, self-contained special classrooms was questioned	Self-contained classes	Researchers questioned the continued practice of educating students with disabilities in separate classes	Academic progress resulting from specialized curricula and techniques was not supported by research
III	1970s	Many students with special needs can benefit from education in general as well as separate classrooms	Primarily resource classrooms, with some education provided in inclusive general classrooms	Many learners may benefit from education in general education classrooms, requiring only some education in a special classroom	Students with special needs should receive the general education curriculum
IV	1980s	Greater emphasis is placed on education in general class-rooms and less emphasis on special classrooms	Primarily inclusive education classrooms; some education provided in resource rooms; consultation among educators	The least restrictive environment for many students with a disabil-ity is in the inclusive education classroom	Many more struggling students may benefit from the general education curriculum if proper adaptations are implemented
V	1990s	Students with special needs are capable of succeeding with full inclusion in general education classrooms	Full inclusion in general education services, classrooms, and curricula; collaboration among educators	The education of most students with disabilities is best achieved in the general education setting; Significant increase in the number of students in special education is questioned, as is the LD Discrepancy formula.	Differentiated classrooms and instruction become the norm rather than the exception in curriculum implementation in inclusive education settings
VI	2000s	Diverse needs are to be met in inclusive settings	Reaffirmation of full inclusion for all students with special needs; collaboration among educators	The inclusive education setting is responsible for meeting an ever-increasing range of needs through tiers/layers of instruction	Prereferral model for curricular and placement decisions is replaced by the multi-tiered RTI model
VII	2010s	Push-in and/or pull-out intervention services are methods of choice for struggling learners	Inclusive education classrooms with supplemental support provided by an interventionist, a coach, or a specialist	All learners are taught using research-based curricula/evidence-based interventions in a multi-tiered structure (i.e., Tier 1–core; Tier 2–supplemental; Tier 3–intensive)	Learning disability eligibility includes consideration of three curricular factors: the gap between expected and actual level of achievement; the rate of progress; and the level of proficiency

Several factors must be considered in implementing the curriculum in multi-tiered RTI models. Teachers must understand how they tend to view or define curriculum. This is important to consider, as it affects their curriculum decision making. The three types of curriculum operating simultaneously in every classroom, along with the five critical components, are integral to effective implementation of the curriculum.

The application of these curricular factors in multi-tiered RTI provides the foundation for meeting the needs of all learners. In applying this knowledge, it is important for teachers to do the following:

- Discuss your definition of curriculum and how it impacts your curriculum decision making in the classroom.

- Analyze the ways in which each type of curriculum (explicit, hidden, absent) is found in your classroom; evaluate the extent to which the hidden or absent curriculum affects learners' progress.

- Give examples of the five curricular components found in your classroom; determine the extent to which they operate collectively in your curriculum implementation.

- Discuss with your school's multi-tiered RTI team the influences of the five curricular components and the three types of curriculum on a student who is struggling to achieve benchmarks.

FORM 1.1 Classroom Analysis of Evidence of Each Curriculum Type

Purpose: The purpose of this guide is to assist in analyzing each curriculum type found in the classroom.

Instructions: Document evidence of each curriculum type found in the classroom for the identified content area.

Name: _____ Grade: _____ Date: _____

<u>Content Area</u>: ___ Reading/Language Arts   ___ Mathematics
                    ___ Science   ___ Social Studies
                    ___ Other—Specify: _____

Explicit Curriculum—Summarize key explicit curricular elements in the classroom for the content area:

Hidden Curriculum—Summarize key hidden curricular elements or examples experienced as a result of teaching the explicit curriculum in the content area:

Absent Curriculum—Identify 3–4 curriculum items that could be added to enrich the curricular experiences already in place through the explicit curriculum and the hidden curriculum:

1.

2.

3.

4.

Additional Comments on the Role of Each Curriculum Type Found in the Classroom for the Specified Content Area:

Source: Used by permission of John J. Hoover.

Purpose: The purpose of this guide is to assist in analyzing the application of each curriculum component used in the identified content area.

Instructions: Describe aspects within the classroom that reflect each curriculum element for the specified content area. Provide Additional Comments if needed.

Name: _____   Grade: _____   Date: _____

Content Area: ___ Reading/Language Arts   ___ Mathematics
                         ___ Science   ___ Social Studies
                         ___ Other—Specify: _____

I. Content/Skills (Identify the key content topical areas and skills emphasized in the core instruction in the content area):

Primary content topics emphasized (Identify top 3–4 topics):

1.

2.

3.

4.

Additional Comments on Key Topical Areas Addressed in Content Area:

Key skills students are to acquire (Identify top 3–4 skill areas):

1.

2.

3.

4.

Additional Comments on Key Skill Areas Addressed in Content Area:

II. Evidence-Based Interventions (Identify most frequently used interventions to teach core instruction in content area):

1.

2.

3.

Additional Comments on Evidence-Based Interventions Used in Content Area:

III. Instructional Arrangements (Identify length of time for core instruction followed by rank ordering the frequency of use of each instructional arrangement for the core instruction):

Length of time for core instruction in content area: _____ (minutes)

Rank	*Instructional Arrangement*
____	Independent Work
____	Paired Work
____	Small-Group Work
____	Whole-Class Instruction

Additional Comments on Instructional Arrangements Used When Teaching Core Content Area:

IV. Class/Instructional Management (Identify most frequently used strategies for managing behavior and instruction in the classroom during the core instruction time):

1.

2.

3.

4.

5.

6.

Additional Comments on Class/Instructional Management in Content Area:

V. Progress Evaluation (Identify the primary means used in the classroom to regularly monitor student progress in the content area):

1.

2.

3.

4.

Additional Comments on Progress Evaluation in Content Area

Source: Used by permission of John J. Hoover.

CHAPTER 2

Response to Intervention Framework: Research-Based Curricula and Evidence-Based Interventions

▶ Overview

AN UNDERSTANDING OF THE importance of research-based curricula and evidence-based interventions in multi-tiered RTI is essential for all educators. This includes structure, decision-making points, and levels of instruction. Knowledge about the fidelity of implementation of curricula and interventions is required to ensure the highest quality of instruction for all learners. In addition, commitment to the transition from previous prereferral models to contemporary RTI models is essential to facilitate the use of effective schoolwide instructional practices found in RTI models.

▶ Key Topics

- ▶ Tiers or levels of instruction
- ▶ Process of RTI
- ▶ Prereferral, curriculum implementation, and RTI
- ▶ Research-based curricula
- ▶ Evidence-based interventions
- ▶ Fidelity of implementation

▶ Learner Outcomes

After reading this chapter, you should:

1. Be able to describe the structure and main components of multi-tiered RTI models
2. Understand the role and significance of research- and evidence-based instruction
3. Be knowledgeable about several important evidenced-based interventions
4. Understand how to transition from a prereferral to an RTI model
5. Know the key factors to consider in selecting and implementing research-based curricula and evidence-based interventions in the classroom
6. Be able to assess the fidelity of curriculum implementation

SIGNIFICANCE TO CONTEMPORARY CLASSROOM INSTRUCTION

Effective teaching of the curriculum has become the focal point in today's classrooms to meet the needs of all learners. This deviates somewhat from previous procedures used to address academic and/or behavioral needs by first targeting the quality and integrity of classroom instruction in a preventative rather than a reactive manner. The current process, referred to as the *multi-tiered response to intervention,* is based on selecting and implementing research-based curricula and evidence-based interventions. It also emphasizes the principle that all instruction must be delivered as designed (i.e., fidelity). In addition, regular screening and monitoring of learners' progress are critical to successful implementation of RTI. These processes are significant, requiring all teachers to become highly knowledgeable about curriculum, its components, and its effects on learning in multi-tiered RTI models.

Historical Perspective on Multi-Tiered Response to Intervention

The concept and practice of RTI date back to at least the early 1980s. In 1982 a National Research Council Report summarized the efforts to evaluate the special education classification system (Heller, Holtzman, & Messick, 1982). In this report, three criteria were recommended for evaluation of this process:

1. Determine the quality of general education instruction.
2. Monitor progress toward outcomes.
3. Ensure the use of valid and accurate special education assessment procedures.

A key point made was that all three criteria must be met for a valid special education placement to exist. These criteria are identical to the underpinnings of multi-tiered RTI models. In the 1990s, two major educational concerns continued to surface:

Concern 1—The increase in the number of students placed in special education, particularly for a learning disability in reading

Concern 2—The validity of using special education assessment for identifying needs, particularly the IQ–achievement discrepancy for determining a learning disability

These concerns, in turn, led to continued progress toward a system that places greater emphasis on quality of instruction rather than students' intrinsic disorders. The most recent formal event that preceded the widespread use of multi-tiered RTI was the reauthorization of the Individuals with Disabilities Education Act (IDEA) of 2004, in which alternative means for identifying a learning disability were authorized (Bradley, Danielson, & Doolittle, 2007). RTI is one practice that may now be used to identify a learning disability (Mellard & Johnson, 2008). The passage of IDEA was preceded by the passage of the No Child Left Behind Act in 2001, which established several requirements that are incorporated in multi-tiered RTI models, including early identification and interventions (Vaughn, Wanzek, Woodruff, & Linan-Thompson, 2007). As a result of these ongoing efforts to improve education, multi-tiered RTI models have emerged in many school systems across the country as the practice or framework of choice to meet the educational needs of all learners.

Overview of Response to Intervention

RTI is a process grounded in research over several decades designed to apply assessment results systematically in instructional and eligibility decision making (Burns & Gibbons, 2008; Hoover, 2009a; Jimerson, Burns, & VanDerHeyden, 2007).

Mellard and Johnson (2008, p. 1) wrote that RTI "is a promising new process of instruction, assessment, and intervention" that facilitates effective education for all learners. In contrast to the prereferral model for meeting the needs of struggling learners when general and special education function as separate, parallel systems of providing needed services, RTI blends these two forms of education through its emphasis on research-based curriculum, evidence-based interventions, screening, monitoring, and diagnostic procedures. For example, previously, special educators became involved with struggling learners only after formal special education assessment and the identification of a disability; today, RTI allows general and special educators to collaborate to meet the needs of all learners (i.e., those with or without a disability) early in the process and prior to consideration of possible special education.

Defining RTI

Multi-tiered RTI has no one accepted definition. However, although numerous definitions exist, each contains similar elements addressing the basic principles of RTI. Table 2.1 provides a sample of the definitions found in the literature.

As Table 2.1 shows, common themes exist across different definitions: multi-tiered instruction, high-quality and research-based instruction, use of data for making instructional decisions, and an emphasis on meeting the needs of all learners, along with periodic monitoring of progress. As with the differences in definition, no single RTI model exists; however, many models contain similar elements as various definitions are put into practice. A review of numerous RTI model descriptions yielded several common elements, as illustrated in Table 2.2. This table was developed from a review of several research and descriptive sources discussing multi-tiered RTI models, including Brown-Chidsey and Steege (2005), Jimerson et al., (2007), and Mellard and Johnson (2008).

TABLE 2.1 Sample Characterizations of Response to Intervention

The Response to Intervention (RTI) process is a multi-tiered approach to providing services and interventions to struggling learners at increasing levels of intensity. (Pierangelo & Giuliani, 2006, p. 1)

Response-to-Intervention (RTI) is the systematic use of assessment data to most efficiently allocate resources in order to improve learning for all students (Burns & VanDerHeyden, 2006) (Burns & Gibbons, 2008, p. 1)

Response to Intervention is, simply put, a process of implementing high-quality, scientifically validated instructional practices based on learner needs, monitoring student progress, and adjusting instruction based on student's response. (Bender & Shores, 2007, p. 7)

RTI is a multi-tiered framework for preventing reading problems and for intervening in the cases of students who are not successful in the general education curriculum. (Mellard & Johnson, 2008, p. 8)

RTI is an objective examination of the cause–effect relationship(s) between academic and behavioral *intervention* and the student's *response* to the intervention. (Brown-Chidsey & Steege, 2005, p. 2)

TABLE 2.2 Common Elements in Multi-Tiered Response to Intervention Models

1. Multi-tiered framework (typically three tiers but sometimes four)

2. Research-based core curriculum (Tier 1)

3. Evidence-based interventions (Tiers 1, 2, and 3)

4. Implementation of three assessment types: universal screening, progress monitoring, diagnostic assessment

5. Monitoring of progress on a continuous, regular basis

6. Use of data to base instructional decisions

7. Implementation of Tier 2 supports as soon as a need is identified through universal screening and/or progress monitoring

8. Adjustment of instruction based on progress monitoring results

9. Consideration of special education only after the learner does not or cannot make adequate progress with Tier 1 and 2 instruction

RTI Curriculum Framework

RTI is a curricular process that includes layers or levels of instruction, increasing in duration and intensity (Fuchs & Fuchs, 2006; Hoover, 2009a), based on evidence of student progress toward academic and behavioral benchmarks. If screening or monitoring results indicate lack of progress, additional supports and interventions are provided for the learner's education as soon as possible once the need becomes apparent. This procedure is in contrast to previous practice, in which the learner needed to wait an extended period of time until a more significant gap emerged between expected and actual academic or behavioral performance, otherwise referred to as the *wait to fail* method (Howell, Patton, & Deiotte, 2008). As discussed, RTI models include multiple layers or tiers of instruction, typically three (Fuchs & Fuchs, 2006; Hoover, 2009a; Vaughn, 2003). Figure 2.1 illustrates tiered instruction, with emphasis on the curriculum within each tier. Three tiers of instruction are illustrated: core Tier 1 instruction, supplemental Tier 2 instructional supports, and intensive Tier 3 instruction for those with more significant needs. Each tier of instruction in RTI is described below.

> *Tier 1*—The research-based core curriculum provided to all learners
>
> *Tier 2*—Supplemental instruction provided to struggling learners to support Tier 1 instruction through the use of evidence-based interventions
>
> *Tier 3*—Intensive interventions and/or curricula provided to students with significant educational needs, including those with disabilities.

TIER 1: RESEARCH-BASED CORE INSTRUCTION ■ Tier 1 is the research-based core instruction provided to all learners in every grade. It reflects the mandated curriculum that occurs in the classroom as the explicit and hidden curricula are

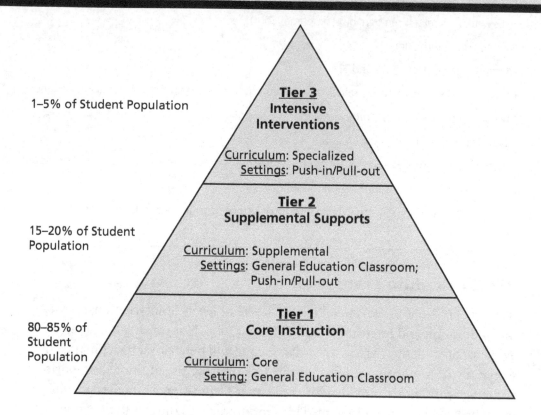

1–5% of Student Population

Tier 3
Intensive
Interventions

Curriculum: Specialized
Settings: Push-in/Pull-out

15–20% of Student
Population

Tier 2
Supplemental Supports

Curriculum: Supplemental
Settings: General Education Classroom;
Push-in/Pull-out

80–85% of
Student
Population

Tier 1
Core Instruction

Curriculum: Core
Setting: General Education Classroom

implemented , as well as any curricular aspects or components that are excluded from implementation of the explicit curriculum (i.e., absent curriculum). Core instruction occurs in the general education classroom, and it is estimated that at least 80% of all learners should make satisfactory progress with this level of instruction (Yell, 2004). If Tier 1 instruction fails to meet the needs of this percentage of students, then Tiers 2 and 3 will become overpopulated, placing great stress on school systems (Howell et al., 2008) and bringing into question the use and implementation of the Tier 1 curriculum. In addition, Burns and Gibbons (2008) wrote that effective Tier 1 implementation of the curriculum "is vitally important because it affects every student and allows approximately 80% of the student population to successfully reach learning objectives" (p. 76).

Therefore, for effective Tier 1 curriculum implementation, that curriculum must be adjusted and/or changed if less than 80% of the students in the class or grade level make adequate progress (e.g., failure of 50% of the students in a class to meet benchmarks requires adjustments in the curriculum and/or in the fidelity of implementation). These adjustments must be made to facilitate learning, so that at least 80% of the students make satisfactory progress, rather than initially providing half of the class with Tier 2 supports. Once this occurs, learners who still make inadequate progress should be considered for Tier 2 supplemental supports.

TIER 2: SUPPLEMENTAL INSTRUCTION ■ For learners who make inadequate progress with Tier 1 instruction, additional support is provided. This support is designed to complement, *not replace,* Tier 1 instruction by providing added instruction in small-group settings within (i.e., push-in) the general education classroom and/or through a pull-out structure (e.g., small-group instruction in the library or another location in the school). A unique aspect of Tier 2 supports is that a variety of educators may provide them (e.g., general educators, special educators, interventionists, speech/language specialist, social worker) without the need to first classify the student with a disability. Tier 2 supports are given to small groups of students for a specified amount of time (e.g., 30 minutes per day for 10 weeks). Estimates are that up to 15–20% of students will need some form of Tier 2 support at some time (Yell, 2004).

In regard to the personnel and location for delivering Tier 2 supports, Burns and Gibbons (2008) wrote that the most efficient method is in the general education classroom by the general class teacher. For example, in a general class of 24 students, 4 of whom require Tier 2 support, the teacher could implement the curriculum in one 30-minute block of time per day, during which the 4 students are instructed by the teacher in a small group while the rest of the students work at learning centers and/or independently to reinforce skills previously taught and learned. It is essential to bear in mind that Tier 2 supports are *in addition to* the Tier 1 curriculum, so no new direct instruction should occur while the Tier 2 supports are being provided. In this example, students in the same classroom are working simultaneously in both Tier 1 and Tier 2 levels of instruction where seamless transitions occur, utilizing the expertise of the general class teacher.

Three other methods for delivering Tier 2 instruction may also be used (Burns & Gibbons, 2008; Hoover, 2009c; Mellard & Johnson, 2008): (1) a pull-out method, (2) push-in support, and (3) schoolwide supports time. The *pull-out* method is the more traditional method for meeting specific learner needs; someone other than the general class teacher pulls the learner out of the general class for a specified time (e.g., 30 minutes per day for 10 weeks, with progress monitored biweekly) and provides supplemental support in a defined area (e.g., reading fluency, mathematics computation). This supplemental support may occur in a resource room, a library, or some other location in the school building. During this time, the general class teacher is providing value-added instruction to knowledge and skills previously taught to the entire class; there is no new instruction that the students receiving Tier 2 support would miss. This arrangement is more labor intensive, removes the learner from the general class, and may lead to a disconnect between Tier 1 and Tier 2 instruction. Therefore, although learners are given value-added Tier 2 support by an educator who specializes in the area of need (e.g., a reading specialist, interventionist, counselor), to be most effective these individuals and the general class teacher must collaborate and communicate regularly to ensure an effective pull-out program.

Rather than pulling the students out of the general classroom, in the *push-in* arrangement for providing Tier 2 support, the specialist goes into the general classroom and works with the students in a paired or small-group setting while the general class teacher provides enrichment for the other students. This blends Tier 1 and Tier 2 instruction in the same classroom while allowing the Tier 2 students to remain with their class. There are two potential problems with this method: (1) students may feel singled out and may be uncomfortable receiving Tier 2 instruction in this manner or (2) too many specialists may need to go into the same classroom if learners' needs are different (e.g., one student needs help with reading fluency, another needs language development, and a third needs mathematics support). A variation of this method is to have students with similar needs in the same grade go to one of the grade-level classrooms and receive push-in support. If this method is used, allowing other students to move to other grade-level classes for enrichment helps to destigmatize the act of changing classrooms for the 30-minute block of time in which Tier 2 support is provided.

Another strategy used in some schools for delivering Tier 2 supports is referred to as *schoolwide supports time*; in this bloc of time, all students simultaneously receive either enrichment within the Tier 1 curriculum or Tier 2 support. In this situation, all students who require Tier 2 supports receive it at the same time of the day (e.g., daily from 11:00 to 11:30 a.m.) while all other students participate in enrichment or value-added tasks. Scheduling difficulty is a potential drawback to this method; however, some schools are implementing it, simultaneously reaching all learners in both Tier 1 and Tier 2 levels of instruction.

TIER 3: INTENSIVE INSTRUCTION ■ Tier 3 intensive interventions are provided to students who cannot make satisfactory progress with Tier 2 supplemental supports (Howell et al., 2008). Up to 5% of students are expected to need Tier 3 interventions. These are students with more significant needs, including those who have a disability; Tier 3 in many school systems includes special education (Mellard & Johnson, 2008). Tier 3 often includes a curriculum different from the one implemented in Tiers 1 and 2 (e.g., Orton-Gillingham, Wilson Reading programs). Tier 3 interventions often involve a pull-out or push-in arrangement similar to those for Tier 2; instruction is delivered by specialists, interventionists, or special educators. Tier 3 interventions may also be part of the schoolwide supports time program used simultaneously with the other tiers at the defined time during the school day.

Tier 3 interventions are the most intensive form of instruction, requiring a lot of time for duration and frequency (Burns & Gibbons, 2008). Tier 3 is a highly systematic process that occurs over an extended period of time (e.g., 60 minutes twice a day for 15 weeks, with progress monitored three times per week). The process and procedures used for Tier 3 interventions are often similar to those used for special education services, with one significant difference: in some multi-tiered RTI models, Tier 3 learners do not need to be

TABLE 2.3 Key Curricular Aspects within Multi-Tiered Response to Intervention

Tier 1 curriculum must be research-based, and at least 80% of students must make adequate progress toward benchmarks.

Tier 1 curriculum implementation includes the use of both general and targeted differentiations prior to determining the need for Tier 2 instruction.

Tier 2 curricular supports include evidence-based interventions and target 15–20% of students in a classroom or grade.

Tier 2 curricular supports add value to, not replace, Tier 1 instruction (i.e., all students receiving Tier 2 supports receive this instruction in addition to all Tier 1 instruction).

Tier 2 supports are determined, in part, by the use of universal screening and/or progress monitoring results (see Chapter 3).

Tier 2 supports should, to the extent possible, be provided in the general education classroom by the general educator, with push-in or pull-out instruction provided as necessary.

Tiers 1 and 2 curriculum implementation is the primary responsibility of general educators (e.g., the general class teacher, interventionist, reading specialist), with collaborative support provided by other professionals (e.g., special educators, a diagnostician).

Tier 3 curriculum implementation is primarily the responsibility of specialists or special educators, with support provided by general educators as appropriate.

Curriculum provided in each tier of instruction must be implemented in the manner in which it was designed to be used (i.e., with fidelity).

Progress toward curricular benchmarks is assessed by universal screening and progress monitoring.

Curriculum implementation for struggling learners should be adjusted as required based on screening and/or progress monitoring results as soon as a need arises.

classified as having a disability to receive services. In other models, Tier 3 is synonymous with special education. In these cases, a disability is identified, adhering to all due process safeguards provided by law.

In RTI, layers or tiers of instruction that increase in duration and intensity based on academic and behavioral needs are provided by a team of skilled, expert educators. This system is based on the selection and implementation of a research-based curriculum, evidence-based interventions, and procedures for more frequently monitoring and screening student progress in which progress data are gathered.

To conclude this section, Table 2.3 summarizes some of the key curricular points discussed above as they pertain to education in multi-tiered RTI models. For a more detailed description of the general structures and components of RTI, the reader is referred to the numerous sources cited the numerous sources cited in the above discussions.

As Table 2.3 indicates, implementation of any model of RTI includes, at minimum, the following six characteristics:

1. Tiers or layers of instruction
2. A research-based curriculum

3. Evidence-based interventions

4. Fidelity of implementation

5. Universal screening and progress monitoring

6. Data-based decision making

Initial efforts to implement a multi-tiered RTI model should include assessment of current structures, supports, and needs. Form 2.1 (*School-Based Multi-Tiered Response to Intervention Evaluation Guide*) provides a checklist for educators to use to ensure that key elements of each tier of instruction are properly implemented.

In addition, Form 2.2 (*School-Based Multi-Tiered Response to Intervention Training Checklist*) is a checklist to target the RTI training needs of school staff. Various school staff members should complete it to provide feedback representing all educators so that the most relevant and comprehensive professional development program can be generated and implemented.

What Is a Research-Based Curriculum?

As indicated, effective education for all learners begins with the selection and implementation of a research-based curriculum in Tier 1. Although most educators are familiar with the use of research in education, its value in selecting and using curriculum in various content areas may be less well understood. Consider the following relative to research-based curriculum (North Central Regional Educational Laboratory [NCREL] Web site):

A research-based curriculum is a curriculum that has:

1. Been tested in educational settings and been shown to achieve what it purports to do (e.g., increase reading fluency, reduce off-task behavior, facilitate more effective study habits, increase knowledge of science concepts)

2. Been designed to be used in specific ways to ensure its effectiveness with students

3. Produced research results demonstrating clear evidence of effectiveness for defined purpose(s) and population(s).

In effect, a research-based curriculum is any curriculum in any content or related area that has been shown to be effective through research. Several Web sites describe the research-based curriculum. The site with the most rigorous standards for evaluating curricula is the government's What Works Clearinghouse (http://www.whatworks.ed.gov). Newly researched curricula are being added to this Web site periodically, and many have already been posted. The reader is encouraged to review this site on a regular basis for updated research information and results concerning many of the more frequently used curricula. This includes entries in the following main categories:

Beginning Reading—Numerous curricula are classified in four general areas: alphabetics, fluency, comprehension, and general reading achievement.

Mathematics—Many programs classified as "mathematical achievement" are described for both elementary and middle school education.

English Language Learners—A variety of programs are described that purport to improve English language development, reading achievement, and mathematics achievement for students in various stages of English language development.

Various curricula and interventions are also provided for dropout prevention, early childhood education, and character education. It should be noted that although several curricula and interventions are listed on the What Works Clearinghouse site, many do not have results from a study and/or results that conform to Clearinghouse standards; therefore, recommendations concerning their effectiveness have not been generated. However, these curricula are described, and even if evidence of effectiveness is not provided, this does not mean that the program does not work; it only indicates that the Clearinghouse currently has no research evidence. Other sites to consider for locating research-based curricula include those of professional organizations, state departments of education, and lists generated by individual school districts. Readers are encouraged to spend time investigating the curricula they are currently using or planning to use by consulting these and similar Web sites.

Curriculum Significance to Educators

Educators must be familiar with the research basis for all curricula used in the classroom. At minimum, they should have a general understanding of the curriculum's stated research effectiveness. This is essential when attempting to understand the lack of progress of struggling learners. A solid understanding of the curriculum also facilitates its implementation with fidelity, another requirement of RTI. A research-based curriculum is the foundation of all RTI models and associated decision making, and educators must understand its effectiveness, proper uses, appropriate populations for usage, and benchmarks directly associated with the Tier 1 core curriculum used in the classroom.

Evidence-Based Interventions

Along with established research-based grade-level curricula (e.g., Investigations, Wilson Fundations, Houghton-Mifflin Reading Program, Saxon Math, Everyday Math), a variety of interventions exist that are used either as part of a research-based curriculum or as additions to facilitate differentiated instruction. RTI requires initial core instruction to be research-based and implemented, along with reasonable and acceptable differentiations. The topic of differentiations and their critical role in RTI is explored in Chapter 6; however, many of the evidence-based interventions discussed here can be used to differentiate instruction effectively in order to run a comprehensive differentiated classroom (see Chapter 6).

Whereas a research-based curriculum is comprehensive, evidence-based interventions are specific techniques with proven effectiveness in meeting various skill or ability needs. These interventions include many of the instructional strategies used in today's classrooms. Sometimes, evidence-based interventions are the basis of the comprehensive research-based curriculum discussed above (e.g., direct instruction, explicit teaching, cooperative learning). Several of these interventions are summarized below. They have been shown to target some of the more common learner needs. Table 2.4, developed from information in Meese (2001), Moran and Malott (2004), and Sabornie and deBettencourt

TABLE 2.4 Evidence-Based Interventions

Intervention	Description	Targeted Learner Need(s)
Direct Instruction	Teaching intervention that systematically develops instructional skills and abilities following established procedures	Structured learning Sequential learning
Task Analysis	Process that identifies discrete components of a task/skill and generates a sequence so that students learn the task/skill more easily	Sequential learning Discrete/ordered tasks
Scaffolding	Teaching intervention that relies on the use of temporary supports that build upon the foundations of acquiring skills and knowledge by providing needed supports to facilitate learning	Discrete steps in learning Initial supports prior to independent learning
Reciprocal Teaching	Teacher–student interactive process in which teacher modeling and guided practice help students develop critical reading skills	Reading comprehension Active engagement
Classwide Peer Tutoring	Peer tutoring strategy in which learners take turns asking/responding to each other's questions to increase acquisition of knowledge and skills	Motivation Active engagement
Sheltered Instruction	Process that gives ELLs greater opportunities for improved class interactions and greater access to the core curriculum while simultaneously supporting the development of English language skills	Language development Curriculum access Retention of learning
Analytic Teaching	Highly structured intervention linking instruction and assessment to assist teachers in making informed curricular decisions	Structured learning Sequential learning
Collaborative Strategic Reading (CSR)	Intervention that blends aspects of cooperative learning and reciprocal teaching to support acquisition of reading comprehension skills	Reading comprehension Motivation
Teacher-Scripted Lessons	A form of explicit instruction in which teachers use developed scripts to teach students in structured and sequential ways	Active engagement Structured learning Sequential learning

(2009), as well as in Echevarria and Graves (2003) and Hoover and Patton (2005), provides an overview of the selected evidence-based interventions discussed in this chapter.

As Table 2.4 shows, selected evidence-based interventions are designed to meet a variety of learning needs. Although not all-inclusive, these interventions can be applied across content areas to meet a broader and more diverse set of needs of all learners. Below is a more in-depth discussion of each intervention, including its process, uses, and curricular significance in RTI models. For additional information, the reader is referred to the sources cited in this section and those used to develop Table 2.3. Also, note that the interventions presented in this section are those that teachers use to implement the curriculum (i.e., teacher interventions); selected interventions that are student directed (i.e., student strategies) are presented in Chapter 8.

Direct Instruction

Overview

Direct instruction is a time-tested intervention that includes the direct teaching of knowledge and skills. Moran and Malott (2004) identified three aspects of direct instruction: (1) a scientific approach that guides decisions on how the curriculum is best implemented, (2) an integrated process that helps learners acquire knowledge and skills in systematic ways, and (3) a sequential process that guides learning from highly directed instruction to independent practice.

Process

Direct instruction includes the application of several steps or procedures in a systematic way (Mercer & Pullen, 2009; Moran & Malott, 2004):

1. It provides clear, explicit directions and instructions.
2. Curricular knowledge and skills are presented in the order in which topics are best introduced, practiced, reviewed, and generalized or combined with other skills.
3. Implementation moves from highly directed to guided practice to independent use through a process of sequencing learning in small steps, building on learner successes, and withdrawing prompts and reducing the level of support as the learner demonstrates success.
4. Learners are provided with guided and independent practice until knowledge or skills are mastered.
5. Periodic brief assessments (i.e., probes) are conducted to determine mastery and graph the results to illustrate progress.

Specific Uses

Direct instruction gives educators a process for smooth, sequential implementation of the curriculum in any content area. It is most appropriate for the student who prefers structured, teacher-directed learning to facilitate the eventual independent use of the skill, along with generalization for use with other acquired abilities.

Significance to Curriculum Implementation in RTI Models

Direct instruction addresses many of the requirements for implementing curriculum within multi-tiered instruction. It includes frequent monitoring of progress, a structured approach that is easily adjusted as necessary, and mastery of prerequisite skills needed to achieve curricular benchmarks, as well as the use of charted data to make informed curricular decisions for each tier of instruction within any RTI model.

Task Analysis

Overview

Task analysis is another time-tested intervention that provides structure to everyday implementation of the curriculum by breaking down tasks into their components (Meese, 2001). It helps educators address learners' needs in a sequential and systematic manner (Mercer & Pullen, 2009).

Process

Task analysis is easy to implement once two types of behavior have been identified:

1. *Outcome Behavior*—Behavior that is desired upon completion of the entire task, which has been broken into discrete steps (e.g., telling time)
2. *Enabling Behaviors*—Prerequisite behaviors that must be mastered to demonstrate the outcome behavior (e.g., knowledge of numbers, number sequencing, digital time that reflects the hour and minutes).

Enabling behaviors are generated by the teacher (or found within the curriculum), who lists all the major behaviors necessary to reach the outcome behavior (Mercer & Pullen, 2009). The enabling behaviors are presented to and mastered by the students in the proper sequence until they eventually reach and master the outcome behavior.

Specific Uses

Task analysis is appropriate for teaching any skill within any curriculum area that can be broken down into discrete steps, where mastery of each step leads to mastery of the broader (outcome) behavior (Meese, 2001). This intervention is most appropriate for educators who initially prefer to teach individual components of broader topics rather than use a more holistic approach in which the study of discrete steps may interfere with the mastery of broader concepts.

Significance to Curriculum Implementation in RTI Models

Task analysis is an evidence-based intervention that meets the most basic needs of curriculum implementation within RTI. It provides a framework for monitoring progress, adjusting instruction, and charting data points to illustrate progress, as well as providing direct, teacher-guided instruction if necessary to meet the needs of learners at any tier of instruction.

Scaffolding

Overview

Scaffolding is a teacher-directed intervention in which instructional supports are provided until the learner is confident in dealing with the material and no longer requires assistance. Scaffolding builds on the concept of supports necessary for successful learning and is used only as long as it is needed. Scaffolding allows learners to be challenged with more complex material as learning is "constructed" by the student (Peregoy & Boyle, 2001).

Process

Ovando, Collier, and Combs (2003) identified three main types of scaffolds that help learners address more complex material: (1) those that simplify the language by providing less wordy directions, using several short sentences rather than one or two longer ones, and avoiding the use of complex terms until the learner becomes more familiar with the material; (2) those that provide a series of responses from which students select answers rather than asking them to generate responses on their own; and (3) those that incorporate visuals such as graphic organizers, charts, figures, or outlines in curricular activities. Application of these three scaffolds significantly increases the opportunities for students to learn challenging curriculum material.

Specific Uses

Scaffolding assists learners with language-related reading needs as curriculum material is presented and studied. In addition, all students benefit from this form of intervention as more complex material is initially studied, providing greater opportunities for success.

Significance to Curriculum Implementation in RTI Models

Providing enough opportunities to learn within a research-based curriculum is fundamental to success with RTI, and scaffolding is especially well suited to this purpose. Use of the three scaffolds described above will assist educators in providing high quality core instruction (Tier 1) as well as supplemental supports and intensive interventions (Tiers 2 and 3, respectively) within RTI.

Reciprocal Teaching

Overview

Reciprocal teaching (Palincsar & Brown, 1984) is a teacher-directed process to help struggling readers with reading comprehension. Although it includes four defined steps, its ultimate purpose is to assist learners in using this strategy to develop their own knowledge through questioning and interactions (Hoover, Klingner, Baca, & Patton, 2008).

Process

Reciprocal teaching includes the development and use of four interrelated strategies by efficient readers (Palincsar & David, 1991):

1. *Questioning*—Teacher and students ask questions about the passage to help focus on the main idea.
2. *Clarifying*—Students identify words and concepts in the passage that are unknown.
3. *Summarizing*—Students summarize the passage in their own words.
4. *Predicting*—Students predict or guess what will occur next in the passage based on what they have just read.

The teacher's role in reciprocal teaching consists of providing scaffolding and guiding the process as students work through the steps. Helping students to understand how interactions and guidance assist them in further developing their own knowledge is key to the success of this intervention.

Specific Uses

Reciprocal teaching was designed for use with groups of students who struggle with reading comprehension. It relies heavily on interactive dialogue to improve the skills necessary to comprehend written material (Meese, 2001). In addition, some researchers have documented the effectiveness of reciprocal teaching with English language learners (ELLs; Hoover et al., 2008).

Significance to Curriculum Implementation in RTI Models

Reciprocal teaching is an intervention consistent with implementation of the curriculum in any tier of RTI instruction. It is easily implemented with small groups of learners who have similar reading comprehension needs. In addition, the effects of reciprocal teaching are easily documented through periodic monitoring of progress based on students' responses to comprehension items after reading the passage.

Classwide Peer Tutoring

Overview

Classwide peer tutoring (CWPT) is a variation of reciprocal teaching in which students are assigned to a tutor–tutee dyad as well as classroom teams designed to increase verbal interactions and involvement among learners (Greenwood, Arreaga-Mayer, Utley, Gavin, & Terry, 2001). CWPT also improves motivation as students gain more confidence through active engagement with the curricular material.

Process

Students are initially assigned to a dyad, and two dyads are paired. Each dyad keeps score of the points awarded for correct responses. Pairs may be selected randomly or assigned based on ability levels (Hoover et al., 2008). CWPT engages the learners through questioning and verbal interactions, and points are awarded for correct responses in a friendly competition between the two dyads. The following process is recommended (Arreage-Mayer, 1998):

1. The teacher uses modeling and role play to prepare students for the various procedures in CWPT, including administering questions, correcting mistakes, providing feedback, and giving positive reinforcement.
2. Each week begins with the teacher directing a mini-lesson on the material to be studied.

3. CWPT is conducted for a minimum of 30 minutes per day, four or five times per week, with the tutor presenting questions on the material to the tutee.

4. If the tutee answers the questions correctly, a reward is provided; if not, the tutor provides the correct response.

5. The tutee writes or says the correct response three times and is rewarded if all three responses are correct.

6. The teacher monitors each dyad's progress by moving around the classroom, making certain to visit each pair.

7. The teacher may use brief (1-minute) probes to provide additional assessment of selected learners' progress in mastering the week's material.

Specific Uses

CWPT was originally developed for culturally and linguistically diverse learners in elementary school (Greenwood et al., 2001). However, it has been used successfully in a variety of subject areas, including reading comprehension and fluency, with students in grades K–12. In addition, it is appropriate for use with students who have mild cognitive disabilities.

Significance to Curriculum Implementation in RTI Models

CWPT is a highly effective evidence-based intervention for use with all learners in grades K–12. RTI methodology requires adjustments to instruction if lack of progress is evident, and CWPT is one intervention that facilitates differentiated instruction. In addition, CWPT emphasizes several interrelated skills that contribute to instructional effectiveness. These include the elements or constructs identified by Gersten and Jimenez (1994) and discussed by Hoover et al. (2008): "challenge, involvement, success, scaffolding/cognitive strategies, collaborative/cooperative learning, feedback, techniques for second language acquisition, and respect for cultural diversity" (p. 202). The use of classroom tutors also gives the teacher additional time to ensure that all learners receive high quality core instruction (i.e., Tier 1), and teachers may use this method to provide supplemental supports (Tier 2).

Sheltered Instruction

Overview

Sheltered instruction helps ELLs achieve greater and more efficient access to the core curriculum (i.e., Tier 1). It also facilitates their development of English language proficiency (Ovando et al., 2003). This intervention provides the instructional language differentiations needed to ensure that all ELLs understand directions, participate fully in instructional tasks, and acquire the knowledge and skills taught in the curriculum.

Process

Sheltered instruction includes the following procedures for effective teaching: (1) speaking clearly, (2) repeating important information such as directions or procedures, (3) defining all key terms using vocabulary familiar to the students, and (4) using a variety of nonverbal cues when communicating verbally to reinforce necessary ideas, concepts, and skills (Hill & Flynn, 2006; Ovando et al., 2003).

Specific Uses

Sheltered instruction should be used with ELLs in any content area where more explicit support for learning is required due to second language acquisition needs. Peregoy and Boyle (2001) also wrote that, when used with related interventions such as paired learning, sheltered instruction promotes deeper understanding of curriculum tasks, skills, and knowledge.

Significance to Curriculum Implementation in RTI Models

Sheltered instruction is important to the implementation of an RTI curriculum, where Tiers 1 and 2 instruction must be relevant and appropriate to the learner prior to determining the need for more intensive or specialized instruction (Tier 3). This intervention helps all teachers to make sure that curriculum implementation within RTI is appropriate for all learners, increasing the possibility of helping ELLs to receive proper Tier 1 core instruction.

Analytic Teaching

Overview

Analytic teaching provides structured learning along with systematic monitoring of progress to inform instructional decisions. This intervention is effective in making necessary differentiations to instruction (de Valenzuela & Baca, 2004). Analytic teaching helps educators to analyze behaviors and learning within the curriculum and make adjustments as needed.

Process

Analytic teaching includes the following steps, derived from information in Hoover (2009b) and Moran and Malott (2004):

1. Identify the current level of performance for a specific skill by selecting and using an activity that targets that skill.
2. Develop two checklists (one for the teacher, one for the student) that reflect the activity the learner must complete to acquire the targeted skill.
3. Observe the learner completing the activity (Item 1 above) and document the behaviors and results; complete the checklists.
4. Compare the results of the teacher and student checklists; summarize the behaviors observed during task completion; determine if the activity facilitated the learning of the identified skill/ability (Item 1 above).
5. If the activity helped the student acquire the skill/ability, the activity should continue, with additional skills/abilities added once the initial ones are mastered.
6. If the activity did not help the student acquire the skill/ability, the activity should be adjusted and then completed.
7. Document results from the adjusted activity; revise it if necessary or continue if progress is observed and documented using the checklists.
8. Plot on a graph the student's progress in acquiring the skill/ability, as well as the results from each checklist over time, to illustrate the student's progress and growth in learning.

Specific Uses

Analytic teaching may be used in any curricular content area where the learning task can be subdivided and taught in sequential order. It is most appropriate for learners who require more structure in the implementation of the curriculum and who are able to learn by breaking down tasks into discrete parts.

Significance to Curriculum Implementation in RTI Models

Analytic teaching is an appropriate educational intervention for use in RTI because it facilitates the breakdown of tasks. It also facilitates decision making concerning adjustments to instruction that are necessary to implement the curriculum in each tier of instruction. Analytic teaching demonstrates how to instruct students using observed results that are linked directly to what is taught.

Collaborative Strategic Reading

Overview

Collaborative strategic reading (CSR) is an intervention that combines cooperative learning principles with reciprocal teaching procedures (Klingner, Vaughn, Dimino, Schumm, & Bryant, 2001). CSR was developed to help students become more confident readers; however, it is also useful in teaching reading comprehension (Hoover et al., 2008). In addition, CSR provides opportunities for students to assist each other with reading comprehension.

Process

CSR gives students opportunities to master content area text (e.g., science, social studies) as they use cooperative learning, facilitating contributions from all group members. Klingner et al. (2001) identified four reading strategies that promote CSR:

Preview—Students preview the text to activate prior knowledge, generate questions about the material, and link to their prior experiences and interests pertaining to the topic.

Click and Clunk—As students preview and read the text, some material is more easily understood, as it "clicks" with them, whereas other material is not as easily comprehended and "clunks." As student groups identify the material that clicks and clunks, they generate strategies to attempt to better understand the clunks. Material not understood is recorded in a journal for future reference.

Get the Gist—This step refers to students' ability to state the main ideas and synthesize information, as well as describe the material in their own words. Students should also be able to write the gist of the material in their own words.

Wrap Up—In this step, students generate questions and summarize the material. They synthesize the various ideas and concepts, demonstrating knowledge of the material.

Specific Uses

CSR can be used with students who have learning disabilities, as well as those who are reading at or above grade level and have specific needs related to understanding content material. CSR helps students to be more confident in learning the curriculum and improves the comprehension of students at all achievement levels in elementary and middle school (Klingner et al., 2001).

Significance to Curriculum Implementation in RTI Models

For learners who struggle with text comprehension, CSR provides interactive opportunities to acquire the skills needed to understand complex or unfamiliar material. This intervention relates directly to RTI curriculum implementation by giving students opportunities to adjust the process for previewing and reading text material in Tier 1 instruction, reducing the need for Tier 2 supplemental supports for some learners.

Explicit Instruction: Teacher-Scripted Lessons

Overview

Teacher-scripted lessons are teacher-generated lessons that draw on the strengths of both task analysis and explicit instruction in teaching and learning. Explicit instruction is a widely accepted intervention that serves as the foundation for several curriculum programs, such as Reading Mastery (Hummel, Venn, & Gunter, 2004). Utilizing explicit teaching principles, teacher-scripted lessons provide a sequential, structured process used to instruct students in various content areas, including reading and mathematics.

Process

Teacher-scripted lessons generally contain seven steps, described below (Hummel et al., 2004). These steps reflect direct and explicit instructional procedures:

1. *Gain Learners' Attention*—Teachers introduce the topic to be studied, clearly stating the purpose and outcomes for the learners.
2. *Review Prerequisite Knowledge/Skills*—Needed prerequisite skills are reviewed through questioning or sharing of prior experiences.
3. *Present New Content/Skill*—New material is task analyzed by being broken down into sequential steps as teachers follow a step-by-step process for modeling the content/skill.
4. *Probe Learning*—Once taught, along with rechecking to be certain that all steps were followed, students' learning is probed to determine the level of acquisition of new material. This is not formal assessment; rather, it is a period of small-group work, oral questioning, verbal rehearsal, or checks on individual responses to determine the level and extent of learning. Topics requiring additional modeling are identified and addressed.
5. *Independent Practice*—Once probing and any reteaching of steps have occurred, students are given independent practice tasks or activities in which more formal, individual assessment of acquired knowledge and

skills is performed. These tasks may occur over the course of several days and provide easy measures for monitoring student progress.

6. *Formal Assessment*—Learners are formally assessed on the material through the use of an assessment device or exam (e.g., multiple-choice test, performance-based assessment). These assessments may also occur over several days as evaluation of different aspects of the material is completed. It is important to be certain that the assessments evaluate the use of higher level thinking skills rather than only memorized material and that what is assessed relates directly to the objectives identified in Step 1. Instruction is adjusted based on the assessment results.

7. *Generalized Practice*—This final step provides learners with experiences that facilitate their application of the material beyond the classroom activities, as well as in conjunction with previously learned material. It promotes the use of higher level thinking skills such as comparing and contrasting or evaluating two or more events. Generalized practice is any type of assignment or task in which students apply and relate what they have learned beyond the classroom setting.

Specific Uses

Teacher-scripted lessons can be generated for any content area where the knowledge and skills to be taught can be sequentially ordered through a process that builds on basic knowledge acquisition and proceeds to higher level thinking (i.e., Bloom, Englehart, Furst, Hill, & Krathwohl, 1956). Scripted lessons can significantly improve teaching and learning for all students, especially those who require more highly directed procedures to initially grasp new concepts and material.

Significance to Curriculum Implementation in RTI Models

Teacher-scripted lessons easily blend into curriculum implementation within RTI in several ways in any tier of instruction. This includes the use of teacher-directed learning, periodic probes to monitor progress, adjustment of instruction based on probing results, and generalization of learned material, as well as individual practice to assist teachers in identifying struggling learners. Teachers may generate scripted lessons to differentiate the Tier 1 curriculum or to use as a foundation for Tiers 2 and 3 interventions.

Implementing the Curriculum with Fidelity

In addition to selecting and using a research-based curriculum and associated evidence-based interventions, teachers need to implement them in a manner consistent with the way each was developed, researched, and validated for effectiveness (i.e., fidelity; Mellard & Johnson, 2008). It is essential that educators follow procedures, steps, proper sequencing, and other elements in both the curriculum and the selected interventions to maintain fidelity in classroom teaching and learning (Bender & Shores, 2007; Sprague, Cook, Wright, & Sadler, 2008).

Fidelity and the Research-Based Curriculum

In general, teachers today use curricula that have been tested and researched in specific content areas and for identified grade levels. To implement research-based curricula with fidelity, at a minimum teachers should do the following:

1. Implement the curriculum in sequence as designed.
2. Teach all required concepts or skills (i.e., avoid eliminating items).
3. Provide sufficient differentiations to meet various needs.
4. Utilize supporting activities provided in the curriculum for enrichment or to assist learners who struggle.
5. Monitor progress in a manner consistent with the development of the curriculum.
6. Spend enough time on each topic to ensure proper acquisition, development, practice, and generalization.
7. Understand the curriculum, how it was developed, with whom it was researched, and provisions for dealing with cultural and linguistic diversity.

To best implement a researched-based curriculum, educators need enough knowledge of the program to understand (1) why the program was developed, (2) who it was designed to serve, (3) content skills and abilities to be acquired, and (4) appropriate differentiations that are consistent with the curriculum's focus. Knowledge of these elements facilitates two of the main aspects of fidelity: consistency and accuracy (Sprague et al., 2008), that is, ensuring that the curriculum is implemented accurately in a consistent manner. Preparation in these and related aspects of curriculum allows educators to make more informed decisions about necessary curricular adjustments and differentiations if learners demonstrate insufficient progress. Form 2.3 (*Fidelity of Implementation of Research-Based Curriculum*) provides a checklist for educators to use in documenting the fidelity of implementation of the research-based curriculum in each tier of instruction.

Fidelity and Evidence-Based Interventions

Fidelity in the use of evidence-based interventions is also essential to ensure proper implementation of multi-tiered instruction (Mellard & Johnson, 2008; Sprague et al., 2008). In Tier 1, differentiated instruction may include the use of various evidence-based interventions to differentiate the core curriculum for at-risk learners who do not yet show the need for Tier 2 supplemental supports. Evidence-based interventions are also an integral component of Tiers 2 and 3 instruction. To implement an evidence-based intervention with fidelity, at minimum the teacher should do the following:

1. Adhere to the clearly defined steps/procedures.
2. Use the intervention in teaching and learning only for the described purpose(s).
3. Use the intervention with populations of learners similar to the research populations.
4. Know the evidence showing the effectiveness of the intervention for its intended/stated purpose(s).
5. Know the intervention's researched conditions, classrooms, and settings.
6. When using the intervention, structure the classroom similarly to the researched classrooms to the extent possible.
7. Know that the intervention has been shown to be effective in a clearly defined school or field-based setting; be certain that the teacher's school or setting is similar.
8. Include only acceptable variations to the implementation of the intervention to accommodate diverse learners' needs while maintaining fidelity.
9. Be certain, to the extent possible, that the classroom population has the characteristics of the population for which the intervention was researched, tested, and shown to be effective, including students with culturally and linguistically diverse needs.

As these items indicate, in selecting and using evidence-based interventions, educators must understand for whom and under what conditions the interventions were designed. Fidelity obviously refers to following all the steps and procedures when using the intervention; however, in addition, fidelity means using the correct evidence-based intervention for the proper purpose. This includes:

1. Making certain that the classroom conditions in which the intervention was developed are generally replicated when used in the teacher's classroom.
2. Selecting and using only those interventions that have been validated for use in the classroom where the interventions are employed.
3. In Tiers 1 and 2, selecting interventions that support, not replace, the knowledge taught in the researched-based core curriculum.
4. Evaluating the effectiveness of the intervention in achieving progress in the area it was designed to impact (e.g., fluency, comprehension, science concepts, mathematics computations).

This is not to say that every intervention must be tested with every type of learner; this is not realistic or necessary. However, interventions that have built-in processes and parameters where learning differences are accommodated simultaneously for various students are best suited to meet the needs of all learners in any tier of RTI instruction. The evidence-based interventions discussed above all provide the opportunity to meet various needs in the same classroom. In addition, flexible, integrated instructional and classroom management greatly increases the potential for successful implementation of evidence-based interventions in conjunction with research-based curriculum. Form 2.4 (*Fidelity of Implementation of Evidence-Based Interventions*) provides a checklist for educators to use in documenting fidelity of implementation in each tier of instruction.

Transitioning from the Prereferral to the Response to Intervention Model

RTI models include a tier of intervention that is synonymous with special education. The highest tier is typically reserved for students with disabilities. In most models this is Tier 3, such as the one Mellard and Johnson (2008) described. Others have written that Tier 3 should include intensive interventions prior to special education, suggesting that a Tier 4 be added for special education serving students with disabilities (Klingner & Edwards, 2006). However, whether a school system employs a Tier 3 or Tier 4 system, the highest tier includes special education and, as such, requires all the due processes mandated by IDEA (2004).

Although RTI, in part, addresses some of the problems associated with previous prereferral models (e.g., waiting to fail, informal progress monitoring, uncertainty about the uses of research- and evidence-based curricula or interventions: Klingner, Hoover, & Baca, 2008), it also must address some of the factors that reflect the process for determining eligibility and placement in special education. As a result, tiered instruction and progress monitoring completed prior to a special education placement become what was previously referred to as *prereferral interventions* (Hoover, 2009a). In support, Kavale and Flanagan (2007) wrote that the "real value of RTI lies in the prospect of providing a systematic and rigorous prereferral process" (p. 134). Table 2.5 compares the components of prereferral and RTI models. The table was developed from information in several sources, including CDE (2008), Hoover (2009a), Hoover et al. (2008), Jimerson et al. (2007), and Klingner, Hoover, and Baca (2008).

As Table 2.5 shows, key practices in an RTI model reflect a more preventative and data-based approach than those used in the prereferral model of the last few decades. Although the prereferral model attempted to meet the needs

TABLE 2.5 Comparison of Prereferral and Multi-Tiered Response to Intervention Models

Prereferral Model	Multi-Tiered RTI Model
Prereferral model includes two primary types of instruction for struggling learners (prereferral interventions and special education)	*RTI model* includes three primary types of instruction for struggling learners (core instruction, supplemental supports, intensive interventions/special education)
School-wide screening of academic and behavioral progress is generally not completed	All learners are screened for academic and behavioral progress, usually three times per year
General class curriculum may or may not be research-based	General class curriculum is required to be research-based
Teaching interventions may or may not be evidence-based	Teaching interventions are required to be evidence-based
Discrepancy between intellectual capacity and actual achievement serves as the foundation for identifying a learning disability	Difference between expected grade-level achievement and actual achievement serves as the foundation for identifying a learning disability
Assessment of struggling learners relies heavily on norm-referenced measures	Assessment of struggling learners relies heavily on curriculum-based measures
Assessment efforts are designed to identify intrinsic disorders within the learner	Assessment efforts are designed to identify instructional effectiveness based on progress toward curricular benchmarks
General class teachers may or may not conduct curriculum-based measurement	General class teachers regularly conduct curriculum-based measurement
Progress of struggling learners is infrequently monitored using primarily informal classroom assessment practices	Progress of struggling learners is regularly monitored using standard measures and procedures
Struggling learners are initially identified through the use of informal classroom assessment results	Struggling learners are initially identified through the use of quantified classroom assessment screening data
Struggling learners who make inadequate progress in the general classroom must receive a comprehensive evaluation for special education prior to being provided targeted supports	Struggling learners who make inadequate progress in the general classroom are given targeted supports prior to making the decision to provide a comprehensive evaluation for special education
Struggling learners are required to exhibit problems for an extended period of time prior to receiving needed supports (i.e., wait to fail)	Struggling learners receive needed supports as soon as problems arise (i.e., prevention)

of struggling learners in the general classroom, these efforts were often less rigorous and structured than those seen in multi-tiered RTI models. Education for all learners within an RTI model is more proactive and preventative, as the needs of all learners, including struggling students and those with disabilities, are more fully addressed through research-based curriculum, evidence-based interventions, ongoing assessment, and associated decision making. In addition, the prereferral model relied heavily on determining a significant discrepancy between learning potential and achievement; in contrast, the RTI model emphasizes the discrepancy between actual and expected achievement along with the rate of progress. This, in turn, places greater emphasis on curriculum-based measurement rather than on the diagnostic testing used extensively in the prereferral model.

In making a successful transition from the prereferral model to an RTI multi-tiered model, several practices are suggested (Hoover, 2009a; Klingner, Mendez Barletta, & Hoover, 2008):

1. Focus on strengthening Tier 1 and Tier 2 curriculum implementation.
2. Conduct ongoing monitoring of student progress.
3. Chart/graph progress monitoring data to illustrate in quantitative terms learner growth or lack of progress.
4. Implement curricular adjustments as necessary in a timely, proactive manner.
5. Eliminate the recurring practice of looking for "deficits" within the learner and focus on instructional effectiveness.
6. Be certain to use only a research-based curriculum and evidence-based interventions.
7. Collaborate with other educators (e.g., general class teachers, special educators, interventionist, speech-language specialist) on a regular and supportive basis.
8. Use school and classroom structures that facilitate integrated learning, including all five components of the curriculum, when making instructional decisions.
9. Be certain that the research-based curriculum and evidence-based interventions are properly implemented (i.e., with fidelity).
10. Bear in mind that the long-term goal of problem-solving or child study teams is to determine the most effective instruction for learners rather than to identify deficits within the students.

The multi-tiered RTI model requires teachers to transition from the previous prereferral model by emphasizing the contemporary goal of meeting the needs of all learners. Table 2.6 provides selected questions and considerations associated with the five curricular components, which may assist educators in moving from the prereferral model to RTI.

As Table 2.6 shows, each of the five curricular components emphasized throughout this book has specific implications for and relevance to multi-tiered RTI models. The key questions and considerations identified in the table are ones that RTI teams should consider when determining the most appropriate tier of instruction.

This chapter concludes with *RTI Curriculum in Practice*, which presents one example of the varied needs and abilities students bring to a classroom that must be addressed simultaneously to transition successfully to the RTI model in the area of reading.

TABLE 2.6 Curricular Components: Transitioning from Prereferral to Response to Intervention

Component	Relevant RTI Questions	RTI Considerations
Content/Skills (Research-Based Curriculum)	Is the learner acquiring the content and skills being taught in the curriculum?	Progress toward content/skills serves as the basis for making curricular decisions
Evidence-Based Interventions	Is the selected evidence-based intervention assisting the learner to acquire necessary content/skills?	Effects of evidence-based interventions (used in a research-based curriculum) on progress toward mastery of content/skills serve as the basis for making curricular adjustments as necessary
Instructional Arrangements	Do the various classroom groupings and instructional settings (i.e., small or large group, independent work, cooperative learning) make it easier for students to use the selected evidence-based interventions and research-based curricula to acquire needed content/skills?	The role of different classroom settings on student progress is essential to know prior to making instructional adjustments
Class/Instructional Management Procedures	Are the classroom and instructional management procedures sufficient to facilitate self-management, increased time on task, and satisfactory progress in acquiring content/skills through the use of selected evidence-based interventions/research-based curricula?	Properly implemented evidence/research-based instruction has a limited chance to succeed if the class or instructional management lacks the necessary structure and consistency
Progress Evaluation	Is the progress being evaluated directly aligned with what is taught in the curriculum?	It is critical to ensure that the content/skills monitored are the same as those taught

RTI CURRICULUM IN PRACTICE

Meeting Second-Grade Classroom Reading Instructional Needs

Description

> Number of Students: 23
>
> Age: 7 and 8 years
>
> Ethnicities include Caucasian, African American, and Hispanic
>
> ELLs: four; all are limited English proficient (LEP)
>
> English Reading Level Ranges: first- through fourth-grade instructional levels

Overview of Curriculum Implementation

1. Implementation consists of highly teacher-directed instruction in which tasks are broken down and taught as sequential parts.
2. Some students learn best through cooperative learning, which facilitates verbal interaction among them.
3. Some students prefer approaches in which concepts and skills are initially taught in a holistic way rather than broken down into discrete parts.

(Continued)

4. Several students have difficulty remaining on task during whole-class, teacher-directed activities.

5. The four ELLs possess basic English reading and writing skills and have the most difficulty grasping and applying new concepts.

Differentiated Needs to Be Addressed

1. Four-grade-level range with instructional reading levels
2. Cultural relevancy to meet the needs of students with diverse ethnicities
3. Student preference for cooperative learning rather than direct instruction
4. Student preference for learning new concepts/skills initially holistically rather than as discrete parts
5. Varied time-on-task abilities
6. English language development needs when introducing/applying new concepts

RTI Curriculum Instructional and Management Issues

It is important to provide enough opportunities for all learners using a research-based reading curriculum by establishing a differentiated classroom and using evidence-based interventions to differentiate instruction to meet students' various needs, including cultural and linguistic needs. Scaffolding, cooperative learning, direct instruction, and self-monitoring, as well as opportunities to learn material in a more holistic way, are methods for differentiating instruction to meet the students' varied needs and preferences for learning.

RTI Curriculum Implementation Challenge

Make certain that students' various needs are initially addressed in Tier 1 (the core curriculum) and subsequently through Tier 2 (supplemental supports) if this is needed. As a result, varied needs should be considered when implementing instruction and assessment and generating informed instructional decisions based on RTI screening, monitoring, and/or diagnostic results.

RTI APPLICATIONS OF KEY CHAPTER CONCEPTS

Multi-tiered RTI is the contemporary model employed in schools to meet the needs of all learners. RTI emphasizes that all students must be given a high quality, research-based curriculum along with evidence-based interventions. In addition, the curriculum and interventions are to be implemented with the student populations and for the purposes for which they were developed, researched, and validated (i.e., fidelity). Numerous evidence-based interventions designed to provide structured, systematic instruction exist and are to be employed throughout the curriculum as Tier 1, 2, and 3 levels of instruction are delivered. The proper selection and use of a research-based curriculum and evidence-based interventions promote the transition from the previous preferral models to contemporary RTI models. This chapter concludes with several suggested tasks to facilitate the application of multi-tiered curricular topics that allows teachers to meet the needs of all learners in today's classrooms.

1. Select two of the evidence-based interventions presented in this chapter with which you are least familiar and implement them to acquire an understanding of each.
2. Evaluate your school's RTI model to determine the extent to which the five components of curriculum discussed in Chapter 1 are addressed in each tier of instruction.
3. Develop or expand your process for implementing a research-based curriculum in Tier 1 instruction (e.g., grade-level peer coaching/observations, schoolwide program).
4. Develop a PowerPoint presentation of the key factors necessary to help your colleagues make a smooth transition to the implementation of an RTI model.

School: _____   Date Completed: _____

Grade Level: ___ Primary (K–3)
(check all that apply)   ___ Intermediate (4–5)
    ___ Middle (6–8)
    ___ Secondary (9–12)

School RTI Leadership Team Members (list primary team members):

_____   _____
_____   _____
_____   _____
_____   _____

Instructions: Check the Multi-Tiered RTI Components currently in place in your school (*check all that apply and provide any relevant comments for each item*):

___ Universal Screening exists for all students (check areas):
    ___ Reading
    ___ Mathematics
    ___ Behavior
    ___ Science
    ___ Social Studies
    ___ Writing
    ___ Other: _____
Comments:

___ Tier 1 Research-Based Core Curriculum is in place for all grades (check areas):
    ___ Reading
    ___ Mathematics
    ___ Writing
    ___ Science
    ___ Social Studies
    ___ Behavior Schoolwide Supports
    ___ Other: _____
Comments:

___ Practices and procedures for providing Tier 2 Supplemental Supports are established
Comments:

___ Practices and procedures for providing Tier 3 Intensive Interventions are established
Comments:

___ School-based multi-tiered RTI decision-making team has been established
Comments:

___ Process (i.e., Decision Rules) for identifying Tiers 2 or 3 instructional needs is clearly established
Comments:

___ District approved Evidence-Based Interventions have been identified
Comments:

___ All instruction includes use of evidence-based interventions
Comments:

___ Fidelity of implementation contains process for corroborating effective instruction using:
    ___ Tier 1 research-based core curriculum
    ___ Tier 2 supplemental supports
    ___ Tier 3 intensive interventions
Comments:

___ Fidelity of implementation contains process for corroborating effective assessment:
    ___ Universal screening
    ___ Progress monitoring
    ___ Diagnostic assessment
Comments:

___ Curriculum-based progress-monitoring procedures exist in all classrooms
Comments:

___ Guidelines for determining an adequate rate of progress are established
Comments:

___ Gap Analysis procedures are defined for each subject and grade level
Comments:

___ Schoolwide data-driven decision-making procedures are clearly articulated
Comments:

___ Procedures for referring a learner for special education are established
Comments:

___ Procedures for determining special education eligibility for learning disabilities are established
Comments:

___ Other (Specify):

_____

Source: Used by permission of John J. Hoover.

School: _____   Date Completed: _____

Grade Level: ___ Primary (K–3)
(*check all that apply*)   ___ Intermediate (4–5)
                                ___ Middle (6–8)
                                ___ Secondary (9–12)

Instructions: Check the multi-tiered RTI training completed with school staff (*check all that apply and provide any relevant comments for each item*):

All educators have received RTI training in the following (check all that apply):

___ Tier 1 Universal Screening
Comments:

___ Schoolwide Behavior Supports
Comments:

___ Curriculum-based progress monitoring procedures (e.g., CBM)
Comments:

___ Procedures for graphing screening and monitoring results
Comments:

___ Multi-Tiered Instruction
        ___ Tier 1
        ___ Tier 2
        ___ Tier 3
Comments:

___ Strategies for implementing curriculum with fidelity
Comments:

___ Procedures for corroborating implementation of curricula with fidelity
Comments:

___ Procedures for corroborating implementation of assessment with fidelity
Comments:

___ Procedures followed by school-based RTI problem-solving team
Comments:

___ Process followed in the identification of students requiring Tier 2 Supplemental Supports
Comments:

___ Process followed in the identification of students requiring Tier 3 Intensive Interventions
Comments:

___ Process and procedures used to make data-driven decisions
Comments:

___ Referral procedures for special education
Comments:

___ Eligibility criteria for learning disabilities
Comments:

___ Other (specify):
Comments:

Source: Used by permission of John J. Hoover.

FORM 2.3 Fidelity of Implementation of Research-Based Curriculum

Title of Research-Based Curriculum: _____

Content/Topic Area Addressed: _____

Primary Method(s) for Completion (Check each that applies):
  ___ Direct Observation by Colleague
  ___ Self-Reporting
  ___ Interview

Instructions: Record evidence that corroborates the extent of implementation of the research-based curriculum. Provide comments as appropriate.

| 1 = Little/None | 2 = Some but Limited | 3 = Adequate | 4 = Extensive |

The extent to which the identified research-based curriculum is . . .

___ Clearly understood by the teacher
Comments:

___ Consistently implemented in the classroom
Comments:

___ Differentiated appropriately to meet a variety of learning needs
Comments:

___ Applied in teaching and learning for the specific purpose(s) for which it was designed
Comments:

___ Implemented using all recommended and prescribed steps and procedures
Comments:

___ Implemented in a manner that facilitates effective teacher–student interactions
Comments:

___ Integrated into the classroom structure by facilitating effective physical proximity between teacher and students
Comments:

Summary of Fidelity of Implementation of a Research-Based Curriculum:

Source: Used by permission of John J. Hoover.

Fidelity of Implementation of Evidence-Based Interventions

Title of Evidence-Based Intervention: _____

Content/Topic Area Addressed: _____

Primary Method(s) Used for Completion (check each that applies):

___ Direct Observation by Colleague   ___ Self-Reporting   ___ Interview

Instructions: Record evidence that corroborates the extent of implementation of the evidence-based intervention. Provide comments as appropriate.

1 = Little/None   2 = Some but Limited   3 = Adequate   4 = Extensive

The extent to which the identified evidence-based intervention is . . .

___ Clearly understood by the teacher
Comments:

___ Consistently implemented in the classroom
Comments:

___ Applied in teaching and learning for the specific purpose(s) for which it was designed
Comments:

___ Implemented using all recommended and prescribed steps and procedures
Comments:

___ Implemented in a manner that facilitates effective teacher–student interactions
Comments:

___ Integrated into the classroom structure by facilitating effective physical proximity between teacher and students
Comments:

Summary of Fidelity of Implementation of Evidence-Based Intervention:

Source: Used by permission of John J. Hoover.

CHAPTER 3

Response to Intervention Assessment to Meet Curricular Needs

▶ ## Overview

RTI MODELS STRESS THE importance of quickly pinpointing learners' needs once they surface in Tier 1 core instruction, as well as the systematic monitoring of progress within Tiers 2 and 3 instruction. This leads to the all-important task of making adjustments to the curriculum to meet a variety of classroom needs for all learners. Informed instructional adjustments are based on the data gathered through three core forms of curricular assessment (universal screening, progress monitoring, diagnostic assessment). In addition, the five curricular components give decision-making teams a more complete picture of the effects of instruction on learners' progress toward academic and behavioral benchmarks. Curriculum-based measurement, performance-based assessment, and functional behavioral assessment are three types of assessment that facilitate the accurate evaluation of student progress by adhering to systematic and standardized procedures. Multi-tiered RTI models present today's educators with the

challenge of accurately and objectively determining all students' progress toward curricular benchmarks. Careful consideration of the total instructional environment is essential to meet this challenge as curricular assessments are conducted with all learners.

Key Topics

- ▶ Universal screening
- ▶ Progress monitoring
- ▶ Diagnostic assessment
- ▶ Process of identifying RTI needs
- ▶ Curriculum-based measurement
- ▶ Functional behavioral assessment
- ▶ Performance-based assessment
- ▶ Managing RTI assessment needs within the curriculum

Learner Outcomes

After reading this chapter, you should:

1. Acquire an in-depth understanding of universal screening and progress monitoring, including gap analysis, rate of progress, cut scores, and decision rules

2. Acquire the skills needed to clarify RTI instructional needs for learners relative to the five essential curricular components

3. Be able to select the proper response to intervention instructional methods

4. Be able to identify how the curricular components are associated with data generated through universal screening, progress monitoring, and diagnostic assessment results

5. Acquire the ability to implement curriculum-based measurement, functional behavioral assessment, and performance-based assessment within RTI models

SIGNIFICANCE TO CONTEMPORARY CLASSROOM INSTRUCTION

Perhaps the most critical multi-tiered decision for all learners is determining curricular needs once lack of progress has been identified. Within the multi-tiered structure, three types of assessment are generally conducted (universal screening, progress monitoring, diagnostic), and each of them yields assessment results that relate specifically to curriculum implementation. Stated simply, the correct curricular need(s) must be identified and adjusted for multi-tiered RTI to be successful for all students, especially struggling learners. For the proper identification of curricular needs, the assessment process and procedures must be valid, reliable, and standardized. This is extremely important because some learners with inadequate progress may eventually be referred to special education. Therefore, assessment must be accurate in identifying RTI progress toward curricular benchmarks/objectives to best assist all learners.

Overview of Assessment within Response to Intervention

Coupled with selecting and implementing a research-based curriculum and evidence-based interventions is the process of determining the effects of those efforts on student progress towards benchmarks and related objectives (Hoover, 2009a). RTI models are mainly designed to ensure that students receive high quality teaching in each tier of instruction. This includes the need to closely monitor learners' progress based on grade- and age-level proficiency achievement and behavioral data. Therefore, although effective curriculum implementation is the foundation for RTI, assessment data provide the basis for making tiered curriculum implementation decisions. This includes the use of regular screening and monitoring of progress by determining (1) the student's actual level of proficiency (i.e., above or below the district-established cut score); (2) the magnitude of the gap between expected and actual level of achievement if the latter is below the cut score; and (3) the student's rate of progress even if the level of achievement is below cut score expectations (Fuchs & Fuchs, 2006; Mellard & Johnson, 2008). Each of these aspects of assessment is discussed below, with emphasis on the link between RTI assessment and curriculum implementation.

Assessment Continuum and Curriculum Implementation

RTI emphasizes the use of three primary types of assessment associated with each tier of instruction. These are:

1. *Universal Screening*—Assessment of all learners to identify those who may be at risk for or finding it difficult to achieve grade-level academic and/or behavioral benchmarks (i.e., struggling learners). It usually occurs three times per academic year.

2. *Progress Monitoring*—Assessment of selected learners to clarify the effectiveness of instruction by determining levels of proficiency and rate of progress toward grade-level academic and/or behavioral benchmarks. It involves learners who require more frequent monitoring of progress toward growth (e.g., monthly, biweekly).

3. *Diagnostic*—Assessment conducted on an individual basis to further clarify learners' needs for the purpose of providing more individualized instruction and/or determining eligibility for special education due to a disability. It usually involves students who have greater needs; however, it may also be used in conjunction with progress monitoring to further clarify suspected educational needs.

Like curriculum implementation, assessment within each tier increases in duration and intensity based on students' needs, as illustrated (Hoover, 2009a):

Universal Screening	Progress Monitoring	Diagnostic Assessment
Tier 1	*Tiers 1, 2, 3*	*Tiers 2, 3*

Each type of assessment is discussed briefly below; more detailed descriptions are found in other literature sources, and the reader is referred to those cited in this section. In the following discussions, the primary purpose is to clarify when and under what conditions each assessment type should be employed. The reader will gain a greater understanding of the connection between RTI assessment and curriculum implementation. This connection must be clearly understood to successfully educate all learners within multi-tiered RTI models.

UNIVERSAL SCREENING ■ The first step in determining the effectiveness of Tier 1 core instruction within an RTI model is to screen all learners for progress toward curricular benchmarks (Fuchs & Fuchs, 2006). This type of assessment is referred to as *universal screening* because it screens all learners, not simply those who already demonstrate potential learning problems. The purpose of universal screening is to identify early in the school year those students who are showing signs of struggling or otherwise making inadequate progress toward the grade-level benchmarks (Howell et al., 2008). Specifically, universal screening (1) provides evidence of the effectiveness of the core curriculum (i.e., Tier 1) and (2) identifies learners who are making inadequate progress in the Tier 1 core curriculum. Note, however, that universal screening must initially show that approximately 80% of all students in the school, grade, or classroom are making adequate progress toward curricular benchmarks; if not, the "school must improve the core curriculum and/or the manner in which the curriculum is delivered" (SERC, 2008).

Also, according to the National Association of State Directors of Special Education (NASDSE), an important purpose of universal screening is to identify teachers who may require additional support to implement the Tier 1 core curriculum with fidelity (NASDSE, 2005). A key feature of universal screening when assessing curricular progress is that it "uses short, quick, and easy-to-administer probes that are aligned to the curriculum and measure specific skills a student has achieved" (McCook, 2006, p. 13).

School systems nationwide use a variety of instruments to complete their universal screenings. Below is a list of some of the instruments or processes used, as identified by current research and literature reviews (e.g., the Iris Center Web site, the National Center for Learning Disabilities):

Systematic Screening for Behavior Disorders (SSBD; Walker & Severson, 1990)

Dynamic Indicators of Basic Early Literacy Skills (DIBELS; Kaminsky & Good, 1996)

Developmental Reading Assessment 2 (DRA, 2007)

Phonological Awareness and Literacy Screening-K (Invernizzi, Swank, Juel, & Meier, 2003)

AIMSweb Progress Monitoring and RTI System (http://www.aimsweb.com/)

Curriculum-Based Measurement (CBM; Deno, 1985)

Dynamic Assessment (Compton, Fuchs, Fuchs, & Bryant, 2006)

In addition, some school systems use various subtests in normative diagnostic assessment devices (e.g., Gates-MacGinitie Reading Tests; Woodcock Johnson III) for screening purposes. These screening instruments and processes illustrate the wide variety of methods/devices that may be used for universal screening. However, it is extremely important that the devices/practices be suitable for screening what is directly taught in the curriculum:

If a disconnect exists between what is taught in the curriculum and what is assessed through universal screening, there is a great risk of false positives, leading to increased misinterpretation of universal screening results and the erroneous implementation of Tier 2 supplemental supports.

In summary, whatever device or process is used, several key points must be considered for universal screening to be effective in determining that approximately 80% of the students are achieving benchmarks and identifying those who appear to be struggling. The following list was compiled from several sources, including Fuchs and Fuchs (2006), Hoover (2009a), Klingner et al.

(2008), and Mellard and Johnson (2008). The keys to effective use of universal screening include the following:

1. Devices must be used that match the curriculum being taught to avoid erroneously identifying achievement gaps that do not exist.

2. False positives may be found, emphasizing the need for multiple screenings throughout the academic year.

3. Universal screening should occur three times per year.

4. To avoid unnecessary Tier 2 instruction based on one universal screening test, students whose scores are slightly below the cut score (e.g., less than 1 year) should have their progress monitored more closely for approximately 5–6 weeks to corroborate the universal screening score.

5. Universal screening focuses on *identifying* students who might be struggling rather than *diagnosing* learning problems, and screening scores should be interpreted with this in mind.

6. Universal screening provides evidence early in the school year that a student is at risk or is struggling with learning.

7. Like curriculum implementation, universal screening must be implemented with fidelity.

8. Universal screening leads to one of three curricular decisions: (a) continue with current Tier 1 core instruction; (b) monitor the student's progress more closely for 5–6 weeks to confirm the universal screening scores by implementing targeted differentiations in suspected Tier 1 curricular areas of need; and/or (c) initiate Tier 2 evidence-based interventions because the student is significantly below benchmarks or is making inadequate progress (e.g., the student is 1–2 years below the benchmark).

When universal screening results and subsequent decisions clearly indicate that the learner is below the cut score, is making inadequate progress, and shows a significant gap between expected and actual classroom performance compared to grade- or age-level peers, Tier 2 supplemental supports should be implemented in a timely manner. The second type of assessment along the RTI assessment continuum, referred to as *progress monitoring*, is discussed next.

PROGRESS MONITORING ■ The second level of assessment in RTI is more frequent assessment to monitor learners' progress more closely (Mellard & Johnson, 2008). Whereas universal screening generally occurs three times per year, progress monitoring is done monthly, weekly, or sometimes daily, depending on the level, duration, and intensity of the tiered instruction. For example, Stecker, Fuchs, and Fuchs (2005) suggested that weekly progress monitoring may be needed for some learners.

Whether performed monthly, weekly, or daily, progress monitoring is a major departure from the previous prereferral models. Its purpose is to allow teachers to make necessary curricular adjustments in a timely manner. Progress monitoring becomes necessary once universal screening indicates a potential struggling learner in Tier 1 or when supplemental or intensive supports in Tiers 2 and 3 are considered necessary. Progress monitoring serves several useful functions in the implementation of an RTI model. It:

1. Gives educators more frequent updates on learner progress.
2. Helps educators determine if the research-based curriculum and evidence-based interventions are helping students to make adequate progress and/or reduce the gap between expected and actual achievement.
3. Provides general class educators with additional data to confirm the initial universal screening score.
4. Allows educators to assess more closely and more frequently the connections between what is taught and student learning.

Hoover (2009a, p. 30) described several steps to follow in implementing progress monitoring:

- Identify skill to be monitored (e.g., oral reading fluency, math computation skills).
- Select/develop valid assessment measures to quickly assess skills (i.e., 1–2 minutes) that directly reflect the instruction of the target skills (oral reading [of a] passage at [the] second-grade level).
- Determine monitoring schedule (monthly, weekly).
- Conduct assessment, adhering to the established schedule.
- Graph or chart the results of each assessment.
- Evaluate level of performance and rate of progress (e.g., progress towards developing math computation skills).
- Adjust instruction based on progress monitoring data.
- Continue with ongoing progress monitoring, chart results, and adjust instruction as needed.

Several commercial programs and organizations provide materials and procedures for progress monitoring (e.g., AIMSWeb, Spectrum K12, DIBELS), as well as resources found in most research-based curricula. The reader is referred to these and similar sources.

Although universal screening provides initial data for making screening decisions about the effectiveness of the research-based curriculum, progress monitoring is critical to the success of RTI. It provides the data-driven foundation for determining the effectiveness of evidence-based interventions, especially in Tiers 2 and 3. Below are three examples of the proper application of progress monitoring in curriculum implementation.

▶ **Scenario 1:** The universal screening score (e.g., September screening) indicates a potential struggling learner who is less than 6 months below the expected achievement level. Because the learner is not too far behind, he may simply need more time to demonstrate adequate growth in the Tier 1 core curriculum rather than the immediate use of Tier 2 services. In this situation, the learner continues to receive the Tier 1 core curriculum for a brief, specified period of time (e.g., 5–6 weeks). In implementing the core curriculum during this time, the classroom teacher should provide differentiations that target the suspected area of need (e.g., fluency, time on task), in addition to the other general differentiations already included in the differentiated classroom structure. The student's progress should be monitored every 10–15 school days. In many situations, simply giving the learner additional time, along with targeted Tier 1 differentiations, is enough to help the learner make the same progress as his or her grade- and age-level peers. If, after the 5- to 6-week period, results show that the student is still not making progress, the teacher has corroborated the universal screening score, leading to the consideration of Tier 2 supplemental support. However, if sufficient progress is shown, then Tier 2 supplemental supports are not necessary for this student at this time. In this scenario, universal screening and progress monitoring are used together in Tier 1 core instruction to identify students who require Tier 2 supplemental supports. This serves several key needs within RTI. It (1) provides Tier 2 or 3 interventions only if necessary, (2) keeps the student's education within the Tier 1 core curriculum as much as possible, (3) reduces the number of students who unnecessarily receive Tier 2 instruction, ensuring that those who need Tier 2 receive it, and (4) maintains the integrity of implementing research-based curricula and evidence-based interventions in preventative ways in the general education classroom.

▶ **Scenario 2:** Universal screening results indicate that a learner is more than 1 year below her grade- and age-level peers and is not making adequate progress toward curricular benchmarks. Unlike the student in Scenario 1, this learner needs Tier 2 supplemental supports immediately; there is no need to give her additional time to corroborate the universal testing score. In Tier 2 instruction, the learner is given additional assistance in targeting the Tier 1 curricular areas of need (e.g., reading fluency, time on task) for a specified period of time (e.g., additional fluency work in a small-group setting for 30 minutes per day for 10 weeks). The learner's progress toward the benchmark in the targeted area is monitored biweekly or monthly, and the results are charted to illustrate progress. It is important to keep in mind that the progress monitoring conducted in conjunction with Tier 2 supplemental supports must directly assess progress toward what is taught, and what is taught in Tier 2 must directly support the development of Tier 1 benchmarks identified as requiring additional assistance. As with universal screening, if Tier 2 supports do not align with the deficit benchmarks in Tier 1, progress monitoring may show progress with Tier 2 supports but may not translate back to progress toward Tier 1 benchmarks given the potential disconnect.

Educators must ensure that both the Tier 2 supplemental supports and the associated progress monitoring are directly aligned with Tier 1 core curricular benchmarks to avoid making progress within Tier 2 instruction that does not relate back to progress within the Tier 1 core curriculum.

In addition, if Tier 2 progress monitoring fails to show adequate progress, then an additional round of supports should be provided with necessary curricular adjustments (Vaughn, 2003). Progress monitoring is continued. If the learner makes adequate progress in Tier 2, and if the support allows sufficient growth and "catching up" toward benchmarks, then Tier 2 supports may be discontinued. However, if not enough progress is demonstrated, then the learner may require more intensive Tier 3 interventions.

▶ **Scenario 3:** The learner has been given at least two rounds of Tier 2 supplemental supports and has failed to make adequate progress or close the gap between expected and actual achievement. At this point in RTI models, more significant needs may be evident and more intensive interventions are warranted, along with closer monitoring of progress. As previously discussed, Tier 3 is reserved for learners who have greater needs and who do not make adequate progress with Tier 2 supports. Tier 3 interventions occur more frequently (e.g., twice daily for 15 weeks in one-one or paired/small-group setting), and progress is monitored and charted much more often (e.g., three times per week). Tier 3 interventions may include the use of alternate research-based curricula and more intensive evidence-based interventions to meet learning or behavioral needs. Although Tier 3 is more intensive than Tier 2, progress monitoring is similar to that described above.

As the three scenarios show, evidence-based interventions and progress monitoring are fundamental to meeting the needs of all students in any tier of instruction. However, two factors warrant additional discussion: (1) frequency of progress monitoring and (2) selection of evidence-based interventions.

FREQUENCY OF PROGRESS MONITORING   Given the many tasks required of today's educators, progress monitoring should occur only as necessary and appropriate to monitor progress; often it is done monthly or every other week. If monitoring is done more often (e.g., daily or weekly), the educator must be sure that this is necessary to obtain valid progress results. This ensures the most effective use of the teacher's valuable time.

SELECTING EVIDENCE-BASED INTERVENTIONS   There may be some confusion about which interventions are most appropriate in different tiers of instruction. More specifically, it is important to avoid artificial restraints by believing that certain evidence-based interventions are only appropriate for a specific tier. For example, direct instruction and scaffolding are both appropriate for use in Tiers 1, 2, and 3. The manner and duration of their use will vary based on learners' needs. Educators should maintain an "inclusion" attitude when making evidence-based decisions, as curricular adjustments are made based on screening, monitoring, or diagnostic results.

However, if progress monitoring continues to indicate a lack of adequate progress and/or lack of sufficient proficiency in the achievement of benchmarks in curriculum that has been properly implemented, then consideration of the third level of assessment may be warranted.

DIAGNOSTIC ASSESSMENT ▪

The most targeted form of assessment in RTI is diagnostic assessment, in which evaluation is more detailed. Diagnostic assessment is often used in a comprehensive evaluation for special education; however, it is also appropriate for other purposes. According to Pierangelo and Giuliani (2006), diagnostic assessment is an individualized form of assessment designed to identify individual student academic/behavioral needs and/or a disability. Building on the progress monitoring results, diagnostic assessment should provide enough information to "diagnose" individual learning needs and strengths and generate recommendations for Tier 3 interventions (e.g., specialized instruction and methods). However, unlike the prereferral models, determining a discrepancy between potential and achievement is not a primary goal of diagnostic assessment.

Diagnostic assessment in the RTI model focuses on pinpointing curricular academic and behavioral needs based on (1) the gap between expected and actual performance, (2) the rate of progress, and (3) the classroom and instructional behaviors exhibited by the learner. Therefore, although instruments such as the Woodcock-Johnson III, the Test of Early Reading Ability, or other standardized general achievement tests may still be used, their purpose in diagnostic assessments in RTI models is to further clarify curriculum instructional and management needs rather than to identify discrepancies between achievement and potential or deficits within the learner. As a result, diagnostic assessment in RTI models achieves three objectives: (1) it further clarifies universal screening and progress monitoring results to specify learning/behavior needs; (2) it helps educators to determine eligibility for special education; and (3) it facilitates the gathering of information to be included in an individualized education plan (IEP) if special education placement is warranted.

RTI models mark a significant advance in student assessment over the prereferral models. Today, emphasis is placed on ensuring that all learners are first given a high quality, research-based curriculum and evidence-based interventions. These must be implemented with fidelity in the general education setting before any suspected disability or learning problem is considered (Bender & Shores, 2007). In addition, the initial assessment for instructional decision making is *followed by* assessment for diagnosis (if necessary) of a suspected disability. This is the reverse of the procedure used over the past few decades (i.e., diagnosis for disability first, then determination of instructional needs on the IEP). Periodic reference to the three types of assessment helps teachers ensure that proper assessment is done in each tier of instruction. It also reinforces the interconnectedness of the three assessment types, along with their relevance in making informed, data-based curricular decisions. To meet the wide-ranging assessment needs of universal screening, progress monitoring, and diagnostic assessment, numerous assessment practices may be used; several of these are described below.

Response to Intervention Assessment Practices

An effective and efficient way to monitor progress or otherwise evaluate curricular effectiveness when students have a variety of needs is to use proven assessment practices implemented directly within the curriculum. This concept is essential to the implementation of RTI models. Table 3.1, developed from information in various sources (Hosp et al., 2007; Moran & Malott, 2004; O'Malley & Pierce, 1996), provides an overview of several such assessment practices. Most classroom teachers are familiar with these practices. They are briefly presented to illustrate how different assessment practices contribute to curriculum implementation within RTI models.

As Table 3.1 shows, a variety of practices may be used for assessment in RTI. Also, as the reader may recall, some of these practices were presented in Chapter 2 as evidence-based interventions. When used for both instruction and decision making, these assessment practices serve two important integrated purposes: (1) assessment for instruction and (2) instruction with embedded assessment procedures. Like curriculum implementation, assessment practices must be used with fidelity to ensure that accurate data are gathered. Fidelity in both assessment and curriculum makes the interconnections between assessment and curriculum implementation meaningful for all learners. Form 3.1 (*Guide for Fidelity of Assessment Devices and Practices*) provides a guide to assist educators to determine the extent to which they use selected assessment devices and practices with fidelity.

Although a detailed discussion of each of the assessment practices is beyond the scope of this book, following is an in-depth description of three of the practices presented in Table 3.1 due to their use and importance in RTI models: curriculum-based measurement, functional behavioral assessment, and performance-based assessment. These methods further illustrate the

TABLE 3.1 Assessment Practices in Response to Intervention Curriculum Implementation

Assessment Practice	Significance to Curriculum Implementation and Decision Making
Task Analysis	Assists in analyzing students' strengths and weaknesses by breaking down tasks into discrete parts and subtasks
Curriculum-Based Measurement	Evidence-based strategy for measuring student progress in a standardized way using valid measures
Performance-Based Assessment	Assessment practice in which student progress is monitored by evaluation of a constructed response or product
Running Records	Record of the reading behaviors of beginning readers while reading for a specified amount of time (e.g., 10 minutes)
Portfolio Assessment	Assessment process in which students compile a collection of work designed to illustrate their educational knowledge, skills, and growth
Functional Behavioral Assessment	A technique based on the idea that behavior serves some meaningful function for the learner
Analytic Teaching	Analyzes the behaviors of learners engaged in a specific task designed to target identified behaviors
Cross-Cultural Interview	The interviewer discusses with the interviewee the cultural and linguistic background of the learner to determine the extent to which the learner's behaviors reflect a diverse background
Language Samples	Documented samples of student uses of language obtained to analyze the student's thinking skills, vocabulary, and contextual uses
Classroom Observations	Provides firsthand knowledge of student academic and socio-emotional behaviors exhibited in the instructional environment
Review Existing Records	Frames learner characteristics in a historical context, determines prior interventions used, and ascertains perceptions of previous teachers
Work Samples Analysis	Identify patterns, consistencies, and strengths of student work

connections between assessment and curriculum implementation in multi-tiered RTI models. The reader is referred to the sources cited in the development of the table for additional information about each of the assessment practices.

Curriculum-Based Measurement (CBM)

Overview

CBM is a standardized method for measuring progress toward benchmarks, objectives, or skills directly related to the curriculum (Deno, 1985; Hosp et al., 2007). It provides educators with "reliable, valid and efficient indicators of academic competence" (Fuchs & Fuchs, 2007, p. 31). CBM measures three different types of performance, each of which may be assessed, depending on the skills/abilities being acquired, as discussed by Hosp et al. (2007).

GENERAL OUTCOME MEASURES (GOMs) ■ Measurement of the learner's performance that includes the use of several related or contributing skills that address several goals within one task is a general outcome measure. A GOM task, by its nature, requires the learner to utilize several skills simultaneously rather than individually. Specifically, "success or improvement on the GOM is assumed to reflect the synthetic application of the contributing skills" (Hosp et al., 2007, p. 11). One frequently used GOM is the assessment of oral reading fluency, in which the interrelated skills of accuracy, rate, and comprehension are blended in one measure (e.g., fluency rate while reading a 100-word passage or number of words read correctly in 2 minutes). An assessment measure such as oral reading fluency is considered a GOM because the learner must simultaneously use a variety of subskills (e.g., letter usage skills, sound–symbol skills, syntax) to complete the task successfully (i.e., inability to use one or more subskills correctly directly influences the fluency rate). Therefore, rather than assessing each subskill, the learner is assessed on the overall result based on the need to use the subskills simultaneously.

▶ **Using GOMs in Curriculum Implementation and RTI Assessment:** The GOM approach within CBM is most appropriate for screening and progress monitoring of student achievement toward year-end benchmarks to assess a student's general level of performance within a broad curricular context (e.g., reading fluency, reading comprehension, mathematics reasoning). Another advantage of using GOMs within CBM is that it requires learners to apply interrelated subskills simultaneously in authentic classroom situations (e.g., using multiple reading subskills to achieve reading comprehension). When used three or four times per year, a GOM approach within CBM provides educators with a systemic approach to measure progress toward year-end benchmarks in which a single task captures the collective use of subskills.

Because a GOM is designed to assess general progress toward benchmarks, it is not appropriate for identifying strengths or weaknesses in the use of specific subskills (Hosp et al., 2007). A GOM will alert a teacher to the possibility, for example, that a learner has poor oral reading fluency or mathematics reasoning abilities. However, it will not pinpoint or specify which subskill(s) need most attention; it will only show that the curriculum must be adjusted to achieve the desired results. Additionally, some sets of skills cannot be adequately assessed through a single task and therefore cannot be measured with a GOM (e.g., various mathematics computation skills, selected science concepts).

SKILLS-BASED MEASURES (SBMs) ■ In some cases, an individual assessment activity, such as reading a single 100-word passage, cannot measure a group or set of skills simultaneously because each subskill may be used or applied at different times based on its intended use. One such content area is mathematics computation, in which several skills are acquired throughout the academic year and no single task requires the use of all of them simultaneously. However, proficiency in all the mathematics computation subskills demonstrates adequate progress toward achievement of the year-end mathematics computation benchmark. Therefore, although the learner must become proficient in all the subksills, a different type of CBM is required than the GOM discussed above. In the mathematics computation situation, the learner completes a series of computations within the same assessment task, but each problem is completed independently of the others (e.g., completion of a page of 15 mathematics computation problems, each assessing a different grade-level skill, yet collectively they represent all the main computation skills to be learned within the specified grade).

▶ **Using SBMs in Curriculum Implementation and RTI Assessment:** When the goal is to assess progress toward a collection of individual abilities and no one task captures all the skills, a skills-based form of CBM is appropriate. SBMs may be used for screening as well as progress monitoring of student proficiency. Like GOMs, skills-based assessment measures progress toward annual benchmarks. As a result, at any given time during the academic year, some of the items on a skills-based device may be too easy, may reflect current instruction, or may be too difficult because they have not yet been taught. However, each skills-based device should reflect a cross section of all the major skills to be taught and learned throughout the school year. When administered three or four times per year, a skills-based CBM will provide timely screening results in which learners systematically demonstrate progress toward overall grade-level skills.

MASTERY MEASURES (MMs) ■ When the goal of the RTI assessment is to determine progress toward discrete subskills, the MM form of CBM should be used. In this type of assessment, proficiency with individual skills is assessed, such as proficiency with capitalization, phonemic awareness, or single-digit addition. This assessment of one skill at a time often reflects an individual learning objective emphasized within the curriculum. MMs are valuable for assessing those skills, which may more easily be measured in isolation to facilitate overall instructional decision making. MMs within CBM assist the progress monitoring of individual skills or subskills, which in turn are used within a broader academic context (e.g., vocabulary knowledge related to reading comprehension).

▶ **Using MMs in Curriculum Implementation and RTI Assessment:** MMs within CBM are valuable forms of progress monitoring when targeted demonstration of skills is desired. When used in the implementation of the curriculum, MMs monitor progress toward individual skills that are necessary for broader application in learning (e.g., phonemic awareness, necessary for reading fluency). MMs are also very useful in pinpointing specific areas of need once GOMs or SBMs indicate overall lack of proficiency or progress toward annual grade-level benchmarks (Hosp et al., 2007). Therefore, MMs are used within CBM to provide specific information on learners' needs, whereas GOMs and SBMs provide a more general view of learners' progress or proficiency.

CBM Process

A major strength of CBM for curriculum assessment in RTI models is its use in the classroom setting to measure progress or proficiency toward year-end benchmarks and a range of specific skills or subskills (Mellard & Johnson, 2008). As a result, CBM can be implemented in a variety of ways in the classroom; however, a standardized process is required to compare performance across time and multiple assessments. Below is a summary of the key components, developed from discussions of CBM in several sources, to include in the implementation of CBM (Fuchs & Fuchs, 2006; Hoover, 2009a; Hosp et al., 2007; Howell et al., 2008):

Proper CBM Procedures During Initial and Subsequent Administrations

- The same directions are given to the learner.
- The same time frame is used for completion of the task (e.g., 1 minute).
- The same task structure is used (e.g., a 100-word passage, 25 mathematics problems).
- The same procedures are used to score the completed task.
- Each CBM task reflects the same set of skills being assessed.
- The material used in subsequent CBM tasks is similar in scope, content, and skills assessed but is not identical to the material in the previous CBM session (e.g., the 100-word passage selected is different from the previous 100-word passage; both passages assess similar skills and abilities, and are equivalent in content and in degree of reading difficulty).
- When CBM is initially used to establish a baseline, this should be determined by averaging the results of the first three administrations.
- CBM results should be consistently charted to illustrate progress over time.

When implementing CBM, it is extremely important to standardize the process so that each administration is completed the same way as the previous one. All that changes from one administration to the next is the use of similar, *not identical*, materials that assess the same skills and abilities. In some instances, CBM procedures are commercially developed, along with standardized instructions and procedures (e.g., AIMSweb, DIBELS); in others, the classroom teacher may need to develop a simple CBM task. In this case, documenting and following a standard process is necessary.

CBM is an efficient and effective means for screening and monitoring the progress of all students, including those who are struggling. Additionally, CBM results may be used in the diagnostic assessment aspects of RTI because all available progress data should be included in a comprehensive assessment. In summary, CBM:

1. Assesses what is taught (i.e., students are tested on material directly related to the classroom curriculum)

2. Assists educators with data-based instructional decision making

3. Is a quick, easy, and time-efficient procedure for screening and monitoring progress and proficiency levels that is research based and has been shown to be effective over time

4. Provides valuable information for making informed decisions about curricular adjustments

5. Helps classroom teachers to effectively communicate student proficiency levels and progress to RTI problem-solving teams

In addition, Form 3.2 (*Fidelity of Implementation of CBM*) is a guide to help ensure that however CBM is implemented, it is used with fidelity.

Functional Behavioral Assessment (FBA)

Overview

Although much attention in RTI has focused on academics, specifically reading, some schools have also developed RTI around positive behavioral supports (PBS) (CEC Today, Sugai, RTI Action Network), a structure coupled with academics to provide the most comprehensive RTI model for all learners. To address social-emotional and behavioral development in an RTI model, FBA should be implemented. FBA helps to clarify and monitor the behavior of students who exhibit social or behavioral needs that appear to require Tier 2 or Tier 3 supports. The underlying premise of FBA is that behavior serves some relevant and meaningful function for the learner (Webber & Plotts, 2008). Stated more directly, "people act the way they do for a reason" (Crone & Horner, 2003, p. 11). Therefore, FBA is a curriculum assessment process that helps educators, parents, and learners to understand and deal with the learner's behavior needs within a multi-tiered instructional model.

FBA Process

As with CBM, the process for implementing FBA is streamlined and highly targeted. It enables educators to understand a behavior, including behavior that occurs just before and after the targeted behavior is exhibited (i.e., ABC: Antecedent–Behavior–Consequence). Using FBA, educators can make informed management and instructional decisions by understanding the elements surrounding a behavior that requires change (Killu, 2008). Cohen and Spenciner (2007) and Crone and Horner (2003) discuss the key components of the FBA process; these are summarized in Table 3.2.

Some of the advantages of using FBA in curriculum implementation within an RTI model include its emphasis on individual needs and its ability to identify various ecological factors that may contribute to the undesirable behavior. Also, FBA results lead directly to curricular adjustments to address

TABLE 3.2 FBA Process

FBA Step	Description
Conduct Interviews	The suspected behavior problem is initially clarified through interviews with those most closely connected to the learner (e.g., teachers, parents).
Conduct Observations	Educators conduct a series of observations in settings in which the behavior occurs most frequently (e.g., 6 consecutive school days), documenting the observations, with specific emphasis on ABCs related to the behavior.
Summarize/ Hypothesize	Once enough interviews and observations have been completed and a more in-depth documentation of the behavior occurs, educators summarize what they have documented and then propose one or more hypotheses that may explain the behavior. These discussions relate specifically to the behavioral antecedents and consequences to help explain the behavior. In addition, the expected rate of occurrence should be identified so that progress is monitored, using data, relative to the rate of progress, along with the actual frequency of the desired behavior.
Problem Solve	Based on the summaries and hypotheses, several potential solutions are explored and prioritized. Eventually, those involved in the decision making (e.g., parents, student, social worker, educators) agree on one or two of the generated solutions and formulate a plan to implement them.
Develop a Behavior Support Plan	A design for implementing and assessing the solutions to help facilitate more appropriate behavior is developed and should include, at minimum, the following: (1) the expected or desired behavior, (2) the conditions in which the desired behavior will probably occur, (3) reinforcement for the learner when the desired behavior occurs, (4) consequences if the learner chooses not to exhibit the desired behavior, (5) timeline and responsibilities of those involved in implementing the behavior plan, (6) progress monitoring procedures to evaluate and chart occurrences and rate of progress of the desired behavior, and (7) specific methods necessary to implement the behavior plan in the context of the total curriculum to facilitate a smooth transition in the use of the plan.
Monitor Progress of Plan	Once implementation begins, the learner's progress resulting from implementing the solutions, the reinforcement, and the consequences are monitored in the manner described in the Behavior Support Plan (e.g., self-management checks every 15 minutes daily for 3 weeks; teacher recording each time the desired behavior is exhibited). Results of the progress monitoring should be charted to illustrate the learner's progress and the effectiveness of the plan.
Evaluate/Revise	The progress monitoring should be reviewed at the end of the initial phase of the Behavior Support Plan (e.g., at the end of 3 school weeks) to evaluate frequency, rate of progress, and effectiveness of solutions. The plan should be continued if adequate progress is achieved or adjusted to promote greater use of the desired behavior.

behavior needs without attempting to assign blame to the learner. Because FBA has been shown to be effective through research (Crone & Horner, 2003; O'Neill et al., 1997), it is very useful in an integrated academic and behavioral RTI model, particularly when providing Tier 2 supplemental supports or Tier 3 intensive interventions. For further information on positive behavioral supports and FBA, the reader is referred to Crone and Horner (2003) and Sugai, Lewis-Palmer, and Hagan (1998).

Performance-Based Assessment

Overview

As discussed in Chapter 1 and emphasized throughout this book, the curriculum and its implementation must be integrated to address all learners' needs. In some cases, an integrated task, rather than assessment of individual abilities in one content area, is necessary to fully understand students' knowledge and skills. Assessment or monitoring in which several interrelated skills and abilities are applied in one task involves performance-based assessment. This type of assessment requires learners to generate a constructed response with several components (Hoover et al., 2008; O'Malley & Pierce, 1996). In addition, Bender (2008) described performance-based assessment as a method that ensures flexibility in both form and response mode (e.g., written paper, videotaped report, PowerPoint presentation) to demonstrate proficiency. Ultimately, the learner demonstrates knowledge and skills in a manner consistent with preferred ways of learning, which leads to more creative and challenging tasks reflecting five key task components (O'Malley & Pierce, 1996):

1. Higher order thinking
2. Authenticity (i.e., alignment with real-world issues/solutions)
3. Demonstrated integration of knowledge and skills across content areas
4. The process followed to construct the response as well as the response itself
5. Depth and breadth

Performance-Based Assessment Process

Figure 3.1 illustrates the five task components of learning that students demonstrate simultaneously in their constructed responses through performance-based assessment. As the figure shows, specific questions have been generated to guide educators and students to ensure that each of the five components is included and addressed in the constructed response. The idea that there can be more than one form of assessment to determine progress and proficiency levels has been discussed by various authors, highlighting the reality that no "one size

FIGURE 3.1 Performance-Based Assessment Elements

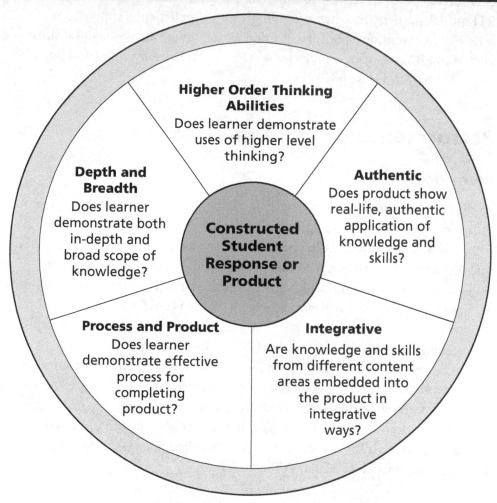

Source: J. Hoover (2009a). *RTI assessment essentials for struggling learners* (p. 75). Corwin Press. Reprinted by permission.

fits all learners" and that students progress at various rates (Allington, 2009; Gregory & Chapman, 2002). Performance-based assessment is a viable option for use in multi-tiered curriculum implementation and associated progress monitoring in any RTI model because it allows students to demonstrate their learning in a relevant and personalized manner.

Cut Score, Gap Analysis, Rate of Progress, and Decision Rules

RTI assessment scores are gathered through one of the three assessment procedures: (1) universal screening, (2) progress monitoring, and (3) diagnostic assessment. However, whichever type is used, three important instructional decisions based on the assessment data concern the following questions: (1) Does the student meet or exceed the established cut score for proficiency? (2) What is the extent of the gap between expected and actual performance? (3) Is the student making adequate progress toward proficiency achievement, even if he or she is below the cut score? (Hoover, 2009a). These decision-making isues are discussed below.

Cut Scores

A *cut score* is a score established by the school or district; any score above it is considered acceptable performance for that grade. Cut scores typically range from the lowest 25% of the class or grade down to the lowest 10% (Bender & Shores, 2007). Students whose scores fall below the established cut score are considered at risk (Mellard & Johnson, 2008), and depending on how far below the cut score the learner falls, he or she may be identified as a struggling learner requiring more intensive instruction (i.e., Tier 2 or 3). Cut scores identify the minimum acceptable proficiency level for all learners if the Tier 1 core research-based curriculum is appropriate for the students and implemented with fidelity.

Gap Analysis

In addition to providing the learner's cut score, the analysis of progress toward curricular benchmarks in RTI models includes determining the size of the gap between expected and actual performance relative to grade-level peers (i.e., reading fluency levels, reading comprehension, mathematics computation). The size of the gap provides additional quantitative data to use in making informed curricular decisions.

A simple procedure is used to complete a gap analysis, as described by the Colorado Department of Education (CDE, 2008) and Shapiro (2008). To perform this analysis, educators should determine:

1. The current standard/benchmark performance level (CL)
2. The expected standard/benchmark performance level (EL)
3. The ratio between current and expected performance levels by dividing the expected level by the current level (EL divided by CL = gap)
4. The gain needed to close the gap

Students with a gap of 2 or more are significantly below their grade-level peers and require immediate multi-tiered supplemental or intensive supports (CDE, 2008). This is further highlighted by the gains needed to catch up to grade-level peers. For example, a student with a gap of 2 must engage in and maintain a very aggressive program reflecting a far greater rate of progress than the typical rate in the Tier 1 curriculum implementation process; this student requires Tier 2 supplemental supports (Hoover, 2009a). The expected time frame for struggling learners to close the gap leads to the third factor to consider when identifying curricular needs: the rate of progress.

Rate of Progress

When evaluating the effectiveness of curriculum implementation in multi-tiered RTI models, it is important to determine the learner's rate of progress toward benchmarks relative to grade-level peers (Knotek, 2007). A student who is achieving below the cut score and has a gap of more than 2 may also demonstrate progress equal to or greater than that of grade-level peers. This indicates that, given sufficient time and supports, the learner will probably catch up to peers. This is significant in the RTI process; failure to achieve at the same level as peers, along with inability to progress at the same rate as peers, may eventually lead to a special education referral for a learning disability (Kovaleski, 2003). These two aspects are referred to as *dual discrepancy* (Fuchs, 2003; Fuchs & Fuchs, 1998); the discrepancy between expected and actual achievement and the discrepancy between expected and actual rate of progress must both be determined.

As with the gap analysis, calculating the rate of progress involves a few simple steps, as discussed by the Colorado Department of Education (CDE, 2008) and Hoover (2009a). The rate of progress is determined by:

1. Identifying the level of progress expected of all students in the grade
2. Establishing the time frame necessary for the learner to achieve the level of progress expected of all learners
3. Considering the feasibility of maintaining the necessary rate of progress for the learner

To establish the expected rate of progress for all learners who progress satisfactorily toward grade-level benchmarks, subtract the beginning-of-year benchmark level (e.g., 10 words per minute) from the end-of-year benchmark level (e.g., 50 words per minute) divided by the number of school weeks (e.g., 35) to obtain the average weekly growth achieved by students who progress satisfactorily throughout the school year (example: $50 - 10 = 40$ divided by 35 = 1.14 words per minute weekly growth).

Table 3.3 provides an example of the total calculation process required to determine the current gap, the expected rate of progress, and the rate of progress necessary to close the gap. The table was derived from similar discussions found in CDE (2008) and Hoover (2009a). It illustrates the process for a student who is struggling in reading and whose progress monitoring (completed at the end of the fall semester) yields the following data.

As Table 3.3 shows, the gap, expected rate of progress, and necessary rate of progress are all calculated. The results are used to make informed, data-based

TABLE 3.3 Gap Analysis and Rate of Progress Determination for a Struggling Reader

Current Performance Level: 25 words per minute (wpm).

Current Expected Benchmark Performance Level: 65 wpm (fall term).

Gap Analysis: 65 divided by 25 = 2.6 (gap is significant: over 2).

Future Expected Performance Benchmark Level: Students should achieve 95 wpm by the next monitoring period (spring term: 15 weeks of instruction).

Expected Growth for Those Achieving the Proficiency Benchmark: 95 – 65 = 30 wpm divided by 15 weeks = 2.0 wpm average weekly expected gain for those who make satisfactory progress.

Gain Needed by Struggling Learner to Close Gap by Next Monitoring Period: 95 – 25 (current level) = 70 wpm needed to close gap by the spring term monitoring.

Rate of Progress Required to Close Gap: Spring term is 15 weeks, so the learner needs to make an average 4.6 wpm weekly gain (70 divided by 15 = 4.6) to close the gap between the end of the fall and spring terms compared to an average weekly gain of 2.0 wpm for the typical learner who is progressing satisfactorily during the same 15-week period.

Growth Time Frame: Typical students making adequate progress will increase the number of words per minute by 30 (i.e., from 65 to 95), or a weekly average increase of 2.0 wpm, whereas our struggling learner must achieve an increase of 70 words per minute (i.e., from 25 to 95) or a weekly gain of 4.6 wpm to close the gap by the next monitoring period (at the end of 15 weeks).

Time Frame Feasibility: The expected growth over 15 weeks for the struggling learner is highly aggressive and a more realistic progress goal should be established. For example, it might be more realistic to have the learner achieve a 3.0 wpm gain per week rather than 4.6 wpm. This gain represents a 30% increase over the gain expected for nonstruggling learners. This results in a 23-week intervention time frame rather than 15 weeks (3 divided into 70 = 23.3 weeks). The decision to reduce the weekly average of 4.6 to 3.0 wpm is made by the RTI assessment team using data, knowledge, and related assessment information about the struggling learner, as well as knowledge of what is expected of nonstruggling students.

decisions concerning the best course of action for implementing Tier 2 supplemental supports. The struggling learner in Table 3.3 is expected to make significant progress in a relative brief period of time to catch up to grade-level peers. A more realistic schedule keeps the learner progressing toward the targeted benchmark; this rate of progress exceeds that of the student's grade-level peers but is more manageable for the student who is struggling.

Another element to consider when interpreting rate-of-progress data is the standard used to base curricular decisions. A learner's level of proficiency—and, more specifically, rate of progress—are determined by comparing the actual scores to one of three types of standards (Shapiro, 1996, 2008; Shinn, 1989; Wright, 2007): (1) research-based national norms, (2) local norms, or (3) criterion-referenced benchmarks. It is important for RTI teams to determine which standard will be followed as a basis for curricular implementation decisions. This refers to *decision rules*, which is discussed later in this chapter. Knowing the strengths and areas of concern for each standard facilitates effective use of whatever standard is applied when interpreting universal screening, progress monitoring, or diagnostic test results. These are summarized below, beginning with an overview of each standard in Table 3.4 (CDE, 2008; Hoover, 2009a; Shapiro, 2008).

As Table 3.4 shows, each of the three types of standards provides a solid basis for making curricular progress decisions. Some additional considerations about the use of each type of standard in curricular implementation decisions are discussed below.

RESEARCH-BASED NORMS ■ National norms are convenient to use; however, these norms may vary significantly from the demographic characteristics of struggling learners in a particular school or district. This must be addressed when measuring rate of progress using national norms.

LOCAL NORMS ■ Norms for specific schools and districts may be more relevant because they directly reflect the school's/district's population of learners. In addition, basing decisions on local norms often allows educators to identify more precisely the gaps/rates of progress of struggling learners by direct comparison to other grade-level classmates. If appropriate, in some situations, the individual school, classroom, or grade-level norms within the district may be the

TABLE 3.4 Standards for Basing Growth Rate Calculations

Standard	Description	Growth Rate Calculation
Research Sample Norms.	Norms derived from scores obtained from a national/state research sample that participates in a study. Scores are actual performance levels in specific areas, such as oral reading fluency or math computations from the research sample (e.g., average year-end oral reading fluency rates for each grade or average weekly gains necessary for satisfactory progress, with an increasing number of words read per minute).	Growth rates are calculated by comparing the current level of performance with the performance of the research sample (i.e., norms), reflecting the expected *level of proficiency* and/ or the expected *rate of progress*. Calculations are often determined by using national/state normed devices and/or curriculum-based measures.
Local School/ District Norms.	Norms that reflect expected and typical scores for specific grade levels in an individual grade, school, or district.	Growth rates are calculated by comparing the current level of performance with the performance seen in classroom, grade, school, or district local norms reflecting the expected *level of proficiency* and/or the expected *rate of progress*. These calculations are often determined by the use of curriculum-based measures, performance-based assessment, or existing standardized devices.
Criterion- Referenced Benchmarks.	Minimum levels of mastery determined for specific skills based on grade level (e.g., 75% accuracy expected in reading fluency, math computation, time on task). Mastery level benchmarks reflect a predetermined standard expected for an acceptable level of proficiency in any curricular area.	Growth rates are calculated by comparing the current level of performance with the predetermined expected performance level based on the learner's grade level. These calculations are often made using a scoring rubric in conjunction with curriculum-based measures.

best standard to use in making progress rate and proficiency level decisions. As with national norms, one issue to bear in mind when using local norms is that within-district average scores may vary significantly from school to school. This may make comparisons across district grade levels difficult; the validity and accuracy of test results may be questionable for some students (e.g., comparing progress between schools with high populations of ELLs with those that do not).

CRITERION-REFERENCED BENCHMARKS ▪ These benchmarks reflect actual performance standards relative to a predetermined level of mastery necessary to prepare students for future success in school (e.g., minimum reading comprehension proficiency level needed in grade 2 for initial success in reading in grade 3). They can be applied to many areas in education (e.g., mathematics computation, science concepts, written expression) and therefore are specific to the curriculum being taught. However, one concern is that these benchmarks may lack formal norms, which may lead to greater subjectivity than experienced with research-based national or local norms.

As discussed above, each of these standards has strengths and concerns. Therefore, RTI school teams should establish guidelines to ensure that the best decisions are made (Burns & Gibbons, 2008). No matter which standard is used, the RTI team must develop a clear, well-defined process for making instructional or eligibility decisions. This refers to the practice of using decision rules to guide RTI decision making.

Decision Rules

Although data are the basis of curricular decisions, problem-solving teams (e.g., data analysis teams) must still use some process for interpreting and applying universal screening, progress monitoring, and diagnostic assessment results. To facilitate this process, each team needs to establish guidelines to follow, often referred to as *decision rules* (Barnett et al., 2007). At minimum, decision rules must be established in the following five areas:

> *Decision Rule 1:* Teams establish the percentile rank below which a learner is believed to be struggling (e.g., the lowest 20% of scores in the class or grade).
>
> *Decision Rule 2:* Teams establish the appropriate level of instruction based on the size of the gap (e.g., a gap of 2 is significant need and requires immediate Tier 2 supplemental supports; a gap of less than 1 requires targeted differentiated instruction within the Tier 1 core curriculum with biweekly progress monitoring).
>
> *Decision Rule 3:* Teams establish the standard on which rate of progress is based (e.g., national research norms, local norms, criterion-referenced benchmarks).

Decision Rule 4: Teams decide on the process necessary to ensure and corroborate fidelity of implementation of both the curriculum and assessment practices (e.g., grade-level teams design a process for their grade in the school; a supervisor observes in the classroom and documents observation of evidence of fidelity; the classroom teacher self-reports evidence of implementation fidelity).

Decision Rule 5: Teams decide how best to implement the comprehensive evaluation if a learner is referred for special education.

Other decision rules may also be needed; however, the primary goal of established decision rules is to identify and adhere to a standard process and set of guidelines as a basis for instructional and diagnostic decisions when implementing the curriculum within RTI (Hoover, 2009a). The established decision rules must be understood by all educators in the school and must be applied in a standard way to all learners to be most effective.

In interpreting RTI data, many schools use a team of educators whose primary purpose is to interpret data scores and generate recommendations concerning tiers of instruction. These teams are referred to as Data Analysis Teams (DATs) (Kovaleski, Roble, & Agne, 2009). These teams may complement the work of a schoolwide RTI team or they may serve as the primary team. However, whether they act as a support team or the primary team, the

---

TABLE 3.5 Tasks of DATs

Assemble the data team.

Clarify cut scores and decision rules for interpreting data.

Distribute data to team members to be evaluated and discussed.

Review the overall performance of entire grade (universal screening—Tier 1).

Identify students who are at risk or currently below benchmarks.

Identify students who require targeted differentiations in Tier 1 and establish a progress monitoring schedule to assess progress more closely; select differentiations.

Identify students who require immediate Tier 2 supplemental supports; establish a program; select evidence-based interventions and establish a schedule, including progress monitoring.

Identify students who require immediate Tier 3 intensive intervention; establish a program; select evidence-based interventions and establish a schedule, including progress monitoring.

Record the responsibilities of different educators for implementing established programs that are developed based on data analysis and interpretations.

Develop a process for follow-up support to ensure that established programs/differentiations are implemented as designed.

Create a schedule for additional meetings to review progress and determine the effectiveness of targeted Tier 1 differentiations and/or Tiers 2 and 3 instruction.

DATs serve a critical function by interpreting data and making recommendations for curriculum implementation. Table 3.5 illustrates key aspects associated with DATs. This table was developed from information in Kovaleski et al. (2009).

Curricular Components and Instructional Adjustments

Given the wide variety of needs, experiential backgrounds, and preferred learning styles, along with the cultural and linguistic diversity seen in today's classrooms, a comprehensive view of the curriculum and its implementation is necessary if all needs are to be met. As discussed, once universal screening and/or progress monitoring data are gathered, educators must interpret the results to make informed instructional adjustments. Central to making curricular adjustments, along with the decision rules, are the five interrelated curriculum components: (1) content/skills, (2) evidence-based interventions, (3) instructional arrangements, (4) class and instructional management procedures, and (5) progress evaluation. Knowing which component requires adjustment, based on the data, is essential to providing effective education for all students:

One or more of the five curricular components may require adjustments to meet the needs of students who are not making adequate progress; adjusting the correct component(s) is key to providing sufficient opportunities to learn.

Table 3.6 provides key questions associated with the five curricular components that should be answered to adequately interpret Tier 1 RTI data and make appropriate instructional adjustments. Answers to these questions also corroborate that all possible Tier 1 efforts have been completed before making the decision to implement Tier 2 and 3 instruction.

The questions in Table 3.6 are designed to provide direction to RTI teams to ensure that all relevant curricular aspects are investigated prior to drawing conclusions about instructional adjustments. Educators should consider these questions to avoid adjusting the wrong curricular component, which may lead to potentially wrong decisions about lack of progress and, more significantly, suspected disabilities. Form 3.3 (*Guide to Interpreting Response to Intervention Data*) provides a checklist that educators can use to develop a more comprehensive decision-making process using RTI data.

This chapter concludes with its *RTI Curriculum in Action* description, which includes an example of skills-based measurement in CBM and suggested instructional adjustments.

TABLE 3.6 Interpreting Response to Intervention Assessment Data: Clarifying Instructional Adjustments

Curriculum Component	RTI Assessment Focus	Key Interpretive Questions
Content/Skills (Research-Based Curriculum)	Extent to which the student acquires knowledge/skills that have been taught through the curriculum	What is the student's current level of performance and rate of progress? Does the student have the necessary experiential background to acquire the content/skills? Does at least 80% of the class/grade achieve at benchmark levels? Are the content/skills too difficult for the student or can these be acquired through the use of different interventions, instructional arrangements, or management procedures? If so, which of these three other curricular elements do you decide to adjust and why?
Evidence-Based Interventions	Extent to which selected evidence-based interventions are successful in providing targeted, differentiated instruction within the Tier 1 curriculum to meet students' needs	Are the selected interventions compatible with students' preferred ways of learning? Was enough time provided for differentiated instruction in Tier 1 to achieve the desired results? Was the selected intervention consistent with those in the Tier 1 curriculum? Have one or more targeted differentiations been attempted to support the Tier 1 curriculum in the general class prior to deciding on the need for Tier 2 support?
Instructional Arrangements	Extent to which the use of groups, paired, or independent structural arrangements in the classroom supports the learning of content/skills or appropriate behaviors	Do the selected structures facilitate or inhibit active participation of the learner? If no adjustments are made to the content/skills or selected interventions and only the instructional arrangements are modified, will this facilitate progress for the struggling learner? On what basis does one decide to change only the instructional arrangement(s) rather than modifying the content/skills or switching to another intervention?
Class/Instructional Management Procedures	Extent to which a differentiated classroom is structured to meet a variety of learning and behavioral needs of all students	Is the classroom sufficiently differentiated to meet the variety of students' needs? Would greater differentiation of the class and the instructional environment better meet the needs of the struggling student and other students in the classroom? Is the classroom sufficiently differentiated to provide opportunities for all students?
Progress Evaluation	Extent to which the evaluation of student academic and behavioral progress is efficiently embedded in the curriculum implementation process	Are the progress-monitoring tasks completed in an efficient and seamless manner or is the process burdensome and cumbersome for students? Do progress-monitoring tasks take into account students' varied needs? In addition to measuring *what* the student has learned (i.e., content/skills), does the progress monitoring measure *how* the student best learns, *under which conditions,* and the *compatibility* between student and teacher in terms of style/preferences?

A Teacher-Developed Skills-Based CBM to Screen for Mathematics Progress and Abilities in a First-Grade Classroom

Description

I am a first-grade teacher in a small independent school. Each year we administer the Iowa Test of Basic Skills (ITBS) to all our students. During the school year I administer informal assessments, chapter tests, and end of the unit tests to my students in math. However, I felt that I needed a more formal way to screen my students' progress during the year towards achieving Tier 1 core mathematics end-of-the-year curricular benchmarks. After reading about universal screening, progress monitoring, and curriculum-based measurement, I decided to give it a try in my classroom. I developed and used the skills-based measurement (SBM) component within CBM procedures.

SBM Procedures

Before the school year began, I gathered all of the posttests from our math curriculum and cut and pasted items from these tests and created four individual, yet equivalent, mathematics assessment measures. Each measure was comprised of a sample of all the math areas of the entire year's curriculum. Items included addition and subtraction of one- and two-digit numbers, regrouping and no regrouping, money, time, measurement, fractions, probability, and problem solving. Each of the four curriculum-based measures included 24 items. I administered the first of these curriculum-based measures to the whole group the second week of school and then subsequently at the end of each trimester, for a total of four annual classroom screenings. Each administered screening followed the same directions and process and, as indicated, included a different, yet equivalent, math problems sheet. Students were instructed to respond to as many of the 24 items as possible. This screening process enabled me to discover which students were beginning to fall behind mastery of year-end mathematics benchmarks and which had already acquired skills yet to be addressed in the classroom instruction.

SBM Analysis

Each test was analyzed, and I used the data to screen each student's progress toward end-of-the year benchmarks. I also calculated the class average on each test and determined how far above and below each student was each time, enabling me to assess individual progress. The students' screening results were charted and shared with their parents at scheduled conferences. Also, results were used to adjust the curriculum as well as give each student the differentiated help needed. Students who were at or above the class average received enrichment, and students who were below the average received targeted differentiations in the needed areas. The parents in my class were very pleased with the knowledge gained from each screening session. By the end of the school year, all students had achieved the mathematics skills expected of our first graders. The periodic screenings alerted me as to who was beginning to fall behind achievement towards annual curricular benchmarks and how far below or above the class average the students were, as well as necessary targeted differentiations to meet needs.

Instructional Adjustments

I was able to analyze each test for specific mathematics knowledge and skills as well as work habits. For example, one student who scored well above the average on our school's annual achievement test (Iowa Test of Basic Skills) worked carelessly when completing the screening measures (e.g., adding instead of subtracting), thus lowering her score on the screenings. Consequently, help was given to improve test-taking skills. Other students who struggled at the beginning of the year were able to close the gap and achieve nearer to the class average due to the differentiations implemented as a result of the periodic screenings. The information was also very useful for writing specific comments on report cards. End-of-the-year

(Continued)

RTI APPLICATIONS OF KEY CHAPTER CONCEPTS

A basic aspect of curriculum implementation in RTI models is the screening and monitoring of learners' progress as the basis of instructional decisions. Universal screening, progress monitoring, and diagnostic assessment are the assessment underpinnings for effective curricular adjustments to meet the needs of all learners. Curriculum implementation in RTI is a multi-tiered process. Levels of instruction are provided to all students, and these levels increase in intensity and duration based on proficiency levels and rate of progress. A variety of RTI assessment practices may be used to screen all learners, monitor the progress of struggling learners, and pinpoint or diagnose specific needs of struggling learners. Of the many assessment practices, curriculum-based measurement (CBM), performance-based assessment, and functional behavioral assessment (FBA) are three that educators will find useful in the implementation and assessment of curriculum in today's classrooms. Determining gaps in achievement and rates of progress is also part of RTI curriculum implementation and decision making. Finally, establishing and adhering to decision rules for making critical instructional decisions and adjustments based on data gathered from standard procedures and established norms is essential in determining RTI curriculum needs.

The following actions will allow educators to meet the needs of all learners in today's classrooms:

- Determine the universal screening and progress monitoring procedures followed in your school, including the methods and standards used for (1) gap analysis, (2) rate of progress, (3) cut scores, and (4) decision rules.

- Review the multi-tiered curriculum implementation and assessment procedures used in your school to determine the most appropriate tier (1, 2, 3) of instruction.

- Discuss how the five curricular components are essential to the determination of RTI curricular progress.

- Select two evidence-based assessments (Table 3.2) with which you are least familiar and acquire the knowledge and skills necessary to use each; apply them in the classroom to monitor student progress (e.g., CBM).

FORM 3.1 Guide for Fidelity of Assessment Devices and Practices

Check Appropriate Item:
___ *Title of Assessment Device:* _____

___ *Title of Assessment Practice:* _____

Primary Method(s) for Completion (check each that applies):
    ___ Direct Observation by Colleague
    ___ Self-Reporting
    ___ Interview

Instructions: Check each item that corroborates the extent of implementation of the assessment device or practice. Provide comments as appropriate.

Assessment device or practice is implemented . . .

___ As described in the manual or guide
Comments:

___ By educator who is sufficiently trained in the assessment used
Comments:

___ With students comparable to the research and development population
Comments:

___ Following all standard procedures and recommendations for proper use
Comments:

___ Only for the specific purpose(s) for which it was designed
Comments:

___ Using proper scoring procedures of results
Comments:

___ By the examiner who provides instructions, directions, probes, steps, etc. that are clearly within the standard procedures for administration (i.e., the examiner does not provide unapproved hints, suggestions, or supports that influence the results)
Comments:

___ Using acceptable assessment accommodations as necessary
Comments:

Source: Used by permission of John J. Hoover.

FORM 3.2 Fidelity of Implementation of CBM

Primary Method(s) for Completion (Check each that applies):
___ Direct Observation by Colleague
___ Self-Reporting
___ Interview

Instructions: Check each item to corroborate its use in the implementation of CBM. Provide comments as appropriate.

CBM . . .

___ Adheres to a standard process for implementation
Comments:

___ Adheres to a standard process for scoring and charting results
Comments:

___ Directly measures progress toward benchmarks/objectives taught in the curriculum implemented
Comments:

___ Is implemented the same way for each repeated measurement
Comments:

___ Provides objective, quantified data scores
Comments:

___ Results are used to determine student's rate of progress compared to that of same-grade and same-age peers
Comments:

___ Material (e.g., reading passage, math problems sheet) is similar in content and scope to previous material used to increase validity from one administration to the next (i.e., the identical reading passage is NOT used more than once to assess the progress of the same learner; rather, a passage similar in scope, content, and skills is used)
Comments:

Summary of Fidelity of Implementation of CBM:

Source: Used by permission of John J. Hoover.

FORM 3.3   Guide to Interpreting RTI Data

Student: _____   Teacher: _____   Date: _____

Type of Assessment Addressed:
___ Universal Screening   ___ Progress Monitoring   ___ Diagnostic

Instructions: Check each item to corroborate its application in the interpretation of RTI screening, monitoring, or diagnostic data results for the identified student. Provide Descriptive Summary comments as appropriate to clarify each item.

Critical Items	*Descriptive Summary*

___ Rate of Progress

___ Gap Analysis

___ Current Level of Proficiency

___ Standard for Basing Decisions
     ___ Research-Based Norms
     ___ Local Norms
     ___ Criterion-Referenced Benchmarks

___ Dual Discrepancy
     ___ Rate of Progress
     ___ Level of Proficiency

___ Assessment results directly reflect progress toward what has been taught in the curriculum

___ Sufficient opportunities to learn have been provided

___ Research-based curriculum is implemented with fidelity

___ Evidence-based interventions are implemented with fidelity

89

___ Tier 1 general and targeted
differentiations have been
implemented with fidelity prior
to considering Tier 2 or 3
instruction

___ Culturally and linguistically diverse
needs have been accommodated
in Tier 1 core instruction
prior to considering Tier
2 or 3 instruction

Source: Used by permission of John J. Hoover.

▶ PART II

Response to Intervention Curricular Supports and Decision Making

THE CHAPTERS IN PART I discussed the foundational aspects of multi-tiered RTI, along with specific considerations in implementing the RTI curriculum in each tier of instruction in both elementary and secondary grades. Another set of knowledge and skills necessary for successful implementation of the multi-tiered RTI curriculum pertains to collaboration and decision-making processes to make the best use of the foundational aspects of RTI and provide the highest-quality research-based curriculum and evidence-based interventions to all learners. Part II covers two interrelated topics that assist educators in making the most informed curricular decisions possible, both in and out of the classroom settings. It presents curricular decision-making models, including procedures and key decision points (Chapter 4), and discusses the importance of collaboration among educators, including interventionists, in multi-tiered RTI models (Chapter 5).

Part II includes the following two chapters:

4. Response to Intervention Curricular Decision-Making Models
5. Collaboration to Meet Response to Intervention Curricular Needs

Response to Intervention Curricular Decision-Making Models

▶ Overview

ONCE UNIVERSAL SCREENING, progress monitoring, and/or diagnostic data are gathered, educators must ensure that these data are properly interpreted and applied. To meet this need, three RTI decision-making models are available to educators: (1) the standard treatment model, (2) the problem-solving model, and (3) the combined standard treatment–problem-solving model. Examination of the critical components of each model, including strengths and areas of potential concern, assists school teams in making the best use of curriculum assessment results. In addition, the roles and responsibilities of RTI school-based decision-making team members must be clearly understood in order to make informed instructional adjustments.

▶ Key Topics

▶ Standard treatment model

▶ Problem-solving model

▶ Combined standard treatment–problem-solving model

▶ Team roles and responsibilities

▶ Learner Outcomes

After reading this chapter, you should:

1. Be able to compare and contrast the standard treatment model with the problem-solving model

2. Be able to implement the combined standard treatment–problem-solving model

3. Know which types of team members are critical to effective RTI decision making

4. Know the roles and responsibilities of each member of the decision-making team

5. Be able to evaluate the effectiveness of the decision-making models

SIGNIFICANCE TO CONTEMPORARY CLASSROOM INSTRUCTION

A basic component of RTI is the process that educators use in making critical curricular decisions. In RTI, three decision-making models have emerged, each with its own strengths and potential concerns. The model used to make RTI decisions in today's schools is critical because of the importance of meeting the student's needs early rather than waiting until the student is significantly behind age and grade-level peers in academic and/or social-emotional development. In addition, research shows that school teams that adhere to a structured process with defined decision rules are best able to make informed instructional decisions based on RTI assessment data. Such decisions are critical to the successful implementation of RTI models, and school RTI teams must ensure that curricular decisions are made efficiently and effectively to best meet the needs of all learners.

Note: The decision-making process described in this chapter is performed by a team of educators who may be referred to in various ways (*child study team, teacher assistance team, data analysis team, student support team,* etc.). Recognizing that different schools refer to their teams in unique ways, in this book the school team is called the *RTI team.* This term may be used interchangeably with terms referring to these and other similar school teams responsible for making RTI decisions.

Overview of Response to Intervention Decision Making

There are four primary tasks in the proper implementation of a multi-tiered RTI curriculum: (1) use of a research-based curriculum and evidence-based interventions; (2) implementation with fidelity; (3) selection and use of general and targeted curricular differentiations; and (4) universal screening, progress monitoring, and diagnostic assessment to determine progress toward curricular benchmarks by documenting levels of performance and rate of progress. Although each of these tasks provides critical information about teaching and learning for all students, the way that information is applied in making informed curricular decisions determines the effectiveness of multi-tiered RTI curriculum implementation. The information, no matter how accurately acquired, is only as good as its interpretation and application to support effective teaching and learning for all students. As a result, educators, working as a team, must make interpretations about levels of proficiency, rate of progress, gap analysis, and instructional and assessment fidelity, as well as decisions concerning the effects of curricular differentiations and adjustments on student progress, to provide the most appropriate tier of instruction for all students.

In regard to efficiency in decision making, at least three decision levels typically exist:

> *Level 1: General Classroom Teacher*—decision making in the implementation of the Tier 1 core curriculum. Decisions at this level are made primarily by the general class teacher, with or without input from other educators. The decisions tend to be those necessary to implement (1) the Tier 1 curriculum with fidelity; (2) a differentiated classroom; (3) additional targeted curricular differentiations supporting those already implemented to meet ongoing needs; and (4) procedures to screen/monitor the needs of learners who do not respond to the general differentiated classroom or targeted differentiations.

> *Level 2: RTI Team*—decisions made by a team of professionals using universal screening and progress monitoring results to determine the most appropriate tier of instruction to meet the needs of learners requiring Tier 2 supplemental supports (e.g., data analysis team, child study team).

> *Level 3: Comprehensive Evaluation Team*—decisions made by a team of professionals and parents/guardians who perform a comprehensive evaluation to determine the student's eligibility for special education due to a learning disability and/or to provide Tier 3 intensive interventions.

At these three decision-making levels, the five curriculum components must be considered to make informed decisions that meet the needs of all learners.

Curricular Decision-Making Models

In multi-tiered RTI there are three decision-making models, each with strengths and areas of concern. Each model is presented below, based on discussions in several sources (Fuchs & Fuchs, 2006, 2007; Hoover, 2009a; Hoover et al., 2008; Jimerson et al., 2007; Marston, Lau, & Muyskens, 2007). Table 4.1 provides an overview of the three models. These include two core decision-making models, along with a third model that combines elements of the others. Each model is discussed further below, followed by a process for implementing a decision-making model (whichever one is selected) within a structured format to ensure consistency and accountability among educators.

Standard Treatment Protocol Model

The standard treatment protocol is a rigorous model. It helps teachers to accurately identify students with special needs (Fuchs & Fuchs, 2006), thereby reducing misidentification. This method refers to "a common intervention for small groups of children to directly address a particular skill deficit" (Burns & Gibbons, 2008, p. 79). It reflects a more scientific approach to selecting curricular interventions (Bender & Shores, 2007). The common element is the need for

TABLE 4.1 Multi-Tiered Response to Intervention Curriculum Implementation Decision-Making Models

Model	Description	Analysis
Standard Treatment	Use of the same treatment for all learners with similar needs (e.g., phonemic awareness; self-monitoring); Instructional decisions are based primarily on data resulting from the standard treatment intervention	More rigorous and accurate in identifying special needs than Problem Solving Model; Procedure is more selective and may miss identifying some students with special needs
Problem-Solving	Process of identifying individual needs followed by development of implementation program; Instructional decisions are made by Problem Solving Team using additional ecological information about individual learner to clarify and pinpoint needs	Less rigorous than Standard Treatment method yet is able to include most/all students with special needs; Runs risk of misidentifying some students as having special needs when they do not
Combined Standard Treatment/Problem-Solving	Process in which elements of both models are used to make decisions and provide appropriate level of instruction; Decisions are made by problem-solving team using standard treatment data and other related information to best understand learner needs	Draws upon strengths of both models, which allows problem solving teams to base instructional decisions on standard treatment data along with considerations of other ecological variables; More time-intensive than other models

Source: RTI assessment essentials for struggling learners by John J. Hoover (2009). Thousand Oaks, CA: Corwin Press. Reprinted by permission.

support in the same skill area (reading fluency, phonemic awareness, mathematical computations, etc). This decision-making model is effective if all the learners in the small group have similar cultural and experiential backgrounds and the selected intervention is designed for that group. However, as we will discuss in Chapter 7, some learners with the same skill deficit may require a different curricular intervention due to cultural, experiential or related differences. In addition, although the standard treatment model is rigorous, it may fail to identify some students with special needs (Fuchs & Fuchs, 2006). Therefore, although this model may be of value to some learners with identical needs and similar backgrounds, research suggests that the sole use of this method may yield limited results (Allington, 2009; Mathes et al., 2005).

Problem-Solving Model

The problem-solving model is one that many educators have used for decades in work related to the prereferral model of intervention (e.g., teacher assistance team, prereferral team). Whereas the standard treatment model promotes the use of the same curriculum intervention and the same progress monitoring procedure and measure, with little consideration of related factors, the problem-solving model emphasizes a more individual approach to meet learning and behavior needs by considering various ecological (i.e., home, school, and community) factors (Bender & Shores, 2007; Hoover, 2009a). In addition, Fuchs and Fuchs (2006) suggested that this method helps educators identify most, if not all, struggling students, especially those with special needs. However, because of its less rigorous approach, some students who do not have special needs may be mistakenly identified. This is one of the reasons for the large increase in the number of students in special education over the past few decades. Also, the problem-solving model has been more loosely implemented than the standard treatment model, mainly with anecdotal documentation and classroom and curriculum progress data generally gathered through informal means. These procedures have raised concerns about the problem-solving model. The suggested enhancement to this model is discussed below.

Combined Standard Treatment– Problem-Solving Model

Various researchers suggest that this model combines the strengths of the standard treatment and problem-solving models (Hoover, 2009a) by adding flexibility in considering other factors (i.e., ecological factors) to the standard treatment process. This provides a more rigorous approach to collecting and interpreting curriculum-based data in the problem-solving model. In a national study, Hoover, Baca, Love, and Saenz (2008) found that most states are using or planning to use some form of a combined model for making RTI decisions.

The combined model also moves away from the "one size fits all" position as variations and differences in learner characteristics, backgrounds, or instructional preferences are recognized. Therefore, because of its adaptability and its emphasis on rigorous implementation, the following discussions focus on the application of the combined model for making effective and efficient multitiered curricular decisions.

Decision-Making Process

Once a decision-making model is selected for making RTI curricular decisions, a systematic process should be followed for best results. Over the past several years, various researchers have suggested different processes for effective decision making (Allington, 2009; Bender & Shores, 2007; Brown-Chidsey & Steege, 2005; Deno, 2005). Figure 4.1 illustrates a decision-making model that includes key aspects of a process for implementing the combined standard treatment–problem-solving model. This process is not new; it includes key elements suggested by various researchers including those cited above.

As Figure 4.1 shows, the six-stage cycle in the decision-making process begins with identification of the problem, proceeds to developing and

---

FIGURE 4.1   Response to Intervention Team Decision-Making Cycle

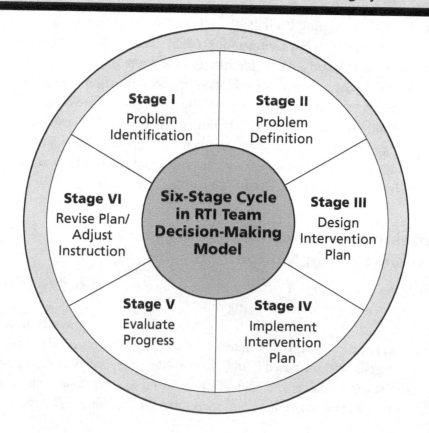

implementing an intervention plan, and is followed by continued monitoring of student progress and making needed curricular adjustments. This process provides a structure for making decisions in multi-tiered RTI models. The following example presents one application of the six-stage cycle. The example illustrates learner needs associated with Tier 2 supplemental supports; however, a similar process can be used with students in the Tier 1 curriculum or those requiring Tier 3 intensive interventions.

1. *Problem Identification.* A struggling learner in the multi-tiered RTI curriculum is first identified by the universal screening data scores. The learner demonstrates a low level of proficiency and/or a low rate of progress compared to grade-level peers and achievement expectations. In addition, the screening corroborates that the learner received the research-based curriculum and evidence-based interventions implemented with fidelity. This includes accommodations for cultural and linguistic diversity.

2. *Problem Definition.* Based on information and data obtained through screening and any related assessments (e.g., FBA, interviews), the specific area of need is clarified (e.g., reading fluency, mathematics computations, self-management). Howell et al. (2008) wrote that when defining the problem, the "emphasis is to break down a broad general issue into specific skills related to the concern" (p. 51). In this stage of the cycle, the various ecological factors (i.e., student, school, home/community) should also be considered to pinpoint needs and interpret results reflecting relevant academic and social-emotional factors. Clearly defining the problem is necessary to develop an intervention plan; using combined standard treatment–problem-solving input provides a comprehensive summary of RTI curriculum needs for struggling learners.

3. *Design Intervention Plan.* Once the need for Tier 2 instruction is determined, a plan for implementing the curricular supports is developed. The intervention plan includes (1) the time frame to implement intervention(s) (e.g., 20 minutes per day, 3 days per week for 12 weeks); (2) selected evidence-based interventions; (3) procedures for monitoring progress, including the devices and practices to be used (e.g., CBM, classroom observation, performance-based assessment); and (4) a timeline for monitoring the learner's progress (e.g., biweekly monitoring). Thus, the RTI team identifies the frequency, intensity, and duration of instruction when designing the implementation plan (Howell et al., 2008). Also included in the plan are the decision rules for making curricular decisions concerning level of achievement and rate of progress as well as educators' responsibilities. See Form 4.1 (*Guide for Designing an Intervention Plan*) for a guide to use in documenting an intervention plan developed to implement Tier 2 or 3 instruction.

4. *Implement Intervention Plan.* The Tier 2 intervention plan is carried out, emphasizing its implementation with fidelity and proper use of the selected evidence-based intervention(s). The learner is taught in the manner described in the plan, with progress monitoring performed as stipulated to determine the student's rate of progress and achievement level. Results of the progress monitoring should be charted to illustrate growth. Procedures for ensuring the plan's implementation with fidelity are also recorded, along with evidence to corroborate its proper implementation.

5. *Evaluate Progress.* Using the progress monitoring data, corroborated evidence indicating that the plan was implemented with fidelity, and other related assessments, the RTI team meets to discuss the student's progress. The established decision rules are adhered to as the student's rate of progress and level of proficiency are evaluated to determine the effectiveness of the plan. Based on the results, one of four decisions are typically made: (1) sufficient progress has been made and the learner no longer requires Tier 2 instruction; (2) some progress has been made but it is not sufficient, and a second round of Tier 2 supports is warranted, with few adjustments to curriculum implementation; (3) little or no progress has been made and a second round of Tier 2 instruction is warranted, with adjustments to curriculum implementation; or (4) Tier 2 supports have led to minimal progress and Tier 3 intensive interventions may be warranted. These decisions lead to the final step in the decision-making cycle.

6. *Revise Plan/Adjust Instruction.* Based on the decisions made in the previous step, the intervention plan may be (1) discontinued due to sufficient progress; (2) continued for a second round of supports with few adjustments; (3) substantially revised and continued for a second round based on progress data; or (4) revised to provide Tier 3 intensive interventions. Key aspects of the RTI team's decision should be recorded, and any revisions to the intervention plan should be documented and implemented. With each decision, the learner's progress is continuously monitored, increasing in duration based on the student's needs. Subsequent team decisions are based on future progress monitoring.

The decision-making cycle described above provides excellent opportunities for combined use of key components of the standard treatment and problem-solving models. In the combined standard treatment–problem-solving model, curriculum-based data gathered in a standardized manner are coupled with information on the student, the classroom, and the student's home/community ecological status to determine the student's needs and design the most appropriate multi-tiered RTI curricular supports. Form 4.2 (*Checklist for Implementing Combined Decision-Making Model*) provides a checklist for educators to use to ensure the proper implementation of the six-step decision-making process.

Decision-Making Team Members and Roles

In addition to following a systematic process for gathering and evaluating curricular data, the composition of the combined standard treatment–problem-solving team is critical. Each team member should have knowledge and expertise directly related to the needs of the learner. Educator expertise is the foundation for accurate interpretation of the curricular data and progress monitoring results. Key educators and others persons with primary roles necessary to make informed multi-tiered RTI curricular decisions are presented in Table 4.2. They have been selected based on the composition of teams from numerous school districts; however, other team members should

TABLE 4.2 Key Response to Intervention Team Personnel and Critical Curricular Contributions

Team Member	Critical Tasks in Multi-Tiered RTI Curriculum
General Educator	Implement Tiers 1 and 2 research-based curriculum and evidence-based interventions Assist with universal screening Gather/chart Tiers 1 and 2 progress monitoring data Determine level of proficiency, rate of progress, and size of gap for struggling learners Implement a differentiated classroom and targeted differentiations for struggling learners Corroborate fidelity of curriculum implementation and associated progress monitoring Present Tier 1 and 2 curriculum implementation efforts and results to the RTI team
Special Educator	Provide special education expertise as necessary Provide general educators with instructional and classroom management ideas to best implement classroom and targeted differentiated instruction Provide Tier 2 supports as necessary to struggling learners Assist with Tier 2 progress monitoring/chart results Implement Tier 3 intensive curricular interventions
School Psychologist/ Assessment Specialist	Provide expertise/support for each aspect of curriculum assessment (i.e., universal screening, progress monitoring, diagnostic assessment) Assist in the Tier 3 comprehensive diagnostic evaluation of a suspected disability Assist in completing gap analysis, determining rate of progress and interpreting results for struggling learners
Content Area Specialist	Provide expertise in content area for struggling learners in each tier of intervention (e.g., reading, mathematics, writing) Provide Tier 2 supplemental support as needed Assist with identifying evidence-based interventions to differentiate instruction in content area in Tiers 1 and 2 Assist with progress monitoring in content area Lead discussions about proper interpretation of progress monitoring and universal screening results Assist in identifying the research-based curriculum appropriate for Tier 3 intensive intervention in content area

(Continued)

TABLE 4.2 (Continued)

Team Member	Critical Tasks in Multi-Tiered RTI Curriculum
Bilingual/ESL Teacher	Provide expertise in the areas of bilingual/ESL education in each tier of instruction Lead discussions and considerations of cultural and linguistic ecological factors when interpreting curriculum screening, monitoring, and diagnostic assessment results Provide leadership in assisting the team to distinguish cultural and linguistic differences from learning disabilities
Speech/Language Specialist	Provide expertise in the areas of speech/language development, differences, and disorders Provide Tier 2 and/or Tier 3 instruction to meet speech and language disorder needs Assist in identifying the research-based curriculum appropriate for Tier 3 intensive intervention in the content area Assist in distinguishing language difference from language disorders when interpreting curriculum screening, monitoring, and diagnostic assessment results
Behavioral Specialist	Provide expertise in social-emotional and behavioral development Assist in the screening, monitoring, and diagnostic assessment procedures (e.g., FBA) Assist general educators with instructional and classroom management procedures and interventions (e.g., positive behavior supports) Implement Tiers 2 and 3 instruction to provide social-emotional and behavioral supports
Social Worker	Provide expertise in the area of social development Assist classroom teachers with suggestions for improving social skills in the classroom Conduct home visits if included in the comprehensive diagnostic assessment for a suspected disability Provide Tier 2 and 3 supports in area of social development
Paraprofessional	Provide a summary of teaching and learning experiences through work with the learner Assist in completing progress monitoring tasks
Parents/Guardian	Provide insight into home/community issues and concerns Assist team in understanding cultural and linguistic values and preferences concerning learning Provide valuable home support to curriculum implementation in the school

be added as necessary. Also, not all of the educators discussed here are or need to be on every RTI team; the composition of the team is based on the needs of the learner. The list of potential team members identified in Table 4.2, along with their critical tasks, was developed from discussions of problem-solving team membership and roles in several sources, including Appelbaum (2009), Howell et al. (2008), and Hoover (2009a).

In the combined standard treatment–problem-solving model, several team members take part in the decision-making process in multi-tiered RTI curriculum implementation and progress monitoring. In this model, the data collected in a standardized manner serve as the basis for decision making. In addition, including the ecological factors relative to the suspected area of need helps the team to make the most informed decisions possible. As previously discussed, the initial decisions are made by the general class teachers to best implement (1) the

Tier 1 core curriculum, (2) a differentiated classroom, and (3) targeted instructional differentiations if screening results identify a potential struggling learner.

However, once insufficient progress with the Tier 1 curriculum is determined and Tier 2 or 3 instruction is considered warranted, the school's RTI team becomes involved to consider all available data and information about the learner's needs. Team members may have expertise in more than one area (e.g., the special educator has assessment and instructional expertise) and therefore may provide support in more than one area if appropriate (e.g., special education, assessment). Other members, including administrators, a vision specialist, or physical and occupational therapists, are included as necessary based on the student's needs. Different individuals may also become involved by providing indirect support (i.e., as consultants) and/or direct support through service on the team (i.e., participating directly in instructional decisions). This section concludes with a summary of when it is essential to include the support and expertise of each educator on the RTI team:

General Class Teachers—Included in all major curricular decisions for learners in their classrooms

Special Educators—Included when a struggling learner is identified based on Tier 1 core curriculum screening or progress monitoring results

School Psychologist/Assessment Specialist—Involved in decisions based on assessment results and when a comprehensive diagnostic assessment is warranted

Content Area Specialist (e.g., in Reading)—Included in decisions that pertain to a struggling learner in a given content area

Bilingual/ESL Teacher—Included whenever the needs of a culturally/linguistically diverse learner are considered

Speech/Language Specialist—Included whenever a speech/language disorder is suspected

Behavioral Specialist—Included when the suspected area of need reflects social-emotional and/or behavioral development needs

Social Worker—Included when home visits are necessary and when social issues are central to the learner's needs

Paraprofessional—Included when the student's needs are considered relative to supports provided by a paraprofessional educator

Parents/Guardians—Included in major RTI decisions made for their child

Form 4.3, developed from the above discussions (*Checklist of Response to Intervention Team Members' Curricular Contributions*), helps RTI teams ensure that the proper members are included and that their input is valued and considered in the decision-making process.

Making Effective Response to Intervention Curricular Decisions

As discussed previously, several principles or practices form the foundation of multi-tiered RTI models:

1. Implementation of the Tier 1 research-based core curriculum with fidelity
2. Screening and monitoring of progress toward curricular benchmarks on a regular basis, adhering to standard administration and scoring procedures
3. Adherence to guidelines established as a basis for curricular decisions (i.e., decision rules)
4. Use of data to base curricular decisions
5. Consideration of (a) level of proficiency, (b) rate of progress, and (c) gap analysis when interpreting data that suggest that a struggling learner may require a more intensive form of instruction (i.e., Tier 2 or 3)
6. Consideration of related factors to best interpret curriculum needs and progress (i.e., ecological factors)
7. Learning accommodations provided in a differentiated classroom and the use of targeted instructional differentiations when necessary

As a result, much is involved in making effective RTI curricular decisions, especially when Tier 2 or 3 instruction seems to be needed. In addition to considering the above factors, RTI teams must keep in mind that Tier 1 core instruction should meet the needs of approximately 80% of learners and allow them to progress toward benchmarks within a grade or class; if not, the Tier 1 curriculum is adjusted to achieve the 80% threshold before Tier 2 or 3 instruction is used.

To give all learners the most appropriate education, both the "what" and the "how" of the curriculum must be assessed and the results interpreted. This brings us back to the significance of considering the five curricular components when evaluating and interpreting screening, monitoring, or diagnostic data, as illustrated in Table 4.3.

As Table 4.3 shows, all five curricular components must be considered when making curricular decisions in multi-tiered RTI models. Focusing on only some of them when determining level of proficiency, rate of progress, and the size of identified gaps in learning may lead to wrong decisions about necessary curricular adjustments. The following examples, derived from research and personal experiences, illustrate unneeded or improper curricular adjustments or differentiations due to the failure to consider all five curricular components:

Example 1: Adjusting the *evidence-based intervention* when all that is needed is adjustment in *instructional arrangement*

TABLE 4.3 Curricular Components and Key Decision-Making Factors in Response to Intervention Models

Component	RTI Curriculum Significance	RTI Decision Making Factors
Content/Skills (Research-Based Curriculum)	Progress toward district content and skill area benchmarks reflecting a research-based curriculum implemented with fidelity serves as the basis for "red-flagging" at-risk or struggling learners	Level of proficiency Rate of progress Benchmarks appropriate for learners (e.g., diverse students) Sufficient opportunities to learn content and skills Fidelity is corroborated Language proficiency considerations
Evidence-Based Interventions	Differentiated classroom strategies and targeted interventions need to be implemented for their intended purposes with fidelity	Differentiated classroom exists Targeted curricular differentiations exist for learner(s) as needed Evidence-based interventions selected are appropriate for learners Cultural/linguistic considerations
Instructional Arrangements	The various classroom groupings and proximity arrangements may have a significant impact on learner progress toward achievement of benchmark content/skills	Instructional groupings reflect differentiated classroom/instruction Instructional arrangements reflect various preferences for learning Teaching/learning preferences are compatible
Class/Instructional Management Procedures	Differentiated classrooms should reflect a variety of management procedures to accommodate the differences typically seen in the classroom (e.g., preferred ways of learning, time-on-task skills, home/community values, self-management skills)	Management procedures reflect various social and behavioral needs Adjustments include changes to instruction and/or class management as necessary Diverse learner abilities, values, and experiential backgrounds are accommodated in the classroom and in instructional management
Progress Evaluation	Regular and standard assessment of learners' progress toward curricular benchmarks occurs with fidelity to produce data scores that serve as the basis for determining level of proficiency, rate of progress, and gap analysis	Appropriate monitoring procedures are used for all learners Cultural and linguistic factors are accommodated in monitoring Progress monitoring is completed with fidelity Progress monitoring is curriculum based following a standard process Monitoring directly reflects what is taught in the classroom

Example 2: Adjustment by *simplifying content* when all that is needed is a more appropriate *evidence-based intervention*

Example 3: Adjustment to *management procedures* when all that is needed is a change in the *instructional arrangement* from a large-group setting to cooperative learning

Example 4: Adjustments to any of the *curricular elements* before using *progress monitoring*

Example 5: Adjustment to the *instructional arrangement* when all that is needed is a change in the selected *evidence-based intervention*

Example 6: Adjustment to the *instructional arrangement* when what is needed is the teaching of skills using a more stepwise, direct instruction process

Other examples exist; however, the basic issue is this: individual educators as well as RTI teams should ensure that the correct curriculum component(s) is adjusted once an insufficient level of proficiency, an insufficient rate of progress, or an achievement gap has been identified through universal screening and/or progress monitoring. Multi-tiered RTI teams should consider these possibilities prior to making curricular adjustments. This will avoid misinterpretation of screening and assessment results, as well as the possible placement of students in the wrong tier of instruction. It is important to remember that although universal screening and progress monitoring data provide specifics concerning progress toward benchmarks and the extent to which the student has learned what has been taught, decisions about specific curricular components(s) that need adjustment often require information about the teaching and learning situation that goes beyond the data scores.

The above examples show that RTI teams must ensure that when screening or monitoring data scores indicate insufficient progress, all five curricular components must be addressed and evaluated to make certain that the proper adjustments are made. This chapter concludes with its *RTI Curriculum in Practice*, describing the results of a research project I recently completed. It was designed to empower RTI school leaders in helping the RTI team develop and/or implement a schoolwide multi-tiered RTI model.

RTI CURRICULUM IN PRACTICE

Empowering RTI School Leaders

During the 2008–2009 academic year, I conducted a project that involved working with teachers in different elementary schools who were selected by their principals and/or districts to serve as their school's RTI leader. In addition to their teaching duties, these leaders were charged with guiding and leading their school's problem-solving teams with the development and implementation of RTI. My work consisted of providing training, support, ideas, and materials to the RTI leaders, who in turn gave the information to their school teams during their regularly scheduled RTI development meetings. This support was in addition to any school, district, or state-initiated RTI trainings that the school staffs received.

This process was very positive: (1) RTI school leaders were empowered to assist their school teams; (2) issues and concerns that arose during team meetings were addressed quickly and immediately; (3) RTI was implemented in an organized, site-based manner, making the process more relevant and effective; and (4) school teams were able to use their time more efficiently to discuss RTI implementation in their schools. Although not all school teams achieved the same level of success, the process helped each team to address RTI issues and concerns regarding their school's unique needs and learner characteristics in a timely manner.

My work in this project reinforced the importance of ensuring that the school's RTI problem-solving team receive support in their collaboration to make effective decisions concerning the development and implementation of RTI. Providing direct support to the school's RTI leader ensured that time was used efficiently, reducing the need for additional team meetings. Also, issues and concerns specific to each school were addressed. This made the RTI implementation process more meaningful, because it was being implemented in a context most relevant to each school. RTI leaders reported progress in their work with individual teachers and/or their school-based RTI teams, further suggesting that empowering RTI leaders helps school teams succeed in their implementation of school-based RTI models.

RTI APPLICATIONS OF KEY CHAPTER CONCEPTS

The importance of a properly assembled RTI team and clearly established procedures for making curricular decisions cannot be overstated. A variety of educators should serve on the team to ensure that sufficient expertise is considered when addressing students' curricular needs. Three decision-making models exist. The combined standard treatment–problem-solving model is the one most frequently used. It provides RTI teams with both standard data and information concerning various ecological factors. Specific contributions that different RTI team members bring to the process must be valued, along with key decision-making factors associated with the five curricular components, to provide effective RTI decision making for all learners.

The application of these curricular topics in multi-tiered RTI provides the foundation for meeting the needs of all learners in today's classrooms. RTI teams should do the following:

- Identify the components of the team problem-solving model followed in your school (Form 4.2).
- Document team members' contributions to your school's RTI decision-making team process (Form 4.3).
- Identify the roles and responsibilities of each member of the decision-making team.
- Prepare a PowerPoint presentation for colleagues addressing the components necessary for effective implementation of an RTI decision-making model.

Student: _____   Teacher: _____   Date: _____

Tier of Instruction for Which Plan Is Developed: ___ Tier 2   ___ Tier 3

Current Gap Analysis Results: _____
Current Level of Proficiency: _____

Instructions: Complete the Guide to document key factors associated with the implementation of Tier 2 or 3 instruction.

Anticipated and Actual Outcomes of Plan:
Expected/Actual Rate of Progress: _____/_____
Expected/Actual Proficiency Level: _____/_____
Expected/Actual Gap Analysis Results: _____/_____

Tier of Instruction Plan

1. Time frame to implement intervention(s) (e.g., 20 minutes/day, 3 days/week for 6 weeks)

2. Selected evidence-based interventions

3. Procedures for monitoring progress, including devices and practices to be used (e.g., CBM, classroom observation, performance-based assessment)

4. Timeline for monitoring learners' progress (e.g., weekly monitoring)

5. Primary educator providing services:

6. Role of general educator in the program:

7. Decision rules for making curricular decisions (i.e., cut score, level of achievement, rate of progress):
_____
_____
_____
_____

Source: Used by permission of John J. Hoover.

Student: _____   Date: _____

Team Members: _____

Instructions: Check each item to evaluate proper implementation of your multi-tiered decision-making model for a student struggling in learning.

1. Problem Identification
___ Universal screening is completed.
___ Identification of potential struggling students is made.
___ Learner's rate of progress is identified.
___ Gap analysis procedures are completed.
___ Follow-up progress monitoring is conducted for suspected at-risk learners.
___ Screening and initial progress-monitoring data are charted to illustrate suspected learning or behavior need.

2. Problem Definition
___ Implementation of Tier 1 instruction with fidelity is confirmed.
___ Fidelity of assessment implementation is confirmed.
___ Validity of interpretation of assessment results is confirmed.
___ Rate of progress is confirmed.
___ Gap analysis results are confirmed.
___ Curricular differentiations previously completed are documented and discussed.
___ Each team member provides expertise to problem-solving process.
___ Specific area of need is clarified and pinpointed (e.g., reading fluency).
___ Standard treatment data and related authentic assessment results are used.
___ Influence of cultural and linguistic diversity needs are considered relative to suspected problem.

3. Intervention Plan Design
___ Need area is defined in terms of progress toward proficiency of benchmark or objective.
___ Expected rate of progress is determined.
___ Gap reduction targets are determined along with reasonable timeline.
___ Appropriate evidence-based assessments are selected.
___ A sufficient number of assessment devices/practices are selected to best monitor progress and explain assessment results (e.g., CBM, work sample analysis, performance-based).
___ Level and duration of support are determined (i.e., Tier 1, 2, 3 level of support).
___ Time frame for implementing support is established (e.g., three days/week for five weeks).
___ Process for monitoring student response to interventions is detailed (e.g., CBM).
___ Roles different educators will assume in implementing supports are clarified.
___ Supports to be provided to general educator are detailed.
___ Process for charting progress-monitoring data is clarified (e.g., computerized, teacher generated, commercial).
___ Implementation requirements necessary to successfully complete progress monitoring are discussed.
___ Procedures for documenting fidelity of assessment implementation are outlined.
___ Date(s) for future discussions to review instructional effects on student progress is established.
___ Established program is culturally responsive for diverse learners.

4. Intervention Plan Implementation

____ Evidence-based interventions are implemented with fidelity.

____ Progress monitoring is completed as designed and with fidelity.

____ Progress-monitoring results are charted over time.

____ Assessments completed relate directly to that which has been taught.

____ Implementation plan is completed the way in which it was designed.

____ Fidelity of assessment is corroborated based on procedures defined in implementation plan.

____ Implemented plan is culturally responsive for diverse learners.

5. Progress Evaluation

____ Team meets to review progress as outlined in implementation plan.

____ Rate of progress is considered along with level of proficiency.

____ Gap analysis is completed and updated based on progress.

____ Classroom-based assessment evidence is carefully considered relative to student rate of progress.

____ All team members apply their expertise to best clarify and interpret assessment results.

____ Effects of instruction are summarized.

____ Standard treatment data are considered along with related authentic classroom results.

____ Cultural responsive implementation is confirmed for diverse learners.

6. Intervention Plan Review/Revision

____ Intervention plan is revised based on progress-monitoring results.

____ Additional supports are provided if necessary.

____ Duration of interventions is extended if necessary.

____ Differentiations are identified as needed.

____ Decision concerning whether student remains with current level of support (i.e., Tier 2; 3) is made.

____ Revised implementation plan is generated.

____ Process for implementing revised plan is outlined including roles and supports to be provided to general educators.

____ Revised plan is implemented and dates to review student progress are determined.

Source: *RTI assessment essential for struggling learners* by John J. Hoover (2009). Thousand Oaks, CA: Corwin Press. Used by permission.

Checklist of Response to Intervention Team Members' Curricular Contributions

Instructions: Check each item once it has been corroborated for each team member.

General Educator
___ Implement Tiers 1 and 2 research-based curriculum and evidence-based interventions
___ Assist with universal screening
___ Gather/chart Tiers 1 and 2 progress monitoring data
___ Determine level of proficiency, rate of progress, and size of gap for struggling learners
___ Implement a differentiated classroom and targeted differentiations for struggling learners
___ Corroborate fidelity of curriculum implementation and associated progress monitoring
___ Present Tier 1 and 2 curriculum implementation efforts and results to the RTI team
___ Other (specify):

Special Educator
___ Provide special education expertise as necessary
___ Provide general educators with instructional and classroom management ideas to best implement general and targeted differentiated instruction
___ Provide Tier 2 supports as necessary to struggling learners
___ Assist with Tier 2 progress monitoring/chart results
___ Implement Tier 3 intensive curricular interventions
___ Other (specify):

School Psychologist/Assessment Specialist
___ Provide expertise/support for each aspect of curriculum assessment (i.e., universal screening, progress monitoring, diagnostic assessment)
___ Assist in the Tier 3 comprehensive diagnostic evaluation of a suspected disability
___ Assist in completing gap analysis, determining rate of progress, and interpreting results for struggling learners
___ Lead discussions concerning proper interpretation of progress monitoring, universal screening, and diagnostic assessment results
___ Other (specify):

Content Area Specialist
___ Provide expertise in content area for struggling learners in each tier of intervention (e.g., reading, mathematics, writing)
___ Provide Tier 2 supplemental support as needed
___ Assist in identifying evidence-based interventions to differentiate instruction in content area in Tiers 1 and 2
___ Assist with progress monitoring in content area
___ Lead discussions concerning proper interpretation of progress monitoring and universal screening results in content area

___ Assist in identifying the research-based curriculum appropriate for Tier 3 intensive intervention in content area
___ Other (specify):

Bilingual/ESL Teacher

___ Provide expertise in the areas of bilingual/ESL education in each tier of intervention
___ Lead discussions and considerations of cultural and linguistic ecological factors when interpreting curriculum screening, monitoring, and diagnostic assessment results
___ Provide leadership in assisting the team to distinguish cultural and linguistic differences from learning disabilities
___ Other (specify):

Speech/Language Specialist

___ Provide expertise in the area of speech/language development, differences, and disorders
___ Provide Tiers 2 and/or 3 instruction to meet speech and language disorder needs
___ Assist in identifying the research-based curriculum appropriate for Tier 3 intensive intervention in content area
___ Assist in distinguishing language difference from language disorders when interpreting curriculum screening, monitoring, and diagnostic assessment results
___ Other (specify):

Behavioral Specialist

___ Provide expertise in emotional and behavioral development
___ Assist in the screening, monitoring, and diagnostic assessment procedures (e.g., FBA)
___ Assist general educators with instructional and classroom management procedures and interventions (e.g., positive behavior supports)
___ Implement Tiers 2 and 3 instruction to provide social-emotional and behavioral supports
___ Other (specify):

Social Worker

___ Provide expertise in the area of social development
___ Provide classroom teachers with suggestions for improving social skills in the classroom
___ Conduct home visits if included in the comprehensive diagnostic assessment for a suspected disability
___ Provide Tier 2 and 3 supports in area of social development
___ Other (specify):

Paraprofessional
___ Provide summary of teaching and learning experiences in working with struggling learners
___ Assist in completing progress monitoring tasks
___ Other (specify):

Parents/Guardians
___ Provide insight into home/community issues and concerns
___ Assist team in understanding cultural and linguistic values and preferences about learning
___ Provide valuable home support to the curriculum implementation in school
___ Other (specify):

Additional Comments to Support Collaborative Team Contributions:

Source: Used by permission of John J. Hoover.

CHAPTER 5

Collaboration to Meet Response to Intervention Curricular Needs

Overview

THE IMPORTANCE OF A school staff working together to develop and implement a schoolwide RTI model highlights the need for continuous collaboration among educators. A process for creating and implementing effective change and applying needed skill sets provides necessary structures for ensuring productive, ongoing collaboration to support learners in each tier of instruction. Although RTI team members are the foundation of this collaboration, the educational interventionist is especially important to its success. This includes procedures and skills to provide push-in or pull-out direct interventions, consultative supports, and monitoring the effects of the instruction on learners' progress.

Key Topics

- Significance of collaboration in RTI
- Interventionist's roles and responsibilities
- Curriculum implementation and the educational interventionist
- Collaboration and the role of the interventionist
- Facilitating change
- Effective communication

Learner Outcomes

After reading this chapter, you should:

1. Acquire the skills necessary to implement collaboration to support a schoolwide RTI model
2. Be able to implement the role of an educational interventionist
3. Acquire the knowledge and skills necessary to help facilitate productive change
4. Understand the various skill sets required to implement a multi-tiered RTI curriculum
5. Be able to collaborate effectively to ensure the selection and use of appropriate tiered curricular interventions

SIGNIFICANCE TO CONTEMPORARY CLASSROOM INSTRUCTION

Collaboration among educators is extremely important given the significant changes that may be needed to meet the many demands of multi-tiered RTI models. It is key to the effective sharing of ideas, time, resources, and staff as various educators provide instruction. Collaboration includes the application of several skill sets for working together to implement the curriculum with fidelity, communicate frequently and effectively, monitor progress, and participate in and/or facilitate RTI team decision making. In RTI, the interventionist provides services to learners and collaborates with other educators. This role includes applying knowledge and skills needed for effective communication, collaboration, and change processes, as well as using evidence-based interventions and progress-monitoring devices and practices. The interventionist's role may be assumed by a variety of educators in addition to a schoolwide designated professional, including general class teachers, special educators, reading specialists, and speech-language specialists, to name a few. Integrating ongoing collaboration with service delivery provided by interventionists is essential for meeting the curricular needs of all learners in a multi-tiered RTI model.

Significance of Collaboration in Response to Intervention Curriculum Implementation

Since the mid-1970s, the roles of general and special educators in meeting the needs of all learners have systematically merged to the point where, today, effective and efficient collaboration is not only encouraged, it is necessary to implement the multi-tiered RTI curriculum. Within the parameters of IDEA (2004), which promotes the use of RTI models, Friend and Cook (2003) wrote that collaboration among educators is often necessary to meet the mandates of federal legislation for students.

Burns and Gibbons (2008) discussed collaboration in RTI and wrote that an efficient collaborative process "involves a sharing of responsibility" (p. 59), in which all concerned have defined tasks, while sharing and receiving needed supports to best meet their responsibilities. Although collaboration in general has many important aspects, three areas are especially important given the complexities of developing and implementing a schoolwide RTI multi-tiered model: (1) abilities and processes associated with creating effective change; (2) application of targeted skill sets; and (3) defining and integrating the role of an educational interventionist within overall collaboration. Each of these areas is discussed below to highlight the importance of collaboration in implementing the multi-tiered RTI curriculum. For additional and more detailed information about collaboration in education, the reader is referred to the sources cited in this chapter.

Facilitating Curricular Changes

The development and implementation of RTI in a school/district requires change in both the way learning needs are identified and the way these needs are addressed in the curriculum. Although far-reaching, the challenges in creating change are best addressed through collaboration among educators. When they consider transitioning to multi-tiered RTI, educators need to address not only the steps or procedures in the transition process but also the factors that contribute to effective change. The model discussed below incorporates factors in creating effective change while addressing the task of changing educational processes and procedures to effectively implement various aspects of RTI.

Change Process

Hall (2008) wrote that the complexities of change require schools/districts to avoid efforts to "launch an RTI initiative without a great deal of consideration" (p. 36). Batsche, Curtis, Dorman, Castillo, and Porter (2007) indicated that effective change best occurs through collaborative efforts and support systems. In regard to RTI change in schools, these authors wrote that "all primary stakeholders must be involved in every stage of the change process" (p. 379). This includes various educators, such as general and special class teachers, bilingual/ESL

TABLE 5.1 Elements for Creating Effective Change

Change Element	Description
1. *Awareness*	Educators must see the possibility that change can occur
2. *Interest*	Educators must have an interest in creating change
3. *Time*	Educators need to be given time to consider the possibility and potential worth of change
4. *Limited Implementation*	The proposed change should initially be implemented on a small, controlled scale
5. *Full Implementation*	Based on the successes and revisions of limited implementation, change is implemented on a larger scale

educators, principals, school psychologists, social workers, interventionists, and counselors. Those most impacted by the change must be part of the process for creating it. Weiner (2003) stated that change involves personal growth and learning, collaboration, and problem solving. Keeping in mind these general change elements, meaningful change for an individual includes, at minimum, the elements described in Table 5.1, developed from information in the above sources.

Whatever the initial outcome of the change, the overall goal is to help educators develop a greater *capacity* for change so that future changes become easier and more manageable. Additionally, "change is often hard on everyone, and doing new things, especially when just learned, is difficult at best" (Fixsen, Naoom, Blasé, & Wallace, 2007, p. 6). To help educators increase their capacity for change, the following qualities should be considered (as discussed by Hoover and Patton, 2005):

- Change happens to individuals.
- Change is a *process*, not a single event.
- Educators in different roles (e.g., general class teacher, principal, special educator, psychologist) perceive the meaning of change differently for the same event or topic.
- Implementation of change is influenced by various factors/events. One must consider what these might be and their effects on the desired change.
- Change and its process can be facilitated.

Therefore, the significance, effects, and process for facilitating the changes required of educators in the transition to RTI are crucial to its success. This comprehensive transition is a process with several defined, sequential stages, reflecting the step-by-step implementation of different aspects of RTI.

Procedures for Initiating/Implementing RTI Curricular Change

Although a variety of RTI models exist or are in development (Jimersson et al., 2007), the process for initiating and sustaining any RTI model has the same general steps or procedures. Batsche et al. (2007) wrote that the best way to implement large-scale endeavors is to use established strategies. This includes following a process that facilitates effective development, implementation, and sustainability. For example, the Florida Department of Education RTI model emphasizes consensus, support, and implementation (Batsche et al., 2007). The Idaho State Department of Education RTI model includes systems evaluation, a problem-solving process, parent involvement, outcomes, and progress monitoring, as well as data-driven decision making and eligibility (Callender, 2007). Ervin, Schaughency, Goodman, McGlinchey, and Mathews (2007) discussed the process for implementing RTI in Michigan. It included creating readiness, initial implementation, institutionalization, and evaluation, as described by Adelman and Taylor (1997).

As can be seen, there are several common elements in the implementation of new initiatives in education, and these provide a framework for success with RTI as a new model requiring changes in both structure and practice. For our purposes, I will discuss an example from the work of Fixsen et al. (2007) and Hall (RTI Action Network Web site), who identified several stages that should be addressed to develop and implement RTI in schools. These have been adapted, building on ideas reflecting the other models discussed above (see Figure 5.1).

FIGURE 5.1 Stages in Implementing and Sustaining a School/District-Based Response to Intervention Model

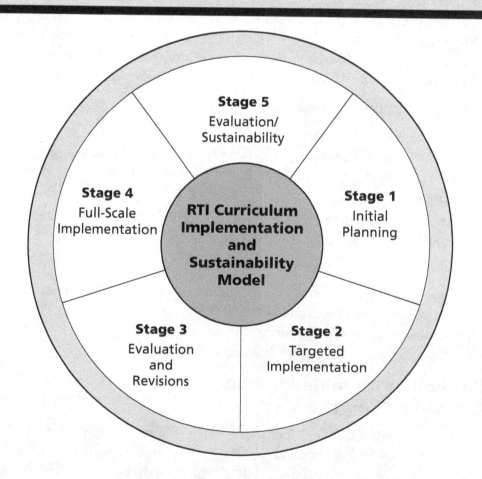

Once the decision to implement RTI in a district or school is made, a model such as the one in Figure 5.1 can serve as a framework to guide those responsible for its development and implementation. In addition, Table 5.2, which was generated from the above sources, summarizes key aspects of each of these stages.

As illustrated in Table 5.2 and Figure 5.1, developing and implementing a multi-tiered RTI model requires much planning, collaboration, evaluation, and revisions to achieve an acceptable level of sustainability. Documentation of efforts in an RTI Action Plan, including evaluation of those efforts, gives RTI leaders an excellent opportunity to incorporate RTI in everyday teaching and learning while facilitating gradual and necessary change. Also, the Guides presented in Chapter 2 may be used to help create a school-initiated RTI development and implementation Action Plan. Each stage in the process is further defined and clarified below, based on discussions in the literature cited above about implementing RTI on a schoolwide basis.

INITIAL PLANNING ■ During the Initial Planning stage, the conditions and parameters are established for developing and implementing an RTI model on both a targeted and a full-scale level. This includes collecting and studying various types of information to determine feasibility and responsibilities in initiating RTI (Fixsen et al., 2007). The following should be documented in the initial planning stage:

- The members of the team charged with developing and implementing RTI
- The vision for full RTI and multi-tiered curriculum implementation

TABLE 5.2 Process for Developing Response to Intervention Models

Stage	Description	Primary Outcomes
1. *Initial Planning*	Gather information about RTI; select RTI team; frame process to implement RTI	RTI leader gathers resources RTI team, consisting of four or five educators who are interested in developing RTI, is assembled An Action Plan necessary to implement RTI is developed RTI tasks are identified and prioritized
2. *Targeted Implementation*	Implement selected RTI tasks	RTI tasks are implemented as prioritized in the Action Plan on a small scale (e.g., in select classrooms or a school; one task is altered to avoid attempting too much change too quickly)
3. *Evaluation and Revisions*	Evaluate small-scale implementation	Evaluation of implementation of RTI tasks is completed; Results documented; Revisions made
4. *Full-Scale Implementation*	Implement RTI on a full scale	RTI as developed and revised based on small-scale implementation is implemented on a full scale (e.g., all classrooms; all schools in the district)
5. *Evaluation/ Sustainability*	Evaluate full-scale implementation	Critical aspects documented in the Action Plan are evaluated Results are documented RTI implementation revisions are made Revisions are incorporated into the full-scale implementation and the RTI process continues, along with additional documentation of evaluation results

- Specific RTI tasks that must be completed to achieve full implementation
- Changes that must occur, including system changes such as enhanced data analysis procedures
- Priorities for developing and implementing RTI tasks
- Projected timeline for completing all RTI tasks (the full RTI model may take 3–5 years to develop)
- School-based RTI Action Plan detailing each task to be addressed
- Evaluation procedures to determine the effectiveness of the RTI team in developing the vision, RTI task sequence, and associated Action Plan(s)
- Procedures for assessing student progress (i.e., universal screening, progress monitoring, diagnostic assessment)

TARGETED IMPLEMENTATION ■ The new RTI tasks implemented at any one time must be limited in scope to provide the best chance for success by not attempting too much too quickly and by allowing issues to arise and be resolved on a limited scale (Fixsen et al., 2007). Building on the developments in the previous stage, the Targeted Implementation stage includes the development and implementation of select, prioritized RTI tasks as outlined in an Action Plan. The following are completed and documented in this stage:

- Timeline for developing the RTI tasks identified in Stage 1
- Process followed to develop tasks needed for multi-tiered curriculum implementation in an RTI model
- Plan to implement developed RTI tasks in a select number of settings and content area(s) (e.g., reading fluency)
- Documented effectiveness of the Action Plan used to implement RTI tasks
- Recording of successes/issues in implementing RTI tasks
- Monitoring of learners' progress using data generated from screening and monitoring procedures

EVALUATION AND REVISIONS ■ As the multi-tiered RTI model is implemented in a targeted manner, progress toward the identified goals, completion of tasks, and results of specific efforts are documented. Once the initial implementation has been completed for the defined time period, its effects are evaluated with specific emphasis on several key factors:

- Completion of tasks as stipulated
- Process followed to involve key educators
- Issues/problems that arose during implementation
- Strategies used to address issues/problems
- Effects of strategies on resolution of issues/problems

- Identifiable changes resulting from targeted implementation efforts
- Effects of the targeted implementation on the RTI curriculum in each tier of instruction

Through review of these key factors, decisions are made concerning any adjustments necessary to facilitate implementation on a larger scale (e.g., school/district-wide; all elementary schools). Revisions are made as necessary in preparation for the next phase in the process.

FULL-SCALE IMPLEMENTATION ■ Once a school or district team has determined that the targeted implementation is successful on a small scale, the evaluation results are considered and the plan is revised as needed. This is followed by full-scale implementation of the multi-tiered RTI model (Hall, RTI Action Network), which involves the following:

- Proper training of all educators involved
- Implementation adhering to the process followed in the Targeted Implementation stage
- Continued evaluation and documentation of implementation efforts
- Determination of the effects of the full-scale process on the fidelity of RTI implementation
- Expansion of the screening and progress-monitoring procedures to determine the effects on student progress once full-scale implementation is completed

As in the Targeted Implementation stage, educators should take part in the ongoing evaluation. Once RTI is implemented for the specified time period, the final stage is considered.

EVALUATION/SUSTAINABILITY ■ During this final stage, the results of the full-scale implementation are summarized and discussed by those leading the RTI efforts to make necessary improvements (Hall, RTI Action Network Web site). Ultimately, the long-term sustainability of the RTI framework and structures is the key indicator of successful RTI implementation on a schoolwide or district level, leading to adequate rates of progress and acceptable levels of proficiency in a multi-tiered RTI curriculum implemented with fidelity.

This overview has focused on some of the key factors to consider in successfully implementing RTI on a schoolwide basis. For a more detailed discussion, the reader is referred to the sources cited in this section. In addition, Form 5.1 (*Guide for Collaboration in the Response to Intervention Change Process*) provides a guide for ensuring that key elements in each phase of implementation are addressed.

Collaboration Skill Sets

In developing and implementing a schoolwide RTI model, educators must collaboratively employ a variety of skill sets targeting the key concepts of a multi-tiered curriculum model. These include (1) implementation with fidelity; (2) frequent monitoring of progress; (3) charting of progress data; (4) increased use of differentiated instruction and classroom management interventions within the Tier 1 core curriculum; (5) knowledge and use of academic and behavioral evidence-based interventions; and (6) application of various instructional accommodations as necessary in the classroom. Given the comprehensive nature of multi-tiered RTI models, collaboration for many educators becomes necessary and desired, highlighting the importance of several critical skill sets required to meet the various learning and behavior needs of students in today's classrooms. These skill sets, discussed by Crone and Horner (2003), Hoover and Patton (2008), Skrtic, Harris, and Shriner (2005), and Vaughn (2003), are summarized in Figure 5.2. There, five major skill sets are

FIGURE 5.2 Collaborative Skills Sets in Multi-Tiered Response to Intervention Curriculum Implementation

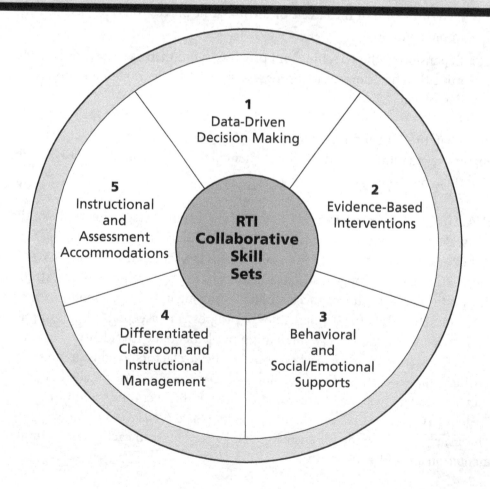

identified. Each of them is discussed in detail below. These skill sets are not all-inclusive; however, proficiency in their use by team members establishes a positive environment for collaborating and sharing responsibilities to implement the multi-tiered RTI curriculum for all learners.

Data-Driven Decision Making

A core element of RTI is the use of data to make informed decisions about curriculum implementation and learners' progress (Vaughn & Fuchs, 2003). As discussed in the previous chapter, in RTI curriculum implementation, data are gathered in three ways: (1) universal screening, (2) progress monitoring, and (3) diagnostic assessment. Each type of assessment yields a score that reflects the student's level of proficiency and rate of progress toward grade-level benchmarks based on national, local, or criterion-based norms. Although other types of ecological information and data may also be gathered, the achievement and behavioral scores serve as the foundation for making important curriculum decisions (i.e., data-driven decisions). To best implement data-based decisions, educators should possess knowledge and skills in a variety of interrelated assessment areas:

- Curriculum-based measurement
- Data graphing and analysis procedures
- Functional skills assessment
- Performance-based assessment
- Functional behavioral assessment (FBA)
- Validity and reliability in assessment

The effective use of screening, monitoring, and diagnostic data helps members of the combined standard treatment–problem-solving teams to make the informed decisions necessary to make appropriate instructional adjustments, select appropriate tiers of intervention, and, if necessary, determine eligibility for special education due to a disability.

Evidence-Based Interventions

Another fundamental element of multi-tiered RTI is the proper use of evidence-based interventions along with the research-based curriculum (U.S. Department of Education, 2002). As previously discussed, evidence-based interventions are specific teaching methods grounded in research and shown to be effective in achievement and/or behavioral development (e.g., direct instruction, cognitive supports, peer tutoring, study and learning strategies). The combined use of evidence-based interventions and the research-based curriculum provides the foundation for effective tiered instruction. This includes the ability to both select the intervention and implement the method as designed (i.e., implementation with fidelity). Some of the key subskill areas associated with this skill set include:

- Direct instruction
- Precision teaching
- Mastery learning
- Task analysis
- Higher order thinking methods
- Progress monitoring with fidelity
- Determination of fidelity of implementation of interventions
- Knowledge of evidence-based interventions as used in core disciplines (e.g., reading, mathematics)

Appropriate decisions in RTI implementation are grounded in the effective application of evidence-based interventions within each tier of instruction, together with the research-based curriculum used in Tier 1 instruction. This skill set includes knowledge of evidence-based interventions and (1) their proper steps and procedures, (2) methods to corroborate their use with fidelity, and (3) their use to make curricular adjustments based on screening/monitoring data.

Behavioral and Social-Emotional Supports

RTI is generally discussed when considering learners who struggle with academic subjects; however, social and emotional development is also critical to success in teaching and learning; thus, it requires equal attention in multi-tiered RTI models (Malecki & Demaray, 2007). Many schools and school districts have begun to incorporate behavioral screening, monitoring, and diagnosis into their RTI framework (Howell et al., 2008; Waller, 2009). Knowledge of the interrelationships among academic, social-emotional, and behavioral learning is crucial in implementing a differentiated classroom, targeted differentiations, and a comprehensive RTI curriculum. Therefore, another significant skill set in RTI pertains to various aspects of behavioral and social-emotional supports. Crone and Horner (2003) discuss the importance of implementing positive behavior supports to meet the behavioral/emotional needs of struggling learners, which includes the application of FBA. Incorporating behavioral assessment along with behavioral supports into the multi-tiered RTI curriculum gives learners a more comprehensive tiered instructional experience. It also gives members of RTI teams valuable behavioral information that may assist them in accurately interpreting screening or progress monitoring data scores.

Select key subskills associated with this RTI skill set include (Crone & Horner, 2003, Hoover, 2009a):

- Differentiated classroom management
- FBA
- Applied behavioral analysis (ABA)
- Student self-management strategies
- Interactions of academic and social-emotional/behavioral progress in teaching and learning (i.e., the five curricular components)
- Positive behavioral supports

This skill set is essential to meet the academic and social-emotional needs of all learners, especially struggling learners in each tier of instruction. Additionally, when combined with academic progress data, social-emotional/behavioral data provide the combined standard treatment–problem-solving team with much needed information to ensure that the most appropriate curriculum component(s) is adjusted, if necessary.

Differentiated Classroom and Instructional Management

Differentiated classrooms and instructional management procedures are also basic to successful implementation of the multi-tiered RTI curriculum. Vaughn (2003) wrote that differentiated instruction is necessary to meet various needs within RTI. In addition, although many classrooms contain differentiated instructional and management aspects, some learners often require more targeted differentiations in addition to the general differentiations of the classroom. As will be discussed in the next chapter, the use of more targeted, evidence-based, differentiated interventions in the Tier 1 core curriculum prevents some at-risk learners from needing more intensive Tier 2 supports. Key subskills in this important RTI skill set include:

- Knowledge of various evidence-based interventions and their suggested uses in the classroom
- Sheltered instruction
- Scaffolding
- Study and learning strategies
- Time on task and academic learning time
- Various progress-monitoring practices
- Culturally responsive teaching

This skill set helps educators implement the curriculum in creative, structured, and diverse ways to meet the many social, academic, cultural, and linguistic needs of today's students. In addition, this skill set helps educators provide targeted differentiations within the Tier 1 curriculum. This reduces unnecessary Tier 2 instruction by implementing a differentiated classroom and an instructional environment that meet the needs of 80% of students, the guideline established for Tier 1 success in the classroom.

Instructional and Assessment Accommodations

Effective multi-tiered curriculum implementation also requires the educator to select and use instructional and assessment accommodations to ensure that students have the best opportunities to learn and to demonstrate their learning through screening and progress monitoring. *Accommodations* are practices that alter or shape learning and assessment conditions to help the student make progress toward curricular benchmarks (Orosco, 2005). When they are used appropriately in the instructional environment, accommodations blend naturally with differentiated classroom structures and targeted differentiations. When they are used appropriately in universal screening, progress monitoring, and diagnostic assessment, the results more accurately reflect the learner's true knowledge and skills; this information is necessary to make informed RTI curricular decisions in each tier of instruction. Knowledge about and proficiency in using the following five accommodations greatly enhances the curricular implementation and monitoring experiences. These descriptions were developed from information in Orosco (2005) and Thompson (2004).

> *Presentation*—refers to the manner in which instructional and assessment material is presented to the learner, such as more visual or auditory emphasis (e.g., using pictures rather than relying extensively on verbal interactions).
>
> *Response*—refers to the preferred method of response in order to obtain more accurate assessment results, as well as demonstrate proficiency and rate of progress within the curriculum (e.g., performance-based assessment, oral rather than written responses).
>
> *Time*—refers to appropriate modifications of time allotments, such as completing the assessment or learning task in two short sessions rather than one longer one that challenges the student's time-on-task ability.
>
> *Scheduling*—which relates to the time accommodation, refers to altering the schedule for completing learning or assessment tasks in line with the student's attention, self-management, or cognitive abilities.
>
> *Setting*—refers to altering the location where learners complete instructional tasks or assessment practices, such as different areas within the classroom, school library, learning centers, or resource rooms.

This skill set helps to ensure that all students are given sufficient opportunities to learn and to demonstrate their learning by considering their social-emotional, behavioral, self-management, cultural, and linguistic needs and preferences. By applying this RTI skill set in teaching and learning, educators develop greater confidence in their students' universal screening, progress monitoring, and diagnostic assessment results. Form 5.2 (*Collaboration Skill Sets Self-Evaluation Checklist*) provides a guide for educators to evaluate their own collaboration abilities in each of the five skill sets.

Role of Interventionists in Response to Intervention Curriculum Implementation

Many schools use educators with specialized training and/or experiences in targeted curricular areas to assist in meeting multi-tiered instructional demands. These individuals are often referred to as *RTI interventionists*. Their responsibilities include providing support to both teachers and students to help meet the curricular needs of struggling learners. In the multi-tiered RTI curriculum, an interventionist is any educator with the knowledge and expertise to provide either Tier 2 supplemental supports or Tier 3 intensive interventions to struggling learners. Some of the key tasks of an interventionist are those described by Appelbaum (2009) and CDE (2008):

- Expertise in a curriculum area and selected interventions
- Knowledge of the Tier 1 core curriculum in which the learner is struggling
- Expertise in making direct connections between the Tier 1 core curriculum and the selected Tier 2 supplemental supports
- Communication and collaboration skills
- Ability to provide necessary Tier 2 supports with fidelity
- Ability to provide necessary Tier 3 intensive interventions with fidelity
- Knowledge of a variety of interventions for meeting defined Tier 2/3 needs (e.g., direct instruction, applied behavior analysis, precision teaching, study skills/learning strategies)
- Both push-in and pull-out teaching abilities to provide supports in the most transparent and inclusive manner possible
- Strong time management and instructional management abilities to meet a variety of needs on a daily basis
- Effective progress-monitoring abilities

An interventionist can be any educator who possesses the above skills, including the general class teacher, special education teacher, reading specialist, literacy coach, or ESL instructor to give a few typical examples (CDE, 2008; West Virginia Department of Education Web site). In some schools, a specific educator is designated the school's interventionist, and this person provides various supports to struggling learners (e.g., reading, mathematics, behavioral). Tier 2 or 3 instruction may occur in a variety of settings, singly or in combination, including the following:

1. In the general classroom, implemented by the general educator
2. In the general classroom, using push-in supports provided by an interventionist
3. In a pull-out situation, implemented by an interventionist
4. A combined arrangement whereby some Tier 2 or 3 instruction is provided by the general educator in the general classroom, along with push-in or pull-out supports provided by an interventionist

As these four possible situations show, Tier 2 or 3 instruction may involve the collective efforts of the general class teacher and other educators providing intervention services.

The optimum method for addressing both inclusion and the targeted needs of struggling learners is to provide supports as much as possible in the general classroom by the general class teacher and/or another interventionist through push-in or pull-out services.

Sometimes, however, a pull-out arrangement alone may be best to meet the learner's needs, as well as most feasible for some schools. In each of the four interventionist structures, it is essential to keep in mind that all Tier 2 instruction is delivered *in addition to* Tier 1 core instruction; that is, Tier 2 instruction *supports* and does not *replace* Tier 1 instruction. Below is a discussion of six interventionist roles or structures used to provide Tier 2 supports in elementary schools identified through a research project investigating the schoolwide implementation of multi-tiered RTI (Hoover & Love, in review) and the literature sources cited in this section. This is followed by a discussion of several tasks often associated with the implementation of Tier 3 intensive interventions with which educators should be familiar.

Tier 2 Interventionist—Role 1: Tier 2 Supports Provided by the General Educator in the General Classroom. In this structure, the general class teacher assumes the role of Tier 2 interventionist by providing necessary supplemental supports to the few students (i.e., 15%) in the classroom who require additional instruction in defined areas of academic or behavioral need (e.g., reading fluency, self-management, mathematics reasoning).

Key to this structure is a creative and flexible differentiated classroom and instructional management that allow the teacher to provide necessary Tier 2 supports (e.g., 20 minutes daily of reading fluency support to three or four students) while simultaneously providing enrichment activities (i.e., value-added learning of previously taught material) for the other students (e.g., using learning centers, cooperative learning, paired learning), who work independently while the teacher provides direct Tier 2 supplemental instruction.

Tier 2 Interventionist—Role 2: *Tier 2 Supports Provided by an Interventionist Through Push-In Support in the General Classroom.* In this structure, someone other than the general class teacher (e.g., the school's reading specialist or literacy coach) acts as the Tier 2 interventionist by providing necessary supplemental supports to a few students (i.e., 15%) in a small-group setting within the general education classroom (e.g., 20 minutes daily of reading fluency support to three or four students). The differentiated classroom for this type of intervention requires a structure that allows the interventionist to work in one area of the classroom with a small group of students while the classroom teacher provides value-added enrichment activities to the other students (e.g., using learning centers, cooperative learning, or paired learning).

Tier 2 Interventionist—Role 3: *Tier 2 Supports Jointly Provided by an Interventionist Through Push-In Support and by the Classroom Teacher in the General Classroom.* This structure combines those of Roles 1 and 2. For example, to meet a need for Tier 2 support (e.g., 20 minutes daily of reading fluency support to three or four students), this structure may include push-in services for 3 days while the general class educator provides supplemental support for the other 2 days. A differentiated classroom and instructional management, as for Roles 1 and 2, should exist to facilitate this type of Tier 2 support.

Tier 2 Interventionist—Role 4: *Tier 2 Supports Provided by an Interventionist Through Pull-Out Support.* In this structure, someone other than the general class teacher (e.g., the school's designated interventionist, a reading specialist or literacy coach) provides the Tier 2 supplemental supports to a few students (i.e., 15%) in a small-group setting outside of the general education classroom. This structure is consistent with the resource room model that has been implemented for several decades. It may be the method of choice when a few students from different classrooms in the same grade require Tier 2 supplemental support in the same area of need (e.g., 20 minutes daily of reading fluency support to two or three students from three different second-grade classrooms). However, this interventionist role is disconnected from the general classroom and runs the risk of being implemented *parallel to* rather than *integrated with* the Tier 1 core curriculum in the general education classroom. In addition, if the general class teacher is not directly involved with the Tier 2 supports (such as in Roles 1, 2, and 3), he or she may not know or understand what may be occurring in the pull-out situation. Although close communication and collaboration will help keep the general class teacher informed, more direct involvement is preferred, such as described in the roles above and in Role 5 below. Also, while the learners are being pulled out from the general classroom, the other students in the class should only receive value-added enrichment; they should not be given any new instruction that the pulled-out students would miss.

Tier 2 Interventionist—Role 5: Tier 2 Supports Jointly Provided by an Interventionist Through Pull-Out Support and by the Classroom Teacher. This structure combines those of Roles 1 and 4. For example, to meet the need for Tier 2 support (e.g., 20 minutes daily of reading fluency support to three or four students), this structure may include pull-out services for 2 days while the general class educator provides the intervention support for the other 3 days. Both educators implement the same Tier 2 instruction plan, with consistent use of evidence-based interventions and progress monitoring. A differentiated classroom and instructional management, as discussed for Role 1, should exist to help provide this type of Tier 2 support to struggling learners.

Tier 2 Interventionist—Role 6: Tier 2 Schoolwide Supports Provided at the Same Time to All Struggling Learners. In this structure, all learners who require Tier 2 supports receive instruction at the same time during the day (e.g., daily from 11:00 to 11:30). Meanwhile, all other learners who receive Tier 1 instruction receive value-added enrichment. Any educator who is providing Tier 2 support (e.g., reading, mathematics, social development, writing) gives instruction at the same time every day. The students receiving Tier 2 instruction may move to different settings or may be instructed in their own classrooms. Additionally, any of the above five interventionist roles will fit into a schoolwide simultaneous Tier 2 supports structure. An advantage of this interventionist role is that the potential scheduling problems often associated with push-in and pull-out structures (i.e., the entire school is on the same schedule for Tier 2 support and Tier 1 enrichment at the same time) are reduced. Also, during this time, Tier 3 intensive interventions for those who require them are provided.

Although a variety of educators can act as an interventionist to provide Tier 2 supplemental supports, Tier 3 intensive interventions are generally implemented by a school-designated interventionist and/or the special education teacher, adhering to practices usually provided to those with special needs. These include the following, as discussed by Hall (2008), Howell et al. (2008), and Mellard and Johnson (2008):

- Use of more specialized curricula to meet targeted needs (e.g., the Wilson Reading Program)

- Daily interventions to ensure increased intensity and duration of implementation commensurate with Tier 3 learning needs

- More frequent monitoring of progress (e.g., weekly, twice per week)

- Implementation of interventions for an extended period, such as 15–20 weeks

- Use of explicit evidence-based intervention (e.g., direct instruction, teacher-scripted lessons, master learning)

These and related tasks provide the level of intensity and duration required to meet the greater educational needs of learners who receive Tier 3 instruction. Form 5.3 (*Interventionist Supports Checklist*) provides an easy-to-complete guide to make certain that an educator has a minimum level of expertise to act as an interventionist.

This chapter's RTI Curriculum in Practice describes the collaboration of two educators who assumed the role of interventionist to provide coordinated Tier 1 and Tier 2 instruction in mathematics.

RTI CURRICULUM IN PRACTICE

Collaboration to Meet Tier 2 Supplemental Needs

As a special education teacher, I was always searching for effective ways to provide struggling students greater access to the general education curriculum. Because collaboration is essential for student achievement, I decided to make an effort not only to converse regularly with general classroom teachers about students' needs, but also to commit part of my day to coteaching in the general education classroom. Several of the fourth graders on my caseload required Tier 2 math support, so I went to the fourth-grade math teacher and proposed a coteaching situation in which we would share in the planning, implementation, and facilitation of the Tier 2 instruction. The teacher delightedly accepted, and we began discussing the possibilities immediately.

Collaborating About Students

Our intent was to be as effective as possible in collectively meeting all of the students' needs. Therefore, the lead and support coteaching model, which had been used in the past, would be replaced with a model that allowed for more flexibility and creativity in both of our roles. This gave us the opportunity to interrelate Tier 1 and Tier 2 instruction relative to our professional roles, as well as in regard to the students served. Tier 2 instruction was provided to some students receiving special education services, as well as to those without special needs who required supplemental supports. This group of students differed from unit to unit, even from day to day. For example, one student on my caseload required a great deal of differentiations in order to obtain a conceptual understanding of multiplication and division, but with geometry, he excelled and did not require any additional supports. Through our collaboration, we were both able to identify students' strengths and needs. This kind of flexibility gave us the opportunity to find the delicate balance of providing students with just enough Tier 2 support, not too much and not too little.

(Continued)

Collaborating About Instruction

Instructional Space—As the special education teacher, I was primarily responsible for identifying components of the Tier 1 core curriculum that needed differentiating and for providing alternative activities, assessments, instructional tools, and pull-out work space, if necessary. I provided Tier 2 supplemental supports through both push-in and pull-out structures. This allowed some students to receive Tier 2 support entirely in the general classroom. In other cases, the students would participate during the first portion of the lesson in the general class receiving the day's instruction, and then they would receive supplemental support outside of the classroom while others received enrichment. In rare cases, the Tier 2 support was provided entirely through a pull-out situation.

Instructional Roles—Using the district-initiated math curriculum, the classroom teacher and I planned lessons together, sharing ideas for how to best meet the needs through both Tier 1 and Tier 2 instruction. Although the general class teacher was primarily responsible for Tier 1 instruction, while I managed Tier 2 supports, we made an effort to switch roles periodically so as to keep ourselves familiar with both domains. On occasion, the general class teacher would provide the Tier 2 supports while I facilitated the Tier 1 instruction. This switching gave us the opportunity to bounce ideas off of each other regarding how to keep Tier 2 supports embedded within the Tier 1 core curriculum. Additionally, during large-group instruction, it was not unusual for us to share the lesson, in the sense that rarely did one of us sit and listen while the other presented the lesson. On the contrary, the general class teacher might have been leading the instruction while I was supporting it by showing visual aids or drawing illustrations. Many times we split the class in twos or fours, and each facilitated a "learning station."

Making It Work

All of these coteaching model components could not have been possible without our daily collaboration. As a teacher's planning time has its worth in gold, we had to be creative when finding the time to collaborate. For us, it worked best to touch base frequently and briefly, as opposed to infrequently that required larger blocks of time and therefore intermittently. We'd share ideas before and after school, during times when students were working independently, during a walk to the copy room, or, on rare occasions, over a sandwich in the staff lounge. Ultimately, we shared the commitment to differentiate our instruction so that all students had the best opportunities to learn. Our teamwork gave us the synergy we needed to effectively and efficiently collaborate while providing Tier 2 supplemental supports to those students requiring these services while maintaining education in the inclusive, general class setting as much as possible.

—Amy B. (Special Educator)

In regard to progress monitoring and the role of the interventionist, this task could also be done in one of several ways, depending on the students' needs and the school situation: (1) primarily by the general class teacher; (2) primarily by the push-in or pull-out interventionist; or (3) in cooperative ways, with some of the monitoring being done by the general class teacher and some by the push-in/pull-out interventionist. But regardless of the monitoring strategy followed, the same monitoring device and process should be used with fidelity. If the general class educator is responsible for some or all of the monitoring, then the differentiated classroom structures described in the next chapter should be considered for a transparent and smooth implementation of progress monitoring.

In addition, Tier 2 instruction must directly support the Tier 1 curriculum; Tier 3 intensive interventions should, to the extent possible, do so as well. However, given the more significant needs of Tier 3 (e.g., special education), alternatives to the Tier 1 curriculum and Tier 2 supplemental supports may be necessary. As discussed, in many schools, Tier 3 support is provided primarily by the special education teacher or another designated interventionist using a pull-out structure. However, in Tier 2 instruction, the combination of the general class teacher and the push-in/ pull-out interventionist is preferred; this arrangement provides the most inclusion possible for struggling learners.

This chapter concludes with Table 5.3, which provides selected examples of Tier 2 supplemental supports, along with suggested key roles for the

TABLE 5.3 Interventionist's Role and Curricular Components in Tier 2 Instruction

Curriculum Component	Example: Tier 2 Curricular Needs	Key Roles of Interventionist in Meeting Curricular Needs
Content/Skills (research-based curriculum)	Learner is not making sufficient progress toward benchmarks; gap analysis indicates a gap of 2 or more between expected and actual performance levels	Provide supplemental support to help learner make sufficient progress; reduce gap between expected and actual performance levels; corroborate fidelity of implementation of research-based curriculum
Evidence-Based Interventions	Learner requires additional supports using interventions with demonstrated effectiveness in meeting needs similar to those of the struggling learner	Select targeted evidence-based interventions designed to meet needs of the struggling learner; blend Tier 2 supports with Tier 1 core curriculum in both push-in and pull-out settings; corroborate fidelity of implementation of evidence-based interventions
Instructional Arrangements	Learner requires more flexible, differentiated instructional settings to meet needs, such as cooperative versus competitive learning, paired learning, or learning centers used strategically to provide Tier 2 instruction	Select a variety of ways to alter or adapt classroom instructional settings; implement both Tier 1 and 2 instruction in the general classroom in order to simultaneously meet needs of struggling learners and those making adequate progress; corroborate fidelity of implementation of instructional arrangements in the classroom
Class/Instructional Management Procedures	Learner requires more creative, differentiated classroom management to meet various needs such as time-on-task, self-management, listening, attention, or organization abilities	Select evidence-based management interventions; incorporate differentiated management procedures into Tier 1 and 2 instruction; corroborate fidelity of implementation of management procedures
Progress Evaluation	Learner requires more frequent evaluation of progress to determine most appropriate tier of instruction and associated adjustments to meet academic or social/behavioral needs	Assist in monitoring progress reflecting what is taught in the curriculum; select appropriate monitoring device/measure (e.g., CBM); implement ongoing progress monitoring in the general classroom in a time-efficient and effective manner, incorporating it in the differentiated classroom and instructional management

interventionist addressing the five curricular components. It should also be kept in mind that the roles of the interventionist are appropriate no matter who the interventionist is (general or special class teacher, school-designated educator, reading specialist, etc.) and should be used in the structures where Tier 2 support is provided (e.g., the general classroom, push-in/pull-out arrangements).

As Table 5.3 shows, the educational interventionist has a critical role in implementing the five curricular components to meet the needs of all learners. Whether the interventionist is a designated educator whose primary responsibility is to provide Tier 2 or 3 instruction or an educator with broader responsibilities (e.g., general class teacher, special educator, reading specialist, literacy instructor), this person must provide sufficient opportunities to learn and necessary adjustments to instruction, as well as gathering and charting progress data in collaborative ways.

RTI APPLICATIONS OF KEY CHAPTER CONCEPTS

The multi-tiered RTI curriculum is implemented successfully when (1) educators collaborate and expertise and tasks are shared; (2) the process of change necessary to transition from the prereferral model to the RTI model is systemically addressed in structured ways in order to move forward at a pace consistent with the needs and skills of the staff; and (3) all educators in the school consider themselves capable of providing Tier 2 supplemental supports to the Tier 1 core curriculum through collaboration. The following process within RTI will allow educators to meet the needs of all learners:

- Identify the different educators who act as interventionists to implement Tier 2 supports or Tier 3 interventions.
- Document the location where Tier 2 or 3 services are provided; keep a record of the extent to which these services are provided in the general classroom (by the classroom teacher and/or the push-in interventionist) as well as in pull-out locations.
- Evaluate the extent to which educators collaborate to provide Tiers 1, 2, and 3 instruction and develop a plan to enhance collaboration in each tier.
- Develop a PowerPoint presentation on effective change and communication to implement the multi-tiered RTI curriculum collaboratively; present it to the staff.

FORM 5.1 Guide for Collaboration in the Response to Intervention Change Process

Educator: _____   Date: _____

Instructions: Check each item as it is emphasized in the process of change to an RTI model. Provide relevant comments as appropriate for the *Key Change* section.

Key Change Elements

___ The change is perceived as important.
Comments:

_____

___ Educators collaborate to facilitate effective change.
Comments:

_____

___ Professional growth and training occur as change is completed.
Comments:

_____

___ Problem-solving sessions are task oriented and specific to issues associated with the change being conducted.
Comments:

_____

___ Varying tolerance levels for dealing with change are respected, and different educators' needs and time required for successful change are accommodated.
Comments:

_____

RTI Change Process

The following checked items within each step are included in the change process:

I. Initial Planning

___ Team is charged with developing and implementing RTI
___ Self-assessment of current status in implementation of RTI tasks is completed
___ Long-range vision for full RTI implementation is prepared and documented
___ Specific RTI tasks that must be completed to achieve full implementation are listed
___ Changes that must occur, including system changes such as enhanced data analysis procedures, are recorded
___ Prioritized order for developing and implementing RTI tasks
___ Projected timeline for completing all RTI tasks (it may take 3–5 years for full RTI to be achieved)
___ RTI Action Plan for key RTI tasks to be initially addressed is developed
___ Evaluation procedures to determine the effectiveness of the RTI team in developing the vision, the RTI task sequence, and the associated Action Plan(s) are documented
___ Other (Specify):

Summary of Initial Planning:

II. Targeted Implementation

____ Timeline for developing the RTI tasks identified in Stage 1
____ Process followed to develop RTI tasks
____ Implement developed RTI tasks in a select number of settings
____ Document effectiveness of the Action Plan followed to implement RTI tasks
____ Record successes/issues in implementing RTI tasks
____ Other (specify):

Summary of Targeted Implementation:

III. Evaluation and Revisions

____ Completion of tasks as stipulated
____ Process followed to involve key educators
____ Issues/problems that arose during implementation are documented
____ Strategies used to address issues/problems are documented
____ Effects of strategies on resolving issues/problems
____ Identifiable changes resulting from targeted implementation efforts
____ Effects of the targeted implementation on the RTI curriculum in each tier of instruction
____ Other (specify):

Summary of Evaluation and Revisions:

IV. Full-Scale Implementation

____ Proper training of all educators involved is completed
____ Implementation adheres to the process followed in the Targeted Implementation phase
____ Continued evaluation and documentation of implementation efforts
____ Determination of effects of the full-scale process on the fidelity of RTI curriculum implementation
____ Procedures for determining effects on student progress once full-scale implementation is initiated and in place
____ Other (specify):

Summary of Full-Scale Implementation:

V. Evaluation/Sustainability

___ Full-scale implementation is evaluated
___ Lessons learned are discussed; revisions are made
___ Plan for long-term sustainability is developed
___ Sustainability Plan is implemented
___ Ongoing educator support is identified; professional development is continued
___ Sustainability efforts are evaluated and revised as necessary
___ Other (specify):

Summary of Evaluation/Sustainability:

Source: Used by permission of John J. Hoover.

FORM 5.2 Collaboration Skill Sets Self-Evaluation Checklist

Educator: _____ Date: _____

Instructions: Rate each item to reflect your current level of proficiency using the following scale:

1 = No Proficiency   2 = Little Proficiency
3 = Some Proficiency   4 = High Proficiency

I. Data-Driven Decision Making
___ Curriculum-based measurement
___ Data graphing and analyses procedures
___ Functional skills assessment
___ Performance-based assessment
___ Functional behavioral assessment
___ Validity and reliability in assessment
___ Assessment fidelity
___ Decision rules
___ Other (specify):

Summary of Proficiency with Data-Driven Decision Making:

II. Evidence-Based Interventions
___ Direct instruction
___ Precision teaching
___ Mastery learning
___ Task analysis
___ Sheltered instruction
___ Scaffolding
___ Peer tutoring
___ Higher order thinking methods
___ Progress monitoring with fidelity
___ Determination of fidelity of implementation of interventions
___ Knowledge of evidence-based interventions as used within core disciplines (e.g., reading, math)
___ Fidelity of implementation
___ Other (specify):

Summary of Proficiency with Evidence-Based Interventions:

III. Behavioral and Social-Emotional Supports
___ Differentiated classroom management
___ Distinguishing cultural difference from social-emotional disorder
___ Functional behavioral assessment

___ Applied behavioral analysis
___ Student self-management
___ Interactions of academic and social-emotional/behavioral progress in teaching and learning (i.e., five curricular components)
___ Positive behavioral supports
___ Facilitation of effective transitions in classroom tasks/activities
___ Other (specify):

Summary of Proficiency with Behavioral and Social-Emotional Supports:

IV. Differentiated Classroom and Instructional Management

___ Knowledge of various evidence-based interventions and their suggested uses in classroom and instructional management
___ Cooperative learning
___ Learning centers
___ Peer tutoring activities
___ Efficient use of teacher's time in the classroom
___ Behavior management strategies
___ Study and learning strategies
___ Time on task and academic learning time
___ Various progress monitoring practices
___ Cultural and linguistic diversity in education
___ Culturally responsive teaching
___ Other (specify):

Summary of Proficiency with Differentiated Classroom and Instructional Management:

V. Instructional and Assessment Accommodations

___ Presentation (manner in which instructional and assessment material is presented)
___ Response (preferred method of response in order to obtain instructional or assessment results more accurately)
___ Time (appropriate modifications of time allotments)
___ Scheduling (altering the schedule for completion of learning or assessment tasks)
___ Setting (altering the location where learners complete instructional/assessment tasks)
___ Other (specify):

Summary of Proficiency with Instructional and Assessment Accommodations:

Source: Used by permission of John J. Hoover.

Interventionist: _____   Date: _____   Tier of Instruction: _____

Primary Position of Interventionist:

___ Designated Schoolwide Interventionist   ___ Special Educator   ___ Literacy Coach
___ General Class Teacher   ___ Content Specialist   ___ Other

Instructions: Check each item to ensure proper background/training to meet the needs of learner(s) who require supplemental supports. Provide comments as appropriate for the items.

_____

The Interventionist Possesses:

___ Knowledge of and expertise in research-based curriculum and evidence-based interventions
Comments:

___ Knowledge of the Tier 1 core curriculum in which the learner is struggling
Comments:

___ Expertise in making direct connections between the Tier 1 core curriculum and the selected Tier 2 supplemental supports or Tier 3 intensive interventions
Comments:

___ Effective communication and collaboration skills
Comments:

___ Ability to provide necessary Tier 2/3 instruction with fidelity
Comments:

___ Knowledge of a variety of interventions for meeting the defined Tier 2 needs (e.g., direct instruction, applied behavior analysis, precision teaching, study skills/learning strategies)
Comments:

___ Both push-in and pull-out teaching abilities to provide supports in the most transparent and inclusive manner possible
Comments:

___ Strong time and instructional management abilities to best meet a variety of needs on a daily basis
Comments:

_____

Source: Used by permission of John J. Hoover.

▶ PART III

Meeting Differentiated Response to Intervention Curricular Needs of All Learners

THE FOUR CHAPTERS IN Part III address several RTI-related areas of education necessary to implement comprehensive multi-tiered instruction for all learners in grades K–12. Chapter 6 discusses key aspects of differentiated teaching and learning. Efficient application of differentiations is the cornerstone of effective curriculum implementation in today's classrooms. Chapter 7 reflects the reality that today's classrooms are becoming increasingly diverse; in fact, cultural and/or linguistic diversity is now the norm. Diverse learners stand to gain much from multi-tiered RTI, provided that curriculum implementation reflects the diversity in the teaching and learning situation. Chapter 8 addresses an important aspect of education that has the potential to significantly improve the accuracy of progress monitoring and diagnostic assessment data results, as well as ensure sufficient opportunities to learn. This chapter explores the role, use, and contributions of study skills and learning strategies in RTI curriculum implementation. The final chapter in this part, Chapter 9, addresses a frequently overlooked aspect of RTI: its implementation at the secondary level. As learners progress through school, the need to implement the multi-tiered RTI curriculum in the secondary grades has become increasingly apparent.

Part III includes the following four chapters:

6. Differentiated Classroom and Instructional Management in Response to Intervention Models
7. Culturally Responsive Curriculum for Diverse Learners
8. Strategies to Support Multi-Tiered Curriculum Implementation
9. Response to Intervention and Secondary-Level Curriculum Implementation

Differentiated Classroom and Instructional Management in Response to Intervention Models

▶ Overview

Dᴵꜰꜰᴇʀᴇɴᴛᴵᴀᴛᴇᴅ ᴵɴꜱᴛʀᴜᴄᴛᴵᴏɴ ʜᴀꜱ ʙᴇᴇɴ a cornerstone of effective classroom teaching for many years. Its application is especially significant in RTI models to meet the academic and behavioral needs of all learners. In RTI models, as the duration and intensity of needed instructional modifications increase, four levels of differentiation can be identified: general, targeted, supplemental, and intensive. The need for varying degrees of differentiation requires educators to develop a differentiated classroom structure that facilitates implementation of multiple tiered supports in a consistent and transparent manner. Many educational interventions facilitate the differentiation of curriculum; selecting the correct evidence-based interventions is critical to meet the needs of all learners in RTI models.

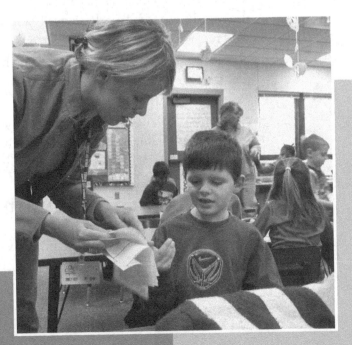

Key Topics

- Differentiated classroom
- Classroom and instructional management strategies and structures
- Differentiation needs in the curriculum within multi-tiered RTI
- Levels of differentiations to meet multi-tiered classroom instructional and management needs
- Teaching and behavior management interventions

Learner Outcomes

After reading this chapter, you should:

1. Acquire the skills and tools to identify differentiated curricular needs
2. Be able to implement differentiated structures in multi-tiered RTI models
3. Understand the significance of differentiated teaching and learning in effective RTI curriculum implementation
4. Apply various instructional and class management practices to meet differing needs simultaneously in multiple tiers of instruction
5. Know various teaching and behavior management techniques to use in implementing general, targeted, supplemental, and intensive differentiations

SIGNIFICANCE TO CONTEMPORARY CLASSROOM INSTRUCTION

Educators today must possess tools to efficiently and effectively identify the differentiation needs of all learners. The success of RTI relies to a great extent on their ability to identify these needs and select appropriate interventions to do so. The greater the ability of teachers to meet these needs simultaneously in the classroom, the more effective they will be in addressing differing instructional and management needs in RTI models, including the use of a variety a evidence-based intervention procedures and structures. This is important in today's classrooms because teachers must find ways to meet the requirements of RTI, reflecting a flexible structure designed to achieve simultaneously different academic proficiency levels and rates of progress.

Overview of Differentiated Teaching and Learning

Differentiated classrooms and instruction have been used for decades to meet a variety of learners' needs. Differentiated learning grew out of the needs and expectations of mainstreaming and inclusion (Hoover & Patton, 2005), as well as

Gardner's work on multiple intelligences (Gardner, 2006). For example, "inclusion efforts over the past few decades have challenged both special and inclusive educators to modify their curriculum to meet diverse needs in the classroom" (Hoover & Patton, 2005, p. 11). Differentiated instruction acknowledges the many needs that students bring to any classroom (Tomlinson, 2001). Differentiated classrooms and instruction represent several aspects of teaching and learning that relate directly to the success of multi-tiered RTI. This includes teachers' recognition that:

- Learners bring a variety of skills, attitudes, cultural values, and expectations to the classroom.
- A variety of instructional interventions may exist to help different students acquire the same content and skills.
- Greater flexibility in classroom management facilitates effective teaching and learning by addressing more needs simultaneously.
- Differentiated classrooms give students a range of acceptable alternatives for addressing tasks and completing assignments.
- Learners bring different preferred or expected learning styles to the classroom.
- Implementation of acceptable variations in the teaching and learning environment has the best chance to reach all students.

These and similar realities in today's classrooms are not new, and as student populations become increasingly diverse, differentiated instruction and classroom management must become more effective. Gartin, Murdick, Imbeau, and Perner (2002) wrote that differentiations include the use of various "strategies that address student strengths, interests, skills and readiness in flexible learning environments" (p. 8). To meet these various needs, differentiated instruction is often discussed as including three general areas (Tomlinson, 1999):

Content—Refers to knowledge and skills to be mastered and applied.

Process—Refers to the way the content is taught and how the learner interacts with it.

Product—Refers to the various ways in which the learner demonstrates acquisition and mastery in learning and using the content.

These aspects of differentiated instruction have been widely discussed in the literature (Bender, 2008; Thousand, Villa, & Nevin, 2007; Tomlinson, 1999, 2001) and will not be reiterated here; rather, the following discussions will build on these three areas and focus on the significance of specific levels of differentiation relative to the tiers of instruction in multi-tiered RTI models. Four levels of differentiation are identified, as illustrated in Figure 6.1.

The four levels progress from general differentiations applied to all learners to specialized differentiations tailored to individual learners. In a

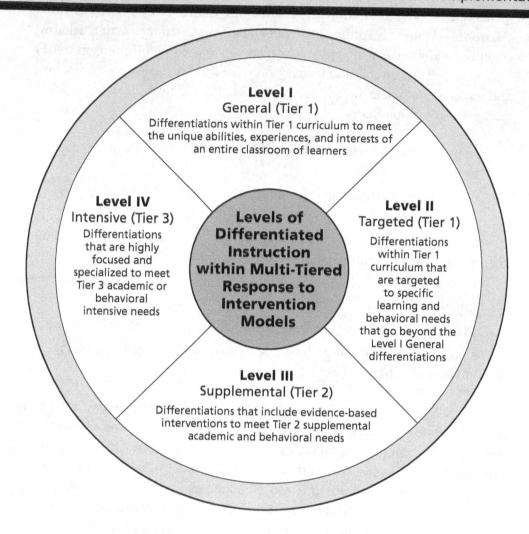

multi-tiered RTI model, two levels of differentiation are most closely associated with the Tier 1 core curriculum, and one level each is most closely connected with Tiers 2 and 3. To provide effective instruction and sufficient opportunities to learn, educators must ensure that these four levels of differentiation are integral to the curriculum implementation process seen in multi-tiered instruction. As curriculum implementation increases in intensity and frequency, along with increases in the assessment of learners' progress toward benchmarks, so must the application of curricular differentiations. To put this into its practical context, Table 6.1 illustrates the interconnections among tiers of instruction, types of assessment, and levels of differentiation.

As Table 6.1 shows, the concept of increased levels of intensity and duration in RTI models applies to the interactions among curriculum implementation, assessment, and differentiation. Although it is important to understand that these may overlap, as previously discussed (e.g., core and supplemental; screening and

TABLE 6.1 Interactions Among Instructional Tiers, Assessment Types, and Differentiation Levels

Instructional Tier	Primary Assessment Type	Differentiation Levels
1. Core Instruction	Universal Screening	General Targeted
2. Supplemental	Progress Monitoring	Supplemental
3. Intensive	Diagnostic	Intensive

monitoring), and are not confined to any particular curriculum tier, the interactions illustrated in Table 6.1 provide an excellent way to ensure proper implementation of the curriculum for all learners in multi-tiered RTI models.

To provide an appropriate education for all learners in RTI models, the curriculum must be implemented in a comprehensive and consistent manner so that instruction, assessment, and differentiations all receive the proper level of intensity and frequency based on need. For example, learners who are provided Tier 2 supplemental supports must also be given supplemental differentiations and regular progress monitoring in order to receive a consistent education with fidelity in RTI models. Conversely, providing Tier 2 supplemental supports but no associated supplemental differentiations (i.e., using only the general differentiations that did not produce adequate progress) and failing to monitor progress sufficiently defeat the purposes of multi-tiered instruction; the outcome may be less than expected or desired academic or behavioral progress. To ensure that the proper level of differentiations is implemented in each tier of instruction, Figure 6.2 illustrates a continuum of differentiations that reflects the modifications within the tiers of instruction required to meet the needs of all learners.

Each level of differentiation is required for multi-tiered RTI curriculum implementation to meet the needs of all students. This includes needs associated with a variety of learning and classroom factors, such as:

- Compatibility between teacher style and student preferences for learning (e.g., competitive or cooperative; direct or constructivist; rapid response or longer wait time; lecture or hands-on, etc.)

FIGURE 6.2 Continuum of Differentiations

Differentiation Level:	1	2	3	4
Differentiation Type:	General	Targeted	Supplemental	Intensive
Tier of Instruction:	Tier 1	Tier 1	Tier 2	Tier 3

- Varying degrees of self-management abilities
- Differences in experiential backgrounds
- Range of reading levels (e.g., a second-grade class may have students whose reading levels range from first through fourth grade)
- English language proficiency levels
- Varying degrees of self-concept and motivation
- Ability to apply study skills or learning strategies
- Ability to learn in small- and large-group settings
- Skills in learning through independent activities

These and similar examples reflect the many needs that any classroom of students brings to the teaching and learning environment. However, although much research over the past two decades has described the value of differentiated instruction and management, Fuchs, Stecker, and Fuchs (2008) wrote that "there is pervasive evidence that most classrooms are bereft of differentiated instruction" (p. 82). Therefore, because effective differentiated instruction is required for RTI models to succeed, the following discussions will explore the four levels of differentiations.

Level I: General Differentiations—Tier 1

Successful implementation of RTI includes differentiated learning to meet students' many needs (Appelbaum, 2009). The need for differentiated learning is supported by Gregory and Chapman (2002), who emphasized that one form of instruction cannot address all needs; therefore, differentiations must occur. The initial level of differentiations occurs in the Tier 1 core curriculum. It includes the same general modifications that many teachers have used successfully for several years to structure their differentiated classrooms and associated instruction. At this level, the differentiated classroom integrates a variety of practices within the instructional environment to address simultaneously the diversity typically seen in many classrooms (e.g., variations in cooperative styles, learning preferences, self-control, experiential background). Therefore, as research strongly suggests (Bender, 2008, Thousand et al., 2007; Tomlinson, 1999), effective teaching begins by establishing a classroom that integrates general differentiated teaching and learning practices to directly or indirectly address the interests, ability levels, and motivational needs of an increasingly diverse population of learners.

Level II: Targeted Differentiations—Tier 1

General differentiations permeate the classroom and may or may not be targeted to individual learners. However, students who begin to show signs of struggling with the Tier 1 core curriculum are best served by the addition of targeted differentiations designed to meet their needs, thereby adding value to the general differentiations that already exist. Differentiated instruction within Tier 1 includes working on targeted skills (Gersten et al., 2009) and may be applied to any learner based on universal screening data results.

Targeted differentiations in the Tier 1 core curriculum are valuable for learners who simply need additional instructional modifications to demonstrate adequate progress before the decision is made to initiate more intensive Tier 2 supports. Mellard and Johnson (2008) wrote that once learners have been "identified on screening measures as being at risk [they] should be monitored at a more frequent rate" (p. 68)—-rather than automatically deciding that they require Tier 2 supports. For some learners, all that may be needed is more time (e.g., 5–6 weeks) and/or targeted differentiations to demonstrate adequate progress/level of proficiency in the Tier 1 core curriculum. In the RTI framework, this is important to ensure that only those who require Tier 2 supports receive them. Learners who demonstrate lack of progress but not a significant gap between expected and actual achievement should be given more targeted differentiations within the Tier 1 curriculum along with weekly or biweekly progress monitoring for a few weeks. This should occur prior to moving to Tier 2 supplemental supports.

The combination of additional time (i.e., 5–6 weeks), targeted differentiations (in addition to the general differentiations), and increased progress monitoring (i.e., weekly) may be sufficient for learners who demonstrate a slight lack of progress (e.g., a gap of 1 or less) to make sufficient progress without needing Tier 2 supports. Additionally, given the large number of students who may require Tier 2 supports, a process such as the one described above will help to reduce unnecessary Tier 2 instruction while at the same time corroborating those who do through a brief (5- to 6-week) process within more differentiated Tier 1 instruction. Recently, the importance of targeting individual skill needs in the Tier 1 curriculum was suggested by Gersten et al. (2009), who wrote that differentiated instruction in Tier 1 includes grouping learners to address targeted needs and skills.

Level III: Supplemental Differentiations—Tier 2

The use of Tier 2 differentiated supplemental supports is warranted once evidence exists that neither the general nor targeted differentiations produce an expected rate of progress or a minimum level of proficiency in meeting curricular benchmarks. Differentiations at this level are directed at meeting clearly defined needs (e.g., reading fluency, mathematics computation) to support Tier 2 instruction as defined by the RTI or related school-based team. Many of the evidence-based interventions, study skills, and learning strategies discussed in this book are appropriate for implementing differentiations to meet Tier 2 curricular support needs. Ensuring that both *general* and *targeted* differentiations occur, in turn, helps educators identify more accurately those learners who require Tier 2 supplemental supports (e.g., 15–20% of the class or grade).

Level IV: Intensive Differentiations—Tier 3

As many as 5% of students may require Tier 3 interventions, reflecting more intensive differentiated instruction to meet curricular demands. Differentiations at the Tier 3 RTI level may include more extensive use of interventions provided as Tier 2 supplemental supports (e.g., direct instruction, phonemic awareness training) or, for some students, the addition of a different curriculum (e.g., the Wilson Reading Program) and highly specialized instruction (e.g., precision teaching) to meet the greater needs of these struggling learners. Tier 3 differentiations are the most intensive forms of academic and social-emotional or behavioral support; they are implemented for extended periods of time.

When considering the application of these four levels of differentiation, the three types of curricula (i.e., explicit, hidden, absent) must also be addressed to ensure that the most appropriate practices to adjust instruction are selected and implemented. The influences of the three types of curriculum on learners' progress toward benchmarks may provide valuable insights into the most appropriate level and types of differentiations to employ.

Differentiation within Curricular Types

In working to identify the proper curriculum aspects to adjust or differentiate, educators should consider the interrelated aspects of the three types of curricula. To understand effective differentiations, it is important to recognize the following: (1) all three curricula types exist in any teaching and learning environment; (2) failure to acknowledge their existence may contribute to incorrect decisions in adjustment or differentiation of instruction; and (3) success with differentiated instruction depends on differentiating the correct curriculum components(s) within the proper curriculum type.

Differentiation and the Explicit Curriculum

The *explicit curriculum* is the stated, mandated, and documented curriculum adopted by the state, district, or school that teachers are required to teach. Although teachers generally follow some defined scope and sequence, their differentiation decisions concerning the explicit curriculum focus on the extent to which the learner possesses the learning skills to access the curriculum in a meaningful way (Hoover & Patton, 2005; Thousand et al., 2007), such as (an) adequate:

- prior experiential background
- language abilities
- prerequisite skills
- vocabulary level

- comprehension ability
- content-specific ways of thinking
- retention of previously acquired material

Issues, problems, or concerns with these and similar factors reflect the learners' ability to successfully interact with, learn from, and retain the explicit curriculum. Most significantly, these factors help educators understand the extent to which the learner is able to access the curriculum (Thousand et al., 2007). Therefore, in providing differentiations of the explicit curriculum, educators must identify the proper place to provide the best access (i.e., the entry point) for a learner within the scope and sequence, whether the curriculum is spiral or layered, to meet diverse needs simultaneously. What is expected of learners—with the assumption that they have the prerequisite skills and abilities to learn from and interact with the curricula—plays a key role in making needed differentiations to the explicit curriculum. As many of us are aware, many students who are expected to interact with the mandated grade-level curriculum lack one or more key learning skills. This, in turn, leads to inadequate progress toward benchmarks.

Differentiating the explicit curriculum includes ensuring that all learners are provided access to the curriculum at points consistent with their abilities while maintaining integrity in challenging students cognitively in the teaching and learning process.

As a result, one of the first questions that should be considered in differentiating instruction is "Does the student have the experiences and abilities required to make satisfactory progress toward curricular benchmarks?" If the answer is "yes," then the need to differentiate the explicit curriculum is reduced. If the answer is "no," this increases the need to differentiate the explicit curriculum by adjusting instruction to provide more appropriate curriculum access points, vocabulary, or experiences.

Differentiation and the Hidden Curriculum

The hidden curriculum consists of occurrences in the classroom that go beyond the explicit curriculum (Eisner, 2002). This includes (1) daily decisions that teachers make to implement the explicit curriculum and (2) unintended learning or outcomes as a result of implementing the explicit curriculum. Often learners are able to access the explicit curriculum, but they struggle with hidden curriculum factors. Instructional factors controlled by the teacher and used at the teacher's discretion include the following:

- Tone of voice
- Proximity

- Reteaching of material
- Pairing of students in a task
- Classroom management structures
- Wait time for a learner's response
- Recognizing students for participation
- Length of time allotted for completion of specific tasks

These and other factors controlled by the teacher in implementing the explicit curriculum are part of the hidden curriculum. The hidden curriculum represents much of what students learn daily as teachers decide how best to implement the explicit curriculum, resulting in what the curriculum actually teaches students, whether explicitly stated on not (Eisner, 2002). Therefore, whereas differentiations within the explicit curriculum reflect adjustments made to access the curriculum at strategic points based on prerequisite knowledge and skills, the differentiations of the hidden curriculum reflect daily adjustments to practices and decisions to implement the explicit curriculum.

The ability to recognize the hidden curriculum in the teaching and learning environment provides a solid foundation for differentiating the proper factors in the classroom. This includes recognizing that although the focus is on planned learning experiences in the classroom, students will acquire unintended skills and abilities (both desirable or undesirable) because the explicit curriculum cannot control or account for all planned learning experiences and outcomes (Hoover & Patton, 2005). Classroom factors representing the hidden curriculum that may require differentiation to meet the needs of struggling learners reflect the five curricula components: content, evidence-based interventions, instructional arrangement, management, and progress evaluation such as:

- Reward or reinforcement systems
- Overall classroom structures
- Academic and behavioral classroom expectations
- Use of problem-solving abilities
- Use of different instructional arrangements (e.g., independent work, small group, pairs)
- Guided practice
- Enrichment activities
- Direct instruction
- Constructivist learning
- Cooperative learning

These and similar classroom aspects, unless specifically outlined in the explicit curriculum, represent decisions teachers make on a daily basis for all students.

Differentiation decisions about the hidden curriculum focus on adjustments to classroom practices and procedures that students are exposed to, based on teachers' decisions made on a daily basis, in their efforts to acquire and maintain knowledge and skills directly associated with the explicit curriculum.

The educator must consider the many aspects of the hidden curriculum to ensure that the correct component of the curriculum is adjusted. As previously emphasized, differentiating the wrong component may lead to the decision to provide an unnecessary tier of instruction (i.e., Tier 2 or 3) and/or placement for special education services.

Differentiation and the Absent Curriculum

Eisner (2002) stated that decisions about what not to teach represent the null or absent curriculum. What we choose to exclude from the teaching and learning environment may be more important in addressing learners' needs than the explicit or hidden curriculum. Content, evidence-based interventions, instructional arrangements, classroom/instructional management, or progress evaluation practices that could be included in the teaching and learning environment but are not are examples of the absent curriculum. Whether various classroom aspects are excluded because of restrictions in the explicit curriculum, the teacher's decision, lack of sufficient time, or simply because they were not considered or believed to be appropriate, they must be addressed to ensure that proper differentiations are selected and implemented.

Differentiations pertaining to the absent curriculum may require inclusion of aspects such as:

- Native language use for English language learners
- New evidence-based interventions not previously used in the classroom
- Curriculum-based measurement practices to replace informal assessment of progress
- Push-in rather than pull-out services to meet the needs of struggling learners
- Emphasis on direct teaching of study skills or learning strategies
- Replacing competitive learning with cooperative strategies

The addition of these and similar practices, if not already included in the classroom, may be the preferred choice for differentiating instruction:

Decisions to <u>include</u> selected content, interventions, groupings, or assessment practices may be the best way to adjust instruction to meet the needs of some struggling learners.

In RTI models, events within all three curricular types may influence decisions concerning (1) the tier of instruction; (2) interpretation of universal screening, progress monitoring, or diagnostic assessment results; (3) level of proficiency; (4) the most appropriate access point to the explicit curriculum; and (5) realistic expectations for an adequate rate of progress. Sprenger (2008) points out that one ultimate goal of differentiated instruction is to simultaneously meet different needs. To achieve this goal, learners' needs associated with the explicit, hidden, and absent curricula guide the decisions to best provide general, targeted, supplemental, and intensive differentiations within the five curricular components, as indicated by the learner's level of proficiency and progress toward curricular benchmarks.

Identifying Response to Intervention Curricular Differentiation Needs

As discussed above, one of the most important decisions that must be made once a learner is identified as at risk or struggling pertains to which curricular components(s) should be adjusted to best meet the student's needs. Modifying or differentiating the correct curricular components is essential to making future decisions concerning the possibility of a disability. Too often we adjust one area of the curriculum (e.g., evidence-based intervention) when in reality we should adjust another (e.g., the instructional arrangement, moving from a large- to a small-group setting using the same evidence-based intervention). Therefore, determining which curriculum component to adjust is critical to effective multi-tiered RTI curriculum implementation. Figure 6.3, developed from literature sources cited earlier in this chapter and from discussions in Hoover and Patton (2005), illustrates continua for the five curricular components, showing when differentiations should occur.

As Figure 6.3 shows, the need for differentiations depends on the learner's success in the five curriculum components. Table 6.2 provides selected examples of instructional situations that alert the teacher to the need to make differentiations.

As Table 6.2 shows, a student struggling to make progress toward academic and/or behavioral benchmarks or objectives may require adjustment in one or more of the five curricular components. In addition to universal screening and progress monitoring results, two guides have been developed and used in the field by numerous practitioners to help clarify the curricular needs of students who show signs of struggling (see Forms 6.1 and 6.2). Table 6.3 illustrates a completed Form 6.1 (*Differentiation Quick Screen* [DQS]) concerning a curriculum situation recently encountered by a classroom teacher.

FIGURE 6.3 Curriculum Differentiation Needs of All Learners

Curricular Content/Skills—Differentiation Need

Learner's abilities match level of curricular content taught

Learner's abilities do *not* match level of curricular content taught

← *Decreased Need for Differentiations*   *Increased Need for Differentiations* →

Evidenced-Based Interventions—Differentiation Need

Learner's needs are met through intervention

Learner's needs are *not* met through intervention

← *Decreased Need for Differentiations*   *Increased Need for Differentiations* →

Instructional Arrangements—Differentiation Need

Learner's needs are met by selected instructional setting(s)

Learner's needs are *not* met by selected instructional setting(s)

← *Decreased Need for Differentiations*   *Increased Need for Differentiations* →

Class/Instructional Management—Differentiation Need

Learner's needs are met through selected class/instructional management procedures

Learner's needs are *not* met by selected class/instructional management procedures

← *Decreased Need for Differentiations*   *Increased Need for Differentiations* →

Progress Evaluation—Differentiation Need

Progress monitoring accurately assesses learner's knowledge/abilities

Progress monitoring does *not* accurately assess learner's knowledge/abilities

← *Decreased Need for Differentiations*   *Increased Need for Differentiations* →

TABLE 6.2 Curricular Red Flags for Differentiation Needs

Component	Sample Red Flags in Curriculum Implementation
Content/Skills (Research-Based Curriculum)	The content being taught is incompatible with the content the learner is ready to learn (e.g., lack of prerequisite skills)
Evidence-Based Intervention	The selected evidence-based intervention is incompatible with the learner's experiential background or learning preference(s)
Instructional Arrangements	The selected arrangements for learning in the classroom (e.g., independent, small group, large group) do not facilitate adequate progress toward curricular benchmarks/objectives
Class/Instructional Management	The selected instructional and classroom management procedures are incompatible or inconsistent with the management needs of the learner
Progress Evaluation	The selected universal screening and/or progress monitoring devices and practices do not give the learner the best opportunity to demonstrate progress toward curricular benchmarks, or they assess knowledge/skills the student has not had sufficient opportunities to learn

TABLE 6.3 Differentiation Quick Screen (DQS)*

Educator: Mrs. Smith   Student: Jessie   Date: 11/14/2008

Clarification of Current Curriculum Needs and Setting:

Curriculum Area of Need: Oral and Silent Reading Comprehension
Current Level of Proficiency: 70% accuracy with grade-level literal comprehension
questions; 20% accuracy with inferential comprehension questions
Current Rate of Progress: Increases 5% accuracy with literal comprehension questions at
Grade-level every 4 weeks; increases 2% accuracy with inferential comprehension questions every 4 weeks
Gap Analysis Results (Size): Literal comprehension: 15% below grade-level
expectations; inferential comprehension: 65% below grade-level expectations
Class Setting in Which Need Is Most Frequently Evident: Large-group setting
Primary Evidence-Based Intervention(s): Direct Instruction

Based on the above curriculum needs and setting, check appropriate items within each curriculum component.

I. Content/Skills—Learner sufficiently possesses the following:

___ Reading level
_X_ Experiential background
___ Required prerequisite skills
___ Language abilities in language of instruction
_X_ Motivation to learn and study material
___ Higher level abstract thinking abilities
___ Other (specify):

II. Evidence-Based Intervention—Intervention used with learner:

___ Facilitates active student participation
_X_ Does not lead to learner progress or attention to task
___ Is an intervention that is clearly understood by the learner
___ Engages the learner by capturing and maintaining attention to the task
___ Is compatible with student preferences concerning learning
___ Assists learner to acquire content/skills being taught
___ Other (specify):

III. Instructional Arrangements—Effects of arrangement(s) on learner progress:

Independent Work Setting:
___ Independent work is successfully completed
_X_ Independent work is not successfully completed

Small-Group Setting (check all that apply):
___ Facilitates productive learner interactions
_X_ Leads to completion of assignments/tasks
_X_ Maintains learner's attention to task
_X_ Is an appropriate structure for managing learner's behaviors
___ Setting does not lead to learner's progress or attention to task
___ Other (specify):

TABLE 6.3 (Continued)

Large-Group Setting (check all that apply):
___ Facilitates productive learner interactions
___ Leads to completion of assignments/tasks
___ Maintains learner's attention to task
___ Is an appropriate structure for managing learner behaviors
_X_ Setting does not lead to learner's progress or attention to task
___ Other (specify):

Paired/Cooperative Learning Setting (check all that apply):
___ Facilitates productive learner interactions
_X_ Leads to completion of assignments/tasks
_X_ Maintains learner's attention to task
_X_ Is an appropriate structure for managing learner's behaviors
___ Setting does not lead to learner's progress or attention to task
___ Other (specify):

IV. Classroom/Instructional Management—Effects of management procedures on learner's curriculum area of need:

Relative to learner's curriculum need(s), the classroom management facilitates (check all that apply):
_X_ self-management of behavior
___ student's responsibility for own learning
_X_ positive physical and emotional environment
_X_ structured, periodic movement within the classroom
___ efficient time management
_X_ smooth transitions
_X_ differentiation to meet social/behavioral needs
___ effective use of academic learning time
_X_ relevant and meaningful rewards/reinforcement
_X_ consistency in implementation of class rules/routines
_X_ sufficient opportunities to learn
_X_ implementation of class management techniques with fidelity
___ other (specify):

Relative to the learner's curriculum need(s), the instructional management facilitates (check all that apply):
___ effective uses of student groupings
___ proper uses of independent learning
_X_ effective uses of learning centers
_X_ differentiation to meet academic needs
___ learner's activation and application of prior knowledge
_X_ valuing cultural diversity in teaching
_X_ accommodating various language needs and levels of proficiency
_X_ use of direct instruction methodology
___ use of cooperative learning
_X_ implementation of instructional techniques with fidelity
___ sufficient progress towards curricular benchmarks in content/skill area(s)
___ other (specify):

(Continued)

TABLE 6.3 (Continued)

V. Progress Evaluation—Evaluation of the learner's progress in curriculum need area includes the following:

_X_ Appropriate, research-based monitoring measures and practices are used
_X_ Evaluation directly assesses what is taught in the curriculum
_X_ Evaluation directly assesses progress toward curricular benchmarks addressed in the curriculum
_X_ Monitoring device/practice is being used only for what it was designed to measure
_X_ Monitoring device/practice is implemented with fidelity
_X_ Monitoring device/practice is used with learners similar to the research population
_X_ Monitoring device/practice is administered in the learner's most proficient language and/or in English if the learner is bilingual

Summary of Current Curriculum Situation and Differentiation Needs:

Content/Skills: Jessie exhibits similar reading comprehension needs in both oral and silent reading. Jessie possesses sufficient decoding and fluency abilities, which are both strengths to draw upon when requiring comprehension. She also has acquired the skill of answering most literal comprehension questions. Jessie is an English language speaker, and her parents are English speaking as well. Yet, she does possess some limitations in her level and usage of oral and receptive language. These are limitations for her when attempting to complete reading comprehension tasks. When the text is of interest to her, she seems a bit more likely to have higher comprehension; however, Jessie consistently experiences difficulty with inferential comprehension questions.

Evidence-Based Intervention: The content taught within the large-group setting includes primary use of direct instruction. In the small group it includes use of direct instruction along with a degree of differentiation that includes task analysis and scaffolding. The students receive a great deal of modeling and repetition. These are used to meet the goal of helping the student independently comprehend what is read. With the necessary cues and prompts, Jessie responds adequately, especially in the small-group setting. Jessie is not very motivated through use of direct instruction in the large group; however, she is usually motivated if direct instruction is coupled with task analysis and scaffolding procedures. At times, Jessie appears disengaged when she is required to listen to the teacher for more than 5 to 10 minutes at a time. Jessie occasionally participates in whole-group discussions, yet is more likely to contribute when the groups consist of two to four students. She is more likely to acquire the information when it is presented to her in a small group or one on one and when she is actively engaged. Attention to the evidence-based intervention is a factor, as Jessie disengages when she is required to listen for an extended period of time through direct instruction–only methods.

Instructional Arrangement: As suggested, Jessie is able to attend to reading comprehension tasks within instructional arrangements when she is actively engaged. Also, as mentioned, when Jessie is required to listen for even modest periods of time, she will frequently lose focus and begin to look around the room or will draw. Jessie works independently when necessary and seems to enjoy tasks that involve writing. However, when working independently to attempt tasks, she usually fails to successfully complete reading comprehension assignments, frequently making this arrangement less than productive toward achievement in academic progress. Her peer relations are appropriate, as she is friendly and congenial to everyone in most instructional arrangements. However, Jessie appears somewhat withdrawn at times, especially when she is required to learn in a new social context or large-group setting. The small-group learning arrangement seems to facilitate her ability to acquire information, within which she is more likely to be engaged than in a large-group arrangement. She almost never verbally participates in a general classroom setting of 25 to 30 students unless the students are working in pairs or small groups. In general, Jessie's behaviors are appropriate within the context of a small-group or paired instructional arrangement, a setting that yields more productivity, even though the level of progress with oral and silent reading comprehension is insufficient as compared to grade-level expectations.

Class/Instructional Management: The classroom management in Jessie's classes includes implementation of consistent rules and routines, clear expectations, smooth transitions, and an overall positive classroom environment. Within this type of classroom management, Jessie does very well maintaining self-control. She is not overtly impulsive, yet she can show some signs of slightly withdrawn behavior. Jessie has several sufficient self-management techniques such as organization, working quietly and independently, and attention to her tasks; however, she lacks the content skills necessary to correctly complete independent reading comprehension tasks. Therefore, the classroom management facilitates task completion even though Jessie struggles to accurately respond to reading comprehension assignments.

TABLE 6.3 (Continued)

In regard to instructional management, Jessie is provided use of learning centers, direct instruction, scaffolding, and selected differentiations to accommodate her reading comprehension needs. However, when she does not initially understand what is being asked of her she will not respond at all to any questions, even if subsequent questions are scaffolded. She will sit and not respond in any way, verbally or nonverbally. This is less likely to occur in a small-group setting than in a large group. As stated, Jessie completes comprehension assignments on time; however, responses are generally incorrect or incomplete. Jessie struggles to demonstrate certain techniques, such as locating important information, and she has difficulty applying previous experiences to the current content, requiring adjustments to the instructional management to meet these needs.

Progress Evaluation: The maze CBM procedure has been established as reliable and valid for monitoring growth in oral and silent reading comprehension, and it is therefore used to track Jessie's progress. Jessie often requires the accommodation of allowing her to read the passage aloud after she has made her word choices through silent reading. That is, if Jessie reads the passage aloud after she completes the task silently, she often corrects a couple of her incorrect responses. This evaluation procedure allows Jessie the opportunity to recognize errors, particularly syntax errors, in her choices and adjust her responses accordingly. Progress monitoring also occurs informally in small-group and paired instructional settings to determine the types of comprehension questions to which she correctly responds (i.e., literal or inferential), to clarify further the CBM data. These two classroom evaluation procedures (i.e., CBM maze and informal questioning) appear to accurately assess Jessie's oral and silent reading comprehension abilities and growth.

*Development of this table included a contribution by Amy Boele

As Table 6.3 shows, the DQS helped the teacher clarify the extent to which the learner's suspected need area relates to each of the five curriculum components. Although general in nature, the DQS is a process/document for the classroom teacher to use in recording perceptions about the influences of each curriculum component on the suspected problem area. This leads to the second, companion guide (Form 6.2, *Curriculum Differentiation Planning Guide*), which is illustrated in Table 6.4. Like the DQS, the *Curriculum Differentiation Planning Guide* has been completed to further clarify the needs identified on the DQS. The completed forms demonstrate their use and value in making decisions about curriculum differentiation.

As Table 6.4 shows, several questions are provided for each component to help the classroom teacher further clarify which of the five curriculum component(s) is most in need of differentiations. Based on the information recorded on the guide, the learner's needs appear to be most strongly related to the evidence-based curricular component; this is the component that should be differentiated. Clarifying how the suspected problem is reflected in and associated with each curriculum component helps educators to implement differentiations in the greatest area of need.

Information from both the DQS and the *Curriculum Differentiation Planning Guide*, coupled with universal screening and/or progress-monitoring data, gives the RTI team a more complete picture of the classroom's instructional environment and the learner's progress. This information, in turn, empowers educators to make more informed multi-tiered instructional decisions to best implement curricular differentiations.

TABLE 6.4 Curriculum Differentiation Planning Guide*

Instructions: Complete this guide to further clarify targeted, supplemental, or intensive differentiation needs of the learner as identified through classroom screening/monitoring procedures and results from the *Differentiation Quick Screen (DQS)*.

Student: Jessie   Date: 11/14/08   Grade: 5

Content Instructional Need Area: Oral and Silent Reading Comprehension

Teacher: Mrs. Smith

Expected outcomes for student resulting from instruction: Increase literal and inferential reading comprehension abilities through oral and silent reading. Progress monitoring includes curriculum-based measurement of correctly answered oral and silent reading comprehension questions.

Reason for concern: Jessie demonstrates difficulties with literal comprehension questions when wording varies from the printed text, and she struggles with most types of inferential questions. These reading comprehension issues occur in both silent and oral reading. Jessie also has limited vocabulary for her grade level and appears to have receptive language problems.

A. Briefly describe the current classroom/instructional situation for the need area in question:

Content area addressed during this instructional period: Oral/Silent Reading Comprehension.

Evidence-Based Intervention(s) used during this instruction: Direct Instruction is used in both the large- and small-group settings.

Instructional Arrangement(s) used during this instruction: Large group in general classroom; small group in pull-out instruction.

Class/Instructional Management Procedures used during this instruction: Classroom Management includes use of positive behavior supports that complement the schoolwide supports program, implemented in a highly consistently manner facilitating a positive emotional and physical class structure. Instructional Management includes use of direct instruction in large and small groups; cooperative and paired learning and learning centers are used to manage instruction more frequently in the small-group, pull-out setting.

Progress Evaluation used to monitor progress resulting from instruction: The Maze CBM method and informal questioning procedures are used to monitor Jessie's progress and include answering questions in both written and verbal formats; assessing comprehension within a variety of genres and subject matters; and using a chart to monitor her ability to comprehend literal and inferential questions over time. Current levels of proficiency place Jessie 15% below grade-level expectations with literal comprehension and 65% below with inferential comprehension based on her CBM scores as compared to grade-level expectations. The standardized CBM maze procedure is completed weekly as part of the small-group, pull-out instruction. In addition, comprehension is monitored daily within the small-group arrangement through informal questioning and observations of her involvement in responding to questions during the small-group instruction.

B. Respond to each curricular element relative to the described situation above:

I. Curriculum Element: Content/Skills

1. *Does the learner possess sufficient reading abilities to be successful with the instruction?* Jessie possesses grade-level oral reading fluency and decoding skills. She is able to correctly answer literal comprehension questions with 70% accuracy for passages at grade level.

2. *Has the learner acquired prerequisite skills necessary to be successful with the instruction?* She has mastered prerequisite objectives of literal comprehension of fourth-grade level text (one grade level below).

   If not, which prerequisite skills does the learner lack? She lacks inferential comprehension skills and literal comprehension abilities when the wording of the question is not identical to the wording/syntax of the sentence(s) in the text.

3. *Does the learner possess sufficient language development skills to be successful with the instruction?* Jessie is a monolingual English speaker. She receives language support from the speech/language therapist. Her language needs primarily emphasize below-age-level vocabulary knowledge and receptive language skills.

TABLE 6.4 (Continued)

4. *Does the learner possess the academic experiences needed to comprehend concepts associated with the instruction?* She needs additional academic experiences in which she interacts with a passage sufficiently to comprehend both oral and written material at a critical, evaluative, and inferential level.

Summary of Content/Skill Needs:

Jessie's primary content/skill need is reading comprehension. Her literal comprehension is a relative strength, as she correctly answers literal questions for a grade-level text with 70% accuracy. She struggles to correctly answer literal questions based on paraphrased text. Jessie struggles to correctly answer questions that require making an inference and use of various higher level thinking skills, correctly responding with only a 20% accuracy. Jessie's reading comprehension skills should be taught within a context of interest and choice, particularly regarding the passages she reads, to facilitate and motivate inferential skills development.

II. Curriculum Element: Evidence-Based Intervention(s)

1. *Does the selected evidence-based intervention provide sufficient motivation to the learner?* Direct instruction does not seem to motivate Jessie, especially in instances when she becomes aware of her difficulty in correctly accomplishing the task.

2. *Does the selected evidence-based intervention generate active learner participation in the instruction?* Yes, Jessie does receive the opportunity to actively participate in discussions and in written assignments, but additional opportunities may be necessary. While Jessie participates, she does not appear motivated by direct forms of instruction.

3. *Under what learning conditions is the selected evidence-based intervention MOST effective for the learner?* Jessie seems to benefit the most during peer-guided interactions, which allows scaffolding to occur.

4. *Under what learning conditions is the selected evidence-based intervention LEAST effective for the learner?* Direct instruction is not effective when Jessie is required to listen to instruction for more than 5 to 10 minutes at a time in either a large- or small-group setting.

5. *To what extent does the learner progress satisfactorily toward curricular benchmarks through use of the selected evidence-based intervention?* Already well below grade level in her ability to use higher order thinking skills, Jessie progresses at a very slow rate.

Summary of Evidence-Based Intervention Needs:

The current evidence-based interventions that are highly teacher directed may not be as beneficial to Jessie as is necessary. More interactive and cooperative forms of instruction assist to better engage Jessie in reading comprehension tasks. For example, an intervention such as Collaborative Strategic Reading (CSR) offers reading comprehension instruction through peer collaboration, in which students are assigned roles to provide support with various comprehension strategies. Because Jessie's learning seems to progress best when she is afforded the opportunity to interact with her peers, this intervention may prove to be very useful. Elements of scaffolding and direct instruction should still be present as needed to support a more cooperative, interactive form of instruction.

III. Curriculum Element: Instructional Arrangement

1. *To what extent is the learner capable of working independently in learning the instructional content?* When working independently in both large and small groups, Jessie is quiet and appears focused on the task. When reading silently to herself, Jessie appears to sustain her reading focus for approximately 15–20 minutes, as is expected for her grade level. She completes her work in the area of reading comprehension; however, her responses are frequently incorrect. At times, when the independent paper/pencil task is too difficult for Jessie, she will stop working and draw or read.

2. *To what extent is the learner capable of working in a small-group setting WITH direct teacher guidance in learning the instructional content?* Jessie cooperates with others and tends to attempt to lead group work during tasks with which she is more familiar. When the group discusses information, Jessie listens most of the time. She needs redirection occasionally to remain on task through teacher guidance.

(Continued)

TABLE 6.4 (Continued)

3. *To what extent is the learner capable of working in a small-group setting WITHOUT direct teacher guidance in learning the instructional content?* Jessie's attention to the task is similar with and without teacher supervision. The major difference is that teacher guidance has the potential to ensure that she correctly and successfully completes the comprehension tasks.

4. *To what extent is the learner capable of working in a large-group setting in learning the instructional content?* In the general education classroom, Jessie receives 60 minutes of large-group instruction daily. If she is required to passively listen for more than 10 minutes at a time, her attention appears to wane, as evidenced by eye contact and body language. A large-group setting does not seem to be conducive to her understanding of reading comprehension strategies, compared to her performance in a small-group or paired setting.

5. *To what extent is the learner capable of working cooperatively with one or two classmates without constant direct teacher guidance in learning the instructional content?* When the other student(s) in the large or small groups are at grade level or above, Jessie contributes to the task only by completing whatever is minimally due to be turned in to the teacher. Jessie does not contribute her own ideas or actively engage on her own. In small-group settings, the work is typically initiated by the others; however, with encouragement through peer interactions and/or direct teacher guidance, Jessie contributes more and becomes engaged in the reading comprehension discussions and tasks to a greater degree.

Summary of Instructional Arrangement Needs:

Jessie appears to benefit from reading comprehension instruction in a small-group setting while struggling with large-group direct instruction. Instructional opportunities that provide Jessie with purposeful interactions within a small group of peers with various ability levels facilitate greater progress with reading comprehension. Teacher-guided small-group work is more effective than only peer-initiated interactions; however, both instructional arrangements are more effective than the large-group setting.

IV. Curriculum Element: Classroom and Instructional Management

Class Management (Briefly describe classroom management during the instruction):

Physical Environment: General Class (tables and desks); Small room (two tables, two desks)

Classroom Climate: Students work quietly; students respect each other and follow rules; teacher intervention for behavior is seldom necessary; most students exhibit a desire to learn.

Rules and Routines: As students arrive in the general class or pull-out setting, they are to collect their personal materials from the side counter and bring them to their seat at the table. Personal materials include pencil boxes, folders, and books. On Fridays, students in the pull-out setting know that they are to come in and quietly begin their progress monitoring assessments. At the end of each session, students return their materials and record their self-monitoring behavior points before returning to their general classroom.

Reinforcement and Rewards: Reinforcement is consistent with the schoolwide positive behavior supports program. This includes distributing tickets to students so as to acknowledge their efforts. Students also feel positively reinforced when they experience a sense of self-accomplishment.

Time Management: For a 30-minute pull-out session, students typically receive direct instruction for 10–15 minutes and work cooperatively or independently for the remainder of the time. Occasionally, whole-group interaction occurs for the entire session. In the general class, reading instruction is for approximately 60 minutes, which includes both direct teacher instruction and independent work. Some small-group work may also occasionally occur.

Transition Time: Students pass each other as they return and collect their materials in both the general and pull-out settings. Jessie typically helps remind others to gather their belongings, and occasionally she is the last one to leave because she is cleaning up materials that others have left on the tables.

1. *Identify appropriate behaviors that the learner exhibits during the instruction:* During small- and large-group instruction, Jessie listens quietly.

2. *Identify inappropriate behaviors that the learner exhibits during the instruction:* She appears to be inattentive at times by writing and drawing during instruction, particularly in a large group where extended listening is required.

TABLE 6.4 (Continued)

3. *Describe the learner's behavioral self-management abilities:* Jessie quickly complies and rarely requires behavioral intervention. She self-manages her behavior very well. In a large-classroom setting, she occasionally shows disengaged behaviors such as drawing or reading when she should be listening, yet she is easily redirected with a mere attempt at eye contact from the teacher.

4. *Describe how well the classroom management rewards/reinforcements affect the learner.* Jessie appears to be very motivated to please adults and comply with requests regardless of whether or not the designated positive behavior supports ticket system is in place.

5. *Describe how well the learner makes transitions to different tasks or activities during the instruction.* Jessie complies with all classroom procedures and is typically one of the first students to transition and become prepared for the next activity.

Instructional Management (Briefly describe how you manage your instructional time): Typically, mini-lessons are presented for 10 minutes at the beginning of the 30-minute small-group pull-out period. In the remaining 15 to 20 minutes, students are working independently or in small groups with teacher facilitation. In large group, approximately 30 minutes is devoted to direct instruction, with the remaining time spent in independent work or small groups in the general class.

1. *What percent of the total instructional time does the learner engage in:*
   On-task behavior?   Large Group: 40%   Small Group: 75%
   Off-task behavior?   Large Group: 60%   Small Group: 25%

2. *Describe the extent to which the instruction is provided through Direct Instruction methods:* Direct Instruction occurs approximately two or three times a week within the small-group mini-lessons and daily in the large-group instruction. Reading comprehension strategies are generally presented explicitly rather than in a more experiential manner associated with cooperative types of instruction. In both group settings, students respond to questions in the typical choral, repetitive fashion as well as individually.

3. *Describe the extent to which the instruction reflects the diverse cultural and linguistic needs of the learner.* Jessie is a monolingual English speaker, but her cultural practices are valued in the recognition of her interests and her personal and familial experiences.

4. *Describe ways in which the instruction facilitates the learner's activation of prior knowledge pertaining to the topic.* Facilitating Jessie's prior knowledge can be either beneficial or impeding to her learning when it is used for reading comprehension. It is mostly beneficial when she applies a personal connection to her reading. However, Jessie frequently overfixates on her prior experiences to the point where she is so focused on her own experiences that she has difficulty adapting or acquiring new information, thereby reducing her comprehension.

5. *Describe how the implementation of the instruction is managed through the use of learning centers.* In the general education classroom, learning centers are used in content areas, such as science, social studies, and math. Learning centers provide a context where Jessie's learning can be facilitated socially with her peers. When organized strategically, this setting is very conducive to Jessie's growth with reading comprehension.

Summary of Classroom and Instructional Management Needs:

Jessie's on-task behaviors are extremely dependent upon the instructional arrangement and instructional interventions that are in effect. Small-group, interactive interventions are more effective than large-group, teacher-directed forms of instruction. The classroom management reflects the schoolwide positive behavior supports system, which assists to provide Jessie a positive classroom climate for learning and should remain in place. Instructional management should emphasize interactions and peer-supported learning along with periodic direct teacher guidance.

V. Curriculum Element: Progress Evaluation

1. *Describe how the progress evaluation directly assesses what is taught through the instruction.* Maze CBM activities are used to directly assess reading comprehension addressed in the classroom instruction. Because of Jessie's difficulty with language, including understanding of appropriate syntax, she likely performs lower than if she did not have trouble detecting syntax errors. Informal oral comprehension assessments are also used on a regular basis.

(Continued)

TABLE 6.4 (Continued)

2. *Describe how the evaluation <u>device</u> is appropriate in measuring the learner's progress with the instruction.* CBM maze passages are appropriate in that they are reliable and valid tools for monitoring grade-level comprehension. Because of the aforementioned language syntax issues at play with Jessie, the tool is best used when she reads the passage aloud so that she can hear her word choices in the context of the passage as a whole. However, progress with silent reading comprehension should also be included, as she struggles in both areas.

3. *Describe how the evaluation <u>practice</u> is appropriate in measuring the learner's progress with the instruction.* The CBM Maze procedure used with Jessie is appropriate for monitoring her reading comprehension because it directly relates to that which is taught in the curriculum. It is a standardized procedure that allows for quick monitoring and documentation of her reading comprehension progress.

4. *Is cultural and linguistic diversity accommodated in the selected progress evaluation device and/or practice?* Jessie's cultural practices are accounted for in that she chooses the content of the passage. Passages of her choice provide greater access to the material to demonstrate abilities to her highest potential.

Summary of Progress Evaluation Needs:

Keeping track of Jessie's responses to correctly answer literal and inferential comprehension questions allows for close attention to her progress. CBM Maze is a reliable and valid procedure that has been developed for progress monitoring. Use of these types of passages facilitates effective monitoring of both silent and oral reading comprehension. Standard CBM procedures are supplemented with teacher-generated questions to further support progress evaluation activities. In addition, Jessie requires the accommodation of reading the passage aloud once she has selected her choices through silent reading.

C. Prioritize curricular components requiring differentiation based on the information provided above. Briefly clarify your recommendation for priority of HIGH-ranked items.

Curricular Components	Recommended Differentiation Priority			
	High	Medium	Low	Clarification
Content/Skills			X	
Evidence-Based Intervention	X			Engagement
Instructional Arrangement	X			Small Group
Class/Instruction Management			X	
Progress Evaluation			X	

Summarize Hypothesis for Differentiation(s):

Begin any curricular differentiations by first addressing the evidence-based intervention and the instructional arrangement. Jessie's reading comprehension seems to progress best when she is afforded the opportunity to interact with her peers in cooperative and interactive ways in small-group settings. Collaborative Strategic Reading (CSR) should be initiated as the evidence-based intervention for reading comprehension instruction. Jessie's reading comprehension should be monitored weekly within an independent setting, after she has received the intervention of CSR, using the maze CBM procedures and passages. If necessary, after differentiations to the curricular components of intervention and arrangement are implemented and the effects monitored, revisit the need for addressing the areas of content/skills, progress evaluation, and class/instructional management; however, these do not appear to need differentiations at this time, and the current procedures should be maintained.

*Development of this table included a contribution by Amy Boele

Implementing Curricular Differentiations

As discussed near the beginning of this chapter, the purpose of discussing differentiations and differentiated learning is to highlight their importance in multi-tiered RTI curriculum implementation. To this end, a variety of practices, procedures, and strategies constitute differentiated instruction. This section presents examples of differentiations to facilitate the interrelated components of (1) classroom management and (2) instructional management. Almost everything that occurs in a teaching and learning environment falls under the heading of classroom and/or instructional management. Although these two aspects are considered here individually, in practice they must be viewed together to best differentiate teaching and learning for all students educated in the multi-tiered RTI curriculum. Several frequently used practices discussed below apply to general, targeted, supplemental, and intensive levels of differentiation. These practices were selected from discussions in various sources (Bender, 2008; Hoover & Patton, 2005; Sprenger, 2008; Thousand et al., 2007). The reader is referred to these sources for further information and for additional differentiations for meeting students' needs. The following are examples of ways to differentiate classroom and instructional management to meet the needs of all learners, whether educated in Tier 1, 2, or 3.

Differentiating Classroom Management Procedures

Classroom management refers to the procedures and practices that structure the learning environment to facilitate success in the classroom (Meese, 2001). Classroom management includes everything that is done to create and maintain a positive climate for teaching and learning. Good management provides the structure for all learning in the classroom; poor management leads to ineffective learning even if the research-based curriculum and evidence-based interventions are implemented properly. That is, even the best instruction provided in an ineffectively and inefficiently managed classroom will generally fall far short of learning expectations and projected progress toward curricular benchmarks. Several critical areas of classroom management, which promote effective behavior management, have been identified by Hoover and Patton (2005), Meese (2001), and Sprenger (2008). They include the physical environment, the classroom climate, routines and rules, reinforcements and rewards, self-management, time management, and transitions. Each of these is discussed below.

PHYSICAL ENVIRONMENT ■ The physical environment consists of the physical arrangements in the classroom, such as the location of the students' and teacher's work spaces or desks, proximity of the teacher to learners, students' assigned seating arrangement of desks/tables, traffic patterns for movement in the classroom, and reduction of distractible external stimuli (e.g., outside noise, view of the hallway) (Chapman & King, 2008).

▶ **RTI Differentiation Considerations:**   Effective teaching and learning begin with structuring the classroom environment to increase time on task, reduce distractions, and maintain teacher–student contact. These and related *physical environmental* factors should be initially considered once a learner has been identified as struggling (i.e., simply restructuring one or more of these classroom factors may be all that is needed to make it easier to learn). This should be considered prior to differentiating content or teaching interventions to be certain that the physical environment itself is not significantly impeding student progress.

CLASSROOM CLIMATE ■ *Classroom climate* refers to the "prevailing attitudes of students and teachers toward the process of learning and to prevailing behavioral expectations for students" (Meese, 2001, p. 100). To create a positive classroom climate, the teacher must understand what motivates the learners. According to Sabatino (1987), several practices contribute to a positive classroom climate, including:

■ Providing clear expectations

■ Modeling appropriate and desirable behavior

■ Demonstrating fairness and self-confidence

■ Reducing anxiety-producing activities

■ Recognizing positive student behavior when it occurs

▶ **RTI Differentiation Considerations:**   The classroom climate may be subtle in form, difficult to observe directly yet vital to effective teaching and learning. An effective differentiated classroom has a positive climate that promotes student interactions, learning, and progress. Educators should consider the classroom climate in regard to the needs of all students, especially those who are struggling, in order to accurately interpret screening and progress monitoring data and associated curricular decision making. Sometimes, differentiating aspects that promote a more positive classroom climate may lead to increased progress without changing the intervention or the instructional arrangements (e.g., small group) or differentiating the content. Consideration of the classroom climate helps educators make more accurate and informed decisions for learners who require targeted, supplemental, or intensive differentiations to meet their needs.

ROUTINES AND RULES ■ Consistency in setting classroom expectations, rules, and routines is essential to providing a safe, efficient, and effective teaching and learning environment (Chapman & King, 2008). Effective classroom management includes the development and implementation of class rules and routines (Oliver & Reschly, 2007). To be most effective, Martella, Nelson, and Marchand-Martella (2003) and Colvin, Kame'enui, and Sugai (1993) stated class rules should:

- Be kept to a minimum
- Reflect behaviors that are expected rather than those prohibited
- Be stated in a positive manner
- Support the schoolwide behavior program

Classroom routines should also be clearly stated, taught to students in a systemic manner, and reviewed periodically to reinforce their importance and use in the classroom (Oliver & Reschly, 2007). Although classroom routines, rules, and expectations vary widely, depending on grade level, teacher preference, or student abilities, the most important thing is to employ them in a fair and consistent manner. A classroom structure that students can rely on every day helps to bring out the best in them as they work toward academic and behavioral curricular benchmarks and objectives.

▶ **RTI Differentiation Considerations:** Vague and inconsistent classroom rules and routines contribute to potential problems for many students. As with the areas previously discussed, the extent to which classroom routines and rules relate to lack of progress should be determined prior to changing other aspects of the classroom. This is necessary to be certain that lack of progress or inability to achieve curricular benchmarks is not a result of inconsistency in routines and/or lack of clarity about the teacher's expectations.

REINFORCEMENTS AND REWARDS ▪ Virtually all behavior is reinforced to some degree and is associated with some reward or reinforcement even if these are not explicitly stated or presented. For example, a high grade on a test may reinforce effective study habits, praise from a teacher may reward or reinforce positive behavior, and congratulations from a friend for a job well done reinforces a friendship. Conversely, a negative tone of voice may add to a learner's problems, frequently ignoring a student who wishes to participate may lead to lack of interest in participation, and using activities that do not interest and motivate learners may contribute to lack of academic or behavioral progress.

▶ **RTI Differentiation Considerations:** The manner in which a learner is rewarded or reinforced for positive academic and social-emotional behaviors does much to continue those behaviors. Positive reinforcements and rewards promote positive behaviors. Some students experiencing problems in school may require adjustments in the reinforcements used to motivate learning.

Although the goal is to facilitate intrinsic motivation, use of extrinsic rewards or reinforcements may be necessary to help students develop curricular knowledge and skills. The effects of classroom reinforcement to support teaching and learning should be considered before adjusting the content or differentiating interventions.

SELF-MANAGEMENT ■ A desired outcome of effective classroom management is the development of students' responsibility and accountability for their own learning. Appelbaum (2009) wrote that "self-management skills are a fundamental key to success not only in the classroom, but also in life" (p. 111). Hoover and Patton (2007) stated that self-management skills help students assume responsibility for their own learning and behavior. And the more responsibility students assume, the more flexibility teachers have in managing their classrooms and meeting additional needs of struggling students (see Chapter 8 for a more detailed discussion of self-management).

▶ **RTI Differentiation Considerations:** In interpreting screening and progress monitoring data, the educator should also consider the learner's self-management abilities. An increase in self-management skills may increase academic and/or behavioral progress toward curricular benchmarks without the need to differentiate other curricular components. Ensuring that students assume as much responsibility as possible for their own learning promotes more effective implementation of the curriculum in any tier of instruction.

TIME MANAGEMENT ■ One of the more pressing realities in education today is the need for effective use of classroom time. Chapman and King (2008) wrote that educators should "emphasize the value of time in lessons, activities, and transitions" (p. 26). The efficient use of academic learning time (i.e., quality time on task) within the total allocated learning time (e.g., a 90-minute reading bloc) relates directly to effective learning and student progress toward curricular benchmarks. For example, Meese (2001) wrote that matching student strengths with assigned tasks makes effective use of the allocated learning time, which is key to providing sufficient opportunities to learn that must be corroborated within the RTI decision-making process.

▶ **RTI Differentiation Considerations:** A basic premise of RTI is that the Tier 1 core curriculum is implemented with fidelity and is appropriate for the learner. Once a struggling learner is identified through screening or progress monitoring, it is important to consider the use of learning time to make certain that the student has been given enough opportunities to learn. In considering the potential need to increase the intensity or duration in teaching curriculum content or skills, the educator should assess how the allocated learning time is translated into academic learning time in the Tier 1 teaching and learning environment.

TRANSITIONS ■ Transition is movement within and across classrooms; it is the time when students change from one activity, content area, situation, task, or teacher to another. Transition time is often very brief (e.g., 3 minutes); however, unless it is organized and structured, it may cause confusion and significantly impact the teaching and learning that immediately follow. Meese (2001) wrote that both verbal and nonverbal cues should be used to facilitate smooth transitions. Smith, Polloway, Patton, and Dowdy (2004) discussed some classroom practices that facilitate effective transitions:

■ Carefully plan transition times.

■ Rehearse procedures for transition, if necessary.

■ Use specific recognizable cues to signal the beginning and end of the transition (e.g., using lights or a timer).

■ Minimize excessive movement during transition times.

■ Allocate sufficient time for students to complete transitions.

■ Provide notice prior to beginning/ending transitions.

■ Be certain that students know what they are transitioning to and what the expectations or choices are when they make the transition (e.g., sit at a table, open a textbook, record items from the board, complete a worksheet).

Effective classroom management includes methods for assisting students to move efficiently from one activity or classroom to another.

▶ **RTI Differentiation Considerations:**   As with the other aspects of classroom management discussed in this section, ensuring that transition time does not help to reduce progress is essential in making informed curricula decisions. As students are provided increased levels of instruction, additional movement may be necessary. If transition time is an issue for the learner, it must be addressed to facilitate learning and satisfactory progress toward curricular benchmarks.

A differentiated classroom must be effectively managed to facilitate teaching and learning to meet a variety of needs. At minimum, classrooms should be structured to include the above management components. Form 6.3 (*Classroom Management Components*) is a guide to document how key components within the classroom facilitate effective classroom management.

Differentiating Instructional Management Procedures

Instructional management refers to the opportunities provided to students in teaching and learning specific content knowledge and skills (Hoover & Patton, 2005). Whereas classroom management deals with the physical and emotional climate necessary for managing classroom behavior so that learning can best occur, instructional management consists of specific targeted teaching practices that directly facilitate student learning and progress toward curricular benchmarks. Key instructional management aspects to consider in multi-tiered RTI curriculum implementation include the grouping of students, independent learning, use of learning centers, activation of prior knowledge, the cultural/linguistic context, and direct instruction. Although this list is not all-inclusive, these instructional components are essential to most learning situations when considering the RTI curricular needs of all learners. Each of these components is discussed below, followed by a table of instructional and classroom management techniques that are effective in meeting a variety of needs in the classroom.

GROUPING OF STUDENTS ■ Differentiated instruction includes the use of flexible small and large groups of students along with paired learning (Chapman & King, 2008). In effective instructional management, various groupings are employed strategically to meet different needs associated with the content being studied and the learning preferences of the students. Stated simply, the way students are grouped in teaching and learning can have a significant effect on the acquisition of knowledge and skills (Hoover & Patton, 2005). For example, some students learn best in a paired or small-group setting where they become more actively involved; large-group instruction is passive for many students and does not create sufficient motivation to learn. Teachers use different types of groupings for a variety of reasons in attempting to create relevant and sufficient opportunities to learn.

▶ **RTI Differentiation Considerations:** Because the types of grouping used may have a powerful effect on student learning and progress, their effectiveness should be reviewed for students who exhibit lack of progress or large achievement gaps. Differentiated curriculum implementation groupings are essential to meet various needs in multi-tiered RTI models. When screening or progress monitoring scores identify struggling learners, the instructional groupings associated with their lack of progress should be considered in making the decision to adjust instruction.

INDEPENDENT LEARNING ■ All students are periodically expected to work independently to complete tasks, take tests, or otherwise demonstrate knowledge or progress. Students who struggle in school may be less willing or able to work independently, due in part to poor study skills, learning strategies, or organizational skills (Hoover & Patton, 2005). However, although independent learning is important in school, a student's inability to complete tasks independently should not be the primary reason for deciding to provide Tier 2 supports; using a different type of grouping to help the student learn may lead to more positive results. When used appropriately and within the learner's abilities, independent learning activities complement other instructional arrangements, such as small and large groups or paired learning.

▶ **RTI Differentiation Considerations:** Independent learning abilities include many skills directly related to self-management, responsibility, reinforcement, and monitoring, in addition to having the content knowledge required to work independently. Decisions concerning differentiated instructional management should include independent activities only if they enhance opportunities to learn. If independent learning becomes an issue for the student within the RTI curriculum, it should be scaled back to reduce failure and time off task in learning.

LEARNING CENTERS ■ The use of learning centers in the classroom increases learning opportunities for all students by differentiating teaching and learning within specific content areas (Bender, 2008). Learning centers may be structured in many creative ways to facilitate independent practice, paired or small-group learning, interdisciplinary content learning, or other activities that target a specific content area or skill.

▶ **RTI Differentiation Considerations:** Depending upon the structure of the learning center, various types of activities may be completed. One advantage of a learning center is that it can serve different needs simultaneously, such as independent study time, paired learning, or reinforcement of content and skills. Differentiated instruction that includes the use of learning centers may provide sufficient support in the Tier 1 core curriculum to reduce the need for Tier 2 supplemental instruction. In making decisions concerning the most appropriate tier of instruction for at-risk or struggling learners, educators should consider the role that learning centers play or could play in multi-tiered RTI curriculum implementation.

ACTIVATION OF PRIOR KNOWLEDGE ■ One of the most effective strategies that students use in teaching and learning consists of accessing prior knowledge in the study of new concepts or skills. Differentiations of instructional management should include activities, questioning techniques (e.g., reciprocal teaching), and similar tasks that help learners activate their prior knowledge in relation to new material being studied. Development of future knowledge and skills builds upon previously acquired knowledge and skills, and all educators should incorporate a variety of ways to help students tap into what they already know when developing new abilities (see Chapter 8 for detailed coverage of active processing and related learning strategies).

▶ **RTI Differentiation Considerations:** The ability to acquire new learning is connected to the ability to access and use prior knowledge. In making decisions about the potential need for Tier 2 supplemental support, the educator should consider:

1. The learner's ability to access prior knowledge.
2. Instructional practices that are sufficiently differentiated to give students opportunities to access prior learning.
3. Differentiated instructional management that helps the learner apply the accessed prior knowledge to the learning of the new material.

For some learners, a more contextually appropriate means to access prior learning may be all that is needed to help them acquire new knowledge and skills. It is essential that implementation of the multi-tiered RTI curriculum provide ways for learners to frequently and consistently access and use their prior knowledge.

CULTURAL/LINGUISTIC CONTEXT ■ One population of students who may benefit significantly from multi-tiered RTI curricular structures are culturally and linguistically diverse learners (Hoover, 2009b; Klingner, Hoover, & Baca, 2008). Specifically, the proper implementation of RTI curricula within any tier of instruction may reduce unnecessary referrals to special education by providing more culturally responsive instruction and progress monitoring (Hoover & Klingner, in press). Differentiated instructional management for culturally and linguistically diverse learners includes valuing diverse cultures, utilizing students' first and second languages, promoting functional use of language in teaching and learning, and providing cognitively challenging experiences to all students (Tharp, 1997) (see Chapter 7 for detailed coverage of RTI for diverse learners).

▶ **RTI Differentiation Considerations:** Culturally and linguistically diverse students often are not successful learners because of their insufficient English language skills and/or their differences in cultural values. Historically, these factors have been misinterpreted as learning disorders (Hoover et al., 2008). In implementing the Tier 1 RTI curriculum, educators must be culturally responsive in order to determine whether Tier 2 supplemental supports are warranted. Classrooms containing English language learners should include instructional management differentiations within the Tier 1 core curriculum that reflect cultural/linguistic diversity prior to subjecting these students to Tier 2 supports. Implementation of the multi-tiered RTI curriculum for diverse learners is effective and implemented with fidelity only if it values and accommodates students' cultural/linguistic diversity. Subjecting diverse students to a curriculum that lacks cultural relevance and/or neglects the students' English language skills is inappropriate; the result is the perpetuation of a biased curriculum and associated decision making. Implementing the RTI curriculum with fidelity has the potential to give diverse students a more effective education than they received in the past, provided that the curriculum is culturally responsive and is taught by educators who are culturally competent when implementing Tier 1 core instruction.

DIRECT INSTRUCTION ■ As discussed in Chapter 2, one of the more thoroughly researched instructional interventions shown to be effective is direct instruction (Swanson, 1999). Differentiated classrooms usually contain this practice, especially to assist struggling learners. Direct instruction is explicit instruction that includes the following steps (Slocum, 2004): clearly stated objectives; teacher explanation, demonstration, and support; guided student practice; and independent demonstration and use of the skill by students. The multi-tiered RTI curriculum should include direct instruction, whether as a separate form of instruction or embedded in selected materials or activities. The differentiation of instructional management uses direct instruction in various ways and in different content areas to assist in meeting a variety of learners' needs in RTI models (refer back to Chapter 2 for a detailed description of direct instruction).

▶ **RTI Differentiation Considerations:** Direct instruction not only provides students with structured, consistent, and organized learning, it also can be used in objective, systematic progress monitoring to determine its effectiveness in helping students make adequate progress toward academic or behavioral curricular benchmarks. Each tier in multi-tiered RTI curriculum implementation should include direct instruction to make certain that students receive clear, teacher-directed learning that is integral to differentiated instructional management. Although direct instruction has been shown to be effective for many students, some students prefer more student-driven learning such as constructivist learning (Cohen & Spenciner, 2010). The effects of direct instruction on progress for students whose screening or monitoring results suggest potential problems with Tier 1 core instruction should be determined during the decision-making process. This should occur prior to initiating Tier 2 supports to be certain that the best evidence-based interventions are selected. Form 6.4 (*Instructional Management Components*) is a guide used to document how key classroom components facilitate effective instructional management.

Addressing the key areas discussed above assists educators in creating effective differentiated classroom and instructional management when implementing the multi-tiered RTI model in all grade levels and each tier of instruction. These areas should be considered along with the various evidence-based interventions discussed in Chapter 2 as well as the study skills and learning strategies to be presented in Chapter 8. In addition, Table 6.5, developed from discussions in Hoover (2009b) and Polloway, Patton, and Serna (2007), provides 16 teaching and behavior management techniques to facilitate effective classroom and instructional management.

These techniques complement the evidence-based interventions and study/learning strategies to assist educators in any grade level in implementing general, targeted, supplemental, and intensive differentiations through multi-tiered RTI curriculum implementation. Each intervention includes a brief description of the process, the desired outcomes, and considerations when using it in RTI curriculum implementation.

TABLE 6.5 Classroom and Instructional Management Techniques for Use in Response to Intervention Curriculum Implementation

Instructional Intervention	Overview	Instructional Purpose	RTI Considerations
Learning Center	Designated area where instructional materials are available for use by individuals or small groups of students	Students reinforce learning at their own pace	Center may contain activities that reinforce areas of needed support
Alternative Method for Response	Mode of response is adapted for learners	Students respond to learning in a manner consistent with their needs	Differentiated response modes support varying styles, and these should be respected by teachers
Shortened Assignments	Breaking down longer assignments into shorter, more manageable tasks	Difficult or complex tasks are more easily completed by students	Students with shorter attention spans or those requiring more time to complete tasks in any tier of instruction may initially respond more easily to shorter assignments
Role Playing	Students assume roles and act these out based on their perceptions of the roles	Students acquire a greater understanding of acceptable behaviors in different situations	Role play is one technique used to help learners address social-emotional objectives in any tier of instruction
Providing Choices	Students are given the opportunity to select completion of tasks or assignments given a choice as to the order in which they wish to complete the tasks	Assists students to manage time and organize completion of assignments; reduces anxiety with assignment completion	This intervention allows learners to manage time and organize themselves based on preferred instructional styles and prior experiences with curricular expectations
Contingency Contracting	An agreement between teacher and student concerning academic subjects or behaviors	Improve motivation; support preferred ways of learning; allow students to assume greater ownership in learning	Learning goals may be incorporated into contracts; a variety of academic or behavioral needs can be accommodated through contracts in RTI
Modifying Presentation of Abstract Concepts	Scaffolding; use of specific procedures to help students learn abstract concepts	Abstract concepts are made more comprehensible to learners based on linguistic abilities	This technique helps to build on the student's prior experiences to increase success in learning new, challenging material

TABLE 6.5 (Continued)

Instructional Intervention	Overview	Instructional Purpose	RTI Considerations
Prompting	Providing cues and supports to facilitate learning and response	Support learning to encourage and maintain interest and success	Prompting alerts students to upcoming transitions or the need to manage their time or behavior
Simplifying Reading Levels	Reducing or minimizing the complexities of language and vocabulary in printed material	Provide learners with language and vocabulary commensurate with their English language development	Learners must access the curriculum at points commensurate with their abilities; this technique facilitates appropriate access
Signal Interference	Using nonverbal cues or signals to manage behavior or support student actions	Prevent minor behaviors from becoming more significant without drawing attention away from the classroom instruction; provide a positive gesture to support learners' actions	Signals must be appropriate and meaningful to be effective and must be viewed as positive gestures to advance learning
Proximity Control	Strategic positioning of the student to provide emotional support and/or minimize the potential for behavior problems	Allow students to increase confidence in their abilities and improve their time-on-task behaviors	Comfort in use of personal space or proximity may vary significantly; this must be considered in the implementation of this intervention
Planned Ignoring	Purposely ignoring select minor behaviors	Reduce negative behaviors by not drawing attention to or reinforcing them	Ignoring minor undesired behavior is effective if it reduces the behavior; it may be a simple means of helping learners deal with minor behaviors that need to be changed
Clearly Articulated Expectations	Providing students with a clear set of directions and steps for learning	Minimize frustration or anxiety caused by unfamiliar or confusing academic and behavioral expectations	Many learners require explicit directions and instruction to best meet their academic and social needs; clear instructions should be part of curriculum implementation with fidelity
Planned Physical Movement	Giving students planned opportunities to engage actively in learning activities through movement within the classroom	Generate active participation in learning and reduce behavior problems associated with extensive passive activities	This intervention supports learners' need for active learning and ongoing interactions to facilitate progress within RTI models
Student Accountability	Providing structures that allow students to be accountable for their actions and learning	Students become more aware of their actions and their impact on their learning and behaviors	Student accountability in their own learning and self-management increases efficiency in the implementation of a multi-tiered curriculum in RTI models
Self-Monitoring	Students monitor and evaluate their own learning and behaviors	Encourages positive learning; increase time on task; minimize behavior problems	This intervention helps students assume greater responsibility for their own learning

These teaching and behavior management techniques are presented, in part, to demonstrate that a variety of occurrences or practices in a classroom contribute to learners' progress or lack of progress. Consideration of the five curricular components may help educators put classroom and instructional management within an educational context that clarifies needed differentiations.

Table 6.6 provides a summary of key factors to consider and questions to ask when differentiating the five curricular components. Use of the teaching and behavior management techniques presented in Table 6.5 is helpful in differentiating each curriculum component to provide effective and efficient

TABLE 6.6 Curricular Components and Classroom/Instructional Management

Component	Relevance to Multi-Tiered Instruction	Key Differentiation Questions
Content/Skills (Research-Based Curriculum)	Content area knowledge, skills, ways of thinking, and outcomes are taught through implementation of the research-based curriculum	Does the learner possess an adequate experiential background, pre-requisite skills, and language abilities to successfully engage in the curriculum? Does the content reflect material that is culturally and linguistically relevant?
Evidence-Based Interventions	Teacher and student interventions used in the classroom are grounded in research-based evidence demonstrating their effectiveness for the intended purpose and the population of learners	Are the selected interventions evidence based? Are they used for the purposes for which they were designed? Are they appropriate for learners with different needs and backgrounds (i.e., if the same intervention is used with all learners, is it appropriate to use it with all of them based on research evidence)?
Instructional Arrangements	Differentiated classrooms use various combinations of settings (e.g., groups, pairs, center work) to facilitate progress toward academic and behavioral curricular benchmarks	With which instructional arrangement(s) do the students learn best? Do learners spend a great deal of academic learning time in settings (e.g., small or large group, independent, cooperative) that reflect the structures in which they learn best? Are the instructional arrangements compatible with learners' experiential background, learning preferences, and self-management abilities?
Class/Instructional Management Procedures	Differentiated classroom and instructional management practices implemented in integrative ways form the foundation of effective teaching and learning	Which classroom management practices best address the needs of all students? Is instruction in the classroom managed properly to provide sufficient opportunities to learn? Are the classroom and instructional management practices compatible with learners' experiential background, learning preferences, and self-management abilities? Does instruction that is implemented with fidelity fail to yield adequate progress because of ineffective classroom management?
Progress Evaluation	Systematic and regular monitoring of progress for all learners is a critical aspect of multi-tiered RTI curriculum implementation	Do the selected progress monitoring measures and practices give the learner a fair and appropriate way to demonstrate progress? Would some accommodation(s) to the progress monitoring provide better opportunities for the learner to demonstrate progress? Is there a direct connection between what is taught and what is assessed?

differentiated classroom and instructional management through the integrated application of all five components.

As shown, differentiations within the five curricular components are essential to implementing effective classroom and instructional management in multi-tiered RTI models. Finding answers to the questions in Table 6.6 assists educators to make informed instructional adjustment decisions by making certain that the proper curriculum component(s) is differentiated and emphasized for all learners. The chapter concludes with its *RTI Curriculum in Practice* example, where the use of targeted differentiations in the Tier 1 core curriculum helped a potentially struggling learner make adequate progress, eliminating the need for Tier 2 supplemental supports.

RTI CURRICULUM IN PRACTICE

Use of Targeted Differentiations to Meet Needs of a Struggling Learner in Tier 1 Core Instruction

Description

The role of special education teachers within RTI has become more flexible and dynamic, allowing us to provide assistance to increased numbers of struggling learners in need of additional supports, as well as directly teach students with special needs. This has led to greater opportunities for me to provide increased assistance to more students throughout the school in each tier of instruction, particularly Tier 1. While most classrooms are differentiated to some extent, as educators we sometimes forget that many students in general education need more targeted differentiations, in addition to those already being implemented, to best address all students' needs within the Tier 1 core instruction. An example of the use of more targeted differentiations within Tier 1 instruction occurred for one secondary-level student in the content area of history, which reduced the need for Tier 2 instruction.

Using Targeted Differentiations in Tier 1 Instruction

In a World History class, there was a particular sophomore student who was an excellent listener who could take in and remember information by hearing it once. However, there was more information being presented than the student could take in at one time, leading to his struggles with being able to take notes and keep them organized while listening to the lecture. He became frustrated and eventually shut down, which limited the amount of knowledge he gained through the classroom lecture. Consequently, the teacher was considering requesting Tier 2 supplemental support since he was falling behind. After consulting with the teacher, we decided it would be best to implement a targeted differentiation to teach the student to recognize when he was becoming overwhelmed so he could ask for a break to maintain acceptable behavior. This targeted differentiation for this particular learner was essential in order for the student to continue functioning in the general education classroom. Once the student began to recognize that he was becoming frustrated and was able to calm himself down during his break, he was able to maintain his behavior in the classroom.

In support of this, in order to give the student autonomy, he was included in a brainstorming session to identify assistance with note taking. The student chose to receive direct instruction on note taking so he could more effectively summarize lectures and learn more efficient organization skills. During that process of learning, he also was given permission to record the lectures as well as receive a copy of the notes from a peer to be used in addition to his notes. These targeted differentiations assisted the student to eventually learn how to stay calm when frustrated as well as take notes in an organized fashion. This process

(Continued)

provided one struggling learner with increased assistance in the general education classroom so he could maintain his progress in Tier 1 instruction. Through this experience, I realized the importance of targeted differentiations and that the additional needs of struggling learners can be successfully met in the general education Tier 1 classroom instruction. Often, it is simple solutions, like the ones described above, which assist students who are beginning to struggle to continue to make adequate progress within the Tier 1 core curriculum.

—**Subini A. (Special Educator)**

RTI APPLICATIONS OF KEY CHAPTER CONCEPTS

Differentiated classrooms integrated with flexible instruction provide the foundation for effective implementation of the multi-tiered RTI curriculum in any grade level. The structure for educating all students, including struggling learners, in today's classrooms highlights the need for greater depth and breadth in the implementation and differentiation of the curriculum. The RTI model provides for more intense tiers of intervention once lack of progress is determined through universal screening and/or progress monitoring. By implementing both general and targeted differentiations in the Tier 1 core curriculum, the need for Tier 2 services is reduced for some students, who are provided a small amount of additional time to demonstrate adequate progress. Effective differentiations are also necessary to provide appropriate Tier 2 and 3 instruction, thereby emphasizing the need for supplemental differentiations (Tier 2) as well as intensive differentiations (Tier 3) once general and targeted differentiations (Tier 1) are shown to be insufficient. Selecting and implementing varying degrees of differentiations reduces the need for unnecessary Tier 2/3 supplemental supports and intensive interventions. This, in turn, creates a structure that does not overload any of the tiers of instruction and meets the needs of all learners.

The application of these curricular topics within multi-tiered RTI provides the foundation for meeting the needs of all learners. Educators should do the following:

- Complete the *Curriculum Differentiation Planning Guide* (Form 6.2) for a struggling learner and generate a program to address the identified needs.
- Identify the manner in which you use the various classroom management strategies discussed in this chapter.
- Identify your use of the various instructional management strategies discussed in this chapter.
- Develop a PowerPoint program discussing the need to consider the integrated use of classroom management features along with instructional management features to best determine RTI needs.
- Provide examples of the use of the four types of differentiation (general, targeted, supplemental, intensive) in your school and classroom.

FORM 6.1 Differentiation Quick Screen (DQS)

Educator: _____   Student: _____   Date: _____

Clarification of Current Curriculum Needs and Setting:

Curriculum Area of Need:
Current Level of Proficiency:
Current Rate of Progress:
Gap Analysis Results (Size):
Class Setting in Which Need Is Most Frequently Evident:
Primary Evidence-Based Intervention(s):

Based on the above curriculum needs and setting, check appropriate items within each curriculum component.

I. Content/Skills—Learner sufficiently possesses the following:

___ Reading level
___ Experiential background
___ Required prerequisite skills
___ Language abilities in language of instruction
___ Motivation to learn and study material
___ Higher level abstract thinking abilities
___ Other (specify):

II. Evidence-Based Intervention—Intervention used with learner:

___ Facilitates active student participation
___ Does not lead to learner progress or attention to task
___ Is an intervention that is clearly understood by the learner
___ Engages the learner by capturing and maintaining attention to the task
___ Is compatible with student preferences concerning learning
___ Assists learner to acquire content/skills being taught
___ Other (specify):

III. Instructional Arrangements—Effects of arrangement(s) on learner progress:

Independent Work Setting:
___ Independent work is successfully completed
___ Independent work is not successfully completed

Small-Group Setting (check all that apply):
___ Facilitates productive learner interactions
___ Leads to completion of assignments/tasks
___ Maintains learner's attention to task
___ Is an appropriate structure for managing learner's behaviors
___ Setting does not lead to learner's progress or attention to task
___ Other (specify):

Large-Group Setting (check all that apply):
___ Facilitates productive learner interactions
___ Leads to completion of assignments/tasks
___ Maintains learner's attention to task
___ Is an appropriate structure for managing learner's behaviors
___ Setting does not lead to learner's progress or attention to task
___ Other (specify):

Paired/Cooperative Learning Setting (check all that apply):
___ Facilitates productive learner interactions
___ Leads to completion of assignments/tasks
___ Maintains learner's attention to task
___ Is an appropriate structure for managing learner's behaviors
___ Setting does not lead to learner's progress or attention to task
___ Other (specify):

IV. Classroom/Instructional Management—Effects of management procedures on learner's curriculum area of need:

Relative to learner's curriculum need(s), the classroom management facilitates (check all that apply):
___ self-management of behavior
___ student's responsibility for own learning
___ positive physical and emotional environment
___ structured, periodic movement within the classroom
___ efficient time management
___ smooth transitions
___ differentiation to meet social/behavioral needs
___ effective use of academic learning time
___ relevant and meaningful rewards/reinforcement
___ consistency in implementation of class rules/routines
___ sufficient opportunities to learn
___ implementation of class management techniques with fidelity
___ other (specify):

Relative to the learner's curriculum need(s), the instructional management facilitates (check all that apply):
___ effective uses of student groupings
___ proper uses of independent learning
___ effective use of learning centers
___ differentiation to meet academic needs
___ learner's activation and application of prior knowledge
___ valuing cultural diversity in teaching
___ accommodating various language needs and levels of proficiency
___ use of direct instruction methodology
___ use of cooperative learning
___ implementation of instructional techniques with fidelity

___ sufficient progress toward curricular benchmarks in content/skill area(s)
___ other (specify):

V. Progress Evaluation – Evaluation of the learner's progress in curriculum need area includes the following:

___ Appropriate, research-based monitoring measures and practices are used
___ Evaluation directly assesses what is taught in the curriculum
___ Evaluation directly assesses progress toward curricular benchmarks addressed in the curriculum
___ Monitoring device/practice is used only for what it was designed to measure
___ Monitoring device/practice is implemented with fidelity
___ Monitoring device/practice is used with learners similar to the research population
___ Monitoring device/practice is administered in the learner's most proficient language and/or in English if the learner is bilingual

Summary of Current Curriculum Situation and Differentiation Needs:

Content/Skills:

Evidence-Based Intervention:

Instructional Arrangement:

Class/Instructional Management:

Progress Evaluation:

Source: Used by permission of John J. Hoover.

<u>Instructions</u>: Complete this guide to further clarify targeted, supplemental, or intensive differentiation needs of the learner as identified through classroom screening/monitoring procedures and results from the *Differentiation Quick Screen (DQS)*.

<u>Student</u>:   <u>Date</u>:   <u>Grade</u>:

<u>Content Instructional Need Area</u>:

<u>Teacher</u>:

Expected outcomes for student resulting from instruction:

Reason for concern:

A. Briefly describe the current classroom/instructional situation for the need area in question:

Content area addressed during this instructional period:

Evidence-Based Intervention(s) used during this instruction:

Instructional Arrangement(s) used during this instruction:

Class/Instructional Management Procedures used during this instruction:

Progress Evaluation used to monitor progress resulting from instruction:

B. Respond to each curricular element relative to the described situation above.

I. Curriculum Element: Content/Skills

1. *Does the learner possess sufficient reading abilities to be successful with the instruction?*

2. *Has the learner acquired the prerequisite skills necessary to be successful with the instruction?*

If not, which prerequisite skills does the learner lack?

3. *Does the learner possess sufficient language development skills to be successful with the instruction?*

4. *Does the learner possess the academic experiences needed to comprehend the concepts associated with the instruction?*

Summary of Content/Skill Needs:

II. Curriculum Element: Evidence-Based Intervention(s)

1. *Does the selected evidence-based intervention provide sufficient motivation to the learner?*

2. *Does the selected evidence-based intervention generate active learner participation in the instruction?*

3. *Under what learning conditions is the selected evidence-based intervention MOST effective for the learner?*

4. *Under what learning conditions is the selected evidence-based intervention LEAST effective for the learner?*

5. *To what extent does the learner progress satisfactorily toward curricular benchmarks through use of the selected evidence-based intervention?*

Summary of Evidence-Based Intervention Needs:

III. Curriculum Element: Instructional Arrangement

1. *To what extent is the learner capable of working independently in learning the instructional content?*

2. *To what extent is the learner capable of working in a small-group setting WITH direct teacher guidance in learning the instructional content?*

3. *To what extent is the learner capable of working in a small-group setting WITHOUT direct teacher guidance in learning the instructional content?*

4. *To what extent is the learner capable of working in a large-group setting in learning the instructional content?*

5. *To what extent is the learner capable of working cooperatively with one or two classmates without constant direct teacher guidance in learning the instructional content?*

Summary of Instructional Arrangement Needs:

IV. Curriculum Element: Classroom and Instructional Management

<u>Class Management</u> *(Briefly describe classroom management during the instruction):*

<u>Physical Environment</u>:

<u>Classroom Climate</u>:

<u>Rules and Routines</u>:

<u>Reinforcement and Rewards</u>:

<u>Time Management</u>:

<u>Transition Time</u>:

1. *Identify appropriate behaviors that the learner exhibits during the instruction.*

2. *Identify inappropriate behaviors that the learner exhibits during the instruction.*

3. *Describe the learner's behavioral self-management abilities.*

4. *Describe how well the classroom management rewards/reinforcements affect the learner.*

5. *Describe how well the learner makes transitions to different tasks or activities during the instruction.*

Instructional Management (Briefly describe how you manage your instructional time):

1. *What percent of the total instructional time does the learner engage in:*
   On-task behavior?
   Off-task behavior?

2. *Describe the extent to which the instruction is provided through Direct Instruction methods.*

3. *Describe the extent to which the instruction reflects the diverse cultural and linguistic needs of the learner.*

4. *Describe ways in which the instruction facilitates the learner's activation of prior knowledge pertaining to the topic.*

5. *Describe how the implementation of the instruction is managed through the use of learning centers.*

Summary of Classroom and Instructional Management Needs:

V. Curriculum Element: Progress Evaluation

1. *Describe how the progress evaluation directly assesses what is taught through the instruction.*

2. *Describe how the evaluation <u>device</u> is appropriate in measuring the learner's progress with the instruction.*

3. *Describe how the evaluation <u>practice</u> is appropriate in measuring the learner's progress with the instruction.*

4. *Is cultural and linguistic diversity accommodated in the selected progress evaluation device and/or practice?*

Summary of Progress Evaluation Needs:

C. Prioritize curricular components requiring differentiation based on the information provided above. Briefly clarify your recommendation for priority of HIGH-ranked items.

Curricular Components	Recommended Differentiation Priority			
	High	**Medium**	**Low**	**Clarification**
Content/Skills				
Evidence-Based Intervention				
Instructional Arrangement				
Class/Instruction Management				
Progress Evaluation				

Summarize Hypothesis for Differentiation(s):

Source: Used by permission of John J. Hoover.

FORM 6.3 Classroom Management Components

Student: _____   Date: _____

Teacher Completing Checklist: _____

Content Area: _____

Instructions: Check each classroom management component once it has been observed or documented relative to the learner's differentiation needs. Provide a descriptive summary for each item as related to the learner's needs.

Classroom Management Component   **Description Summary**

___ Physical Environment   _____
                                            _____

___ Classroom Climate   _____

___ Routines/Rules   _____
                                            _____

___ Reinforcement/Rewards   _____
                                            _____

___ Self-Management Procedures   _____
                                            _____

___ Teacher Time Management   _____
                                            _____

___ Transition Times   _____
                                            _____

Source: Used by permission of John J. Hoover.

FORM 6.4   Instructional Management Components

Student: _____   Date: _____

Teacher Completing Checklist: _____

Content Area: _____

Instructions: Check each instructional management component once it has been observed or documented relative to the learner's differentiation needs. Provide a descriptive summary for each item as related to the learner's needs.

Instructional Management Component

____ Use of Student Groupings (Small/Large, etc.)

____ Independent Learning Time

____ Instructional Uses of Learning Centers

____ Activation of Prior Knowledge

____ Direct Instruction

____ Cultural and Linguistic Context

Description Summary

_____

_____

_____

_____

_____

_____

_____

_____

_____

_____

_____

_____

_____

_____

Source: Used by permission of John J. Hoover.

CHAPTER 7

Culturally Responsive Curriculum for Diverse Learners

▶ Overview

OVER THE PAST TWO DECADES, culturally and linguistically diverse learners have been the fastest-growing population in our schools, a trend affecting both urban and rural areas in almost every state. These students remain at higher risk for misplacement in special education, resulting in part from the misinterpretation of learning differences as learning disorders. RTI models show significant promise for instructing and assessing diverse learners more accurately; however, culturally responsive education must prevail for RTI to benefit all students. This includes developing knowledge and skills that facilitate cultural competence in the classroom, valuing diversity, and ensuring sufficient and appropriate opportunities to learn. Implementation of a multi-tiered curriculum for diverse learners requires teachers to increase their expertise by expanding their knowledge of different types of curriculum and the five curricular components operating within a classroom that includes culturally/linguistically diverse learners. Thus, culturally

responsive educators become more cognizant of the influences of various ecological factors on development and education, especially because these factors may differ across cultures, languages, and experiential backgrounds.

▶ Key Topics

- ► Ecological educational perspective
- ► Learning differences versus learning disabilities
- ► Culturally responsive teaching
- ► Implementing a culturally responsive tiered curriculum

▶ Learner Outcomes

After reading this chapter, you should:

1. Understand the critical curricular issues to consider in multi-tiered RTI for culturally and linguistically diverse learners
2. Be able to apply ecological principles and practices to meet diverse needs within multi-tiered instruction
3. Be able to assess your cultural competence in teaching and develop an associated personal professional development plan
4. Know the best practices necessary to implement a culturally responsive tiered curriculum for all students

SIGNIFICANCE TO CONTEMPORARY CLASSROOM INSTRUCTION

The fact that our schools and classrooms are becoming more diverse is apparent in most of our more than 15,000 school districts. Diversity brings a global perspective to teaching and learning and must be reflected in curriculum implementation to meet the needs of all learners. It is important to ensure that all students have sufficient opportunities to learn; providing education within a cultural context for diverse learners contributes significantly to a meaningful and relevant curriculum. This becomes especially important in multi-tiered RTI when decisions concerning difference versus disability issues arise in relation to suspected academic or behavioral problems. Meeting the needs of all learners requires the application of ecological principles in teaching and learning, because what occurs in any classroom is directly related to home/community as well as diverse values and norms. This is significant in today's classrooms because core (Tier 1), supplemental (Tier 2), and intensive (Tier 3) curriculum implementation must be appropriate to all learners, including those who bring diverse cultural and linguistic backgrounds to the teaching and learning environment.

Overview of Cultural/Linguistic Curricular Needs in Response to Intervention

Perhaps no learners have a greater stake in the successful implementation of a multi-tiered RTI curriculum than those who bring cultural and linguistic diversity to the classroom (Vanderwood & Nam, 2007). In our initial efforts to meet the needs of all learners (at least 80% of students) within the core Tier 1 curriculum in the general classroom, the ability to address diversity is critical to avoid the erroneous belief that a learning disability exists when in fact the student is exhibiting learning differences. An underpinning of Tier 1 as well as Tier 2 RTI is the implementation of a curriculum shown to be effective with the learners with whom it is being used (i.e., a research-based curriculum and evidence-based interventions).

This highlights several issues that must be addressed when considering the implementation of a curriculum with fidelity for culturally and linguistically diverse learners within multi-tiered RTI:

- Sufficient opportunities to learn that reflect cultural and linguistic diversity
- Use of a research-based curriculum and evidence-based interventions designed and shown to be effective in addressing cultural and linguistic diversity
- Curriculum implementation that reflects students' English language proficiency levels
- Curriculum implementation that reflects students' cultural values and norms
- Compatibility between preferred teaching styles and students' learning preferences
- Curriculum implemented and assessed by a culturally responsive educator (Hoover, 2009b)

These practices facilitate the successful implementation of Tier 1 and Tier 2 curricula for culturally and linguistically diverse learners while avoiding the misrepresentation of "lack of progress" as "lack of opportunity." Each of these issues is further explored below. They must all be addressed satisfactorily within Tier 1; otherwise, decisions concerning Tier 2 may be flawed, which in turn directly affects Tier 3 decision making.

Sufficient Opportunities to Learn

To determine the effectiveness of instruction within any tier for culturally/linguistically diverse learners, educators must be certain that students have opportunities to learn that are relevant to their experiential backgrounds and current levels of English proficiency. In classrooms or grades that contain a majority of diverse learners, instruction must accommodate their needs to ensure that at least 80% of these students have sufficient opportunities to achieve classroom or grade-level benchmarks. For example, if a majority of the class (e.g., over 50%) demonstrates lack of achievement, then Tier 1 instruction should receive modifications and adjustments to better address students' cultural and linguistic needs rather than immediately moving these students into Tier 2 instruction. Therefore, sufficient opportunities to learn are relative to the context in which students are educated.

Research-Based/Evidence-Based Curriculum and Interventions

An extremely significant question related to the selection and use of a research-based curriculum and evidence-based interventions is "For whom were these developed, researched, and shown to be effective?" McLaughlin (1992) suggested that it is unclear whether we may assume that interventions shown to be effective with English speakers will also be effective with learners from different language backgrounds. As discussed in Chapter 2, both the curriculum and the interventions used in the teaching and learning environment must be grounded in evidence that clearly demonstrates their effectiveness for the population for which they are used and the content area addressed. Therefore, when selecting and using curricula and interventions, their appropriateness for use with culturally and linguistically diverse learners must be considered. To make the proper selection, educators should corroborate that the curricula and interventions used with diverse learners directly reflect or make provisions for accommodating cultural and linguistic diversity. In other words, there should be evidence that selected curricula and interventions can meet diverse learning needs in multi-tiered instruction. This includes considering the significance of cultural values and norms in everyday teaching and learning.

Cultural Values and Norms Reflected in the Curriculum

Bruner (1996) indicated that curricula reflect cultural beliefs, and Joseph et al. (2000) wrote that "curriculum conceptualized as culture educates us to pay attention to belief systems, values, behaviors, language, artistic expression and most importantly, norms" (p. 19). Even general knowledge of a learner's culture and stage of English language acquisition provides significant insight into students' responses to instruction—insight necessary to interpret curriculum implementation results for diverse students. However, according to Baca and Cervantes (2004), most curricula fail to incorporate diverse cultures or accommodate limited English language abilities. In order for multi-tiered RTI to be appropriate for diverse learners, cultural and linguistic differences need to be addressed and accommodated. Otherwise, diverse students will be expected to make adequate progress within a curriculum that is not designed for their success. This leads to misinterpretation of the rate of progress of diverse learners, indicating that they need more intense levels of instruction (i.e., Tiers 2 or 3) when in reality all that is needed is a more appropriate Tier 1 core curriculum that accommodates cultural and linguistic diversity.

English Language Proficiency Levels

Many of today's classrooms include a growing number of students who have limited English proficiency and are in the process of learning English as a second language (Hill & Flynn, 2006). The ability of educators to simultaneously meet curricular and second language needs challenges our educational system. Multi-tiered RTI provides new opportunities to address these needs by implementing culturally responsive teaching and learning. This is vitally important. If the curriculum and interventions reflect cultural values inconsistent with those of diverse learners and/or require use of the English language that is beyond the student's ability, then academic progress is compromised.

Culturally Responsive Teaching and Learning

A culturally responsive educator is able to connect curriculum and interventions with academic progress for diverse learners. Most educators become culturally proficient through a process that systematically blends experience with and knowledge about various cultures (Gay, 2000; Mason, 1993). This experience and knowledge, in turn, is included in curriculum development, implementation, and evaluation so that diverse cultural and linguistic values, norms, and stages of language acquisition are accommodated for all learners. Moore, Armentrout, and Neal (2008) identified several factors that contribute to culturally responsive education. These include understanding:

1. One's own biases
2. One's own values
3. One's own perceptions of society
4. One's own concept of an acceptable school climate
5. Learners' and teachers' expectations
6. One's own preferences concerning the use of various curricular materials and interventions

The extent to which these six factors are consistent with learners' expectations, values, and norms determines the responsiveness of the selected curriculum and interventions to diverse learners' needs. Table 7.1, developed from information in Hoover et al. (2008), provides suggestions for ensuring cultural responsiveness in each of these areas.

As Table 7.1 shows, multicultural perspectives in curriculum implementation provide a solid foundation for making teaching and learning relevant for diverse learners. Although we all have values, perceptions, potential biases, and teaching/learning expectations, no one perception or value is better than

TABLE 7.1 Curricular Considerations for Culturally Responsive Education

Factor	Curricular Consideration	Implications for RTI Implementation
Personal bias	Personal bias influences the implementation of curriculum in both subtle and overt ways	The extent to which personal biases are incompatible with diverse cultural values/norms reflects the potential disconnect between classroom instruction and contextual learning
Values	The values educators bring to the teaching and learning situation are just as important as the values learners bring to the learning environment	The extent of compatibility between educators' and students' values significantly influences academic and behavioral progress
Perceptions of society	The same behavior may be viewed differently by various ethnic and societal groups, reflecting appropriateness (or lack thereof) of those behaviors within the context of curriculum	A general understanding of cultural values/norms goes a long way toward accurately interpreting the behaviors of diverse learners so as to avoid misinterpreting acceptable behaviors in one culture as deviant behaviors in another
Views of an acceptable school climate	The school's attitude toward acceptance of diversity in the implementation of curriculum reflects the level and depth of student–teacher interactions	Realistic schoolwide expectations for all learners facilitate effective curriculum implementation, monitoring of progress, and interpretation of response to instruction
Learners' and teachers' classroom expectations	Clear, consistent student and teacher expectations in the classroom are essential to meeting the needs of diverse learners and to implement a curriculum that is culturally and linguistically responsive; expectations for all learners must be high to ensure a challenging curriculum	Establishing and maintaining realistic and challenging curricular expectations is essential for effective instruction of diverse learners, even if the level of proficiency may be lower than that of other learners yet commensurate with the student's cultural and linguistic needs and stage of English language development
Preferences concerning the use of various curricular materials and interventions	A curriculum that supports a multicultural perspective in teaching and learning provides opportunities for diverse students to learn within a context that is culturally and linguistically relevant	Students who identify with people, concepts, cultural expectations, and other factors that reflect a multicultural society are best able to develop and learn within a meaningful context

another; they may differ, yet they must be respected, at least in general terms, to meet the needs of all learners. Simply disregarding diverse values/norms or expectations because they differ from those of the teacher or school is not acceptable within multi-tiered RTI. Form 7.1 (*Checklist of Culturally Responsive Teaching*) provides a guide to assist educators in evaluating their own responsiveness in teaching diverse learners.

Student Preferences/Teacher Style Compatibility

One of the challenges that cultural and linguistic diversity often creates is that of compatibility between preferred styles of teaching and student preferences concerning learning (Hoover & Collier, 2003). This issue is highly significant in RTI curriculum implementation because research-based curricula and evidence-based interventions have underlying expectations for teaching style and learning style. For example, a highly teacher-directed curriculum assumes that the students learn better through this approach than through a cooperative learning or constructivist teaching approach. A critical issue in the successful implementation of a multi-tiered curriculum is the match between the teaching style embedded in the research-based curriculum and the learning preferences of the students being taught with this curriculum. Compatibility issues surface when the research-based curriculum and evidence-based interventions are inconsistent with the students' cultural values or norms. Form 7.2 (*Checklist of Curriculum Instructional Compatibility for Diverse Learners*) provides a checklist for educators to use in determining the extent of compatibility between student and teacher instructional preferences. This information is essential when progress and the response to instruction are assessed and the results interpreted (i.e., lack of progress may reflect a mismatch between teacher and student instructional preferences rather than the student's ability to learn). This leads directly to one of the more misunderstood aspects of working with culturally and linguistically diverse learners who struggle in school—distinguishing differences from disabilities.

Distinguishing Learning Differences from Disabilities

The education of culturally and linguistically diverse learners brings out many issues among educators, parents, and community members. Ultimately, controversies over formal education for diverse students concern the extent to which these students are required to "fit into" a school structure and curriculum designed for nonminority students. As discussed above, teaching and learning experiences that are consistent and relevant to students have the greatest chance to succeed. We have all struggled with situations or topics that do not interest us or with which we have little or no experience. A similar situation often occurs in the classroom for diverse learners. This frequently leads to misinterpretation of behaviors or abilities as disabilities rather than as what they frequently are—learning differences resulting from different cultural experiences, English language proficiency, or heritages.

Although these misinterpretations have led to overrepresentation of diverse students in special education (Donovan & Cross, 2002), multi-tiered RTI provides a new opportunity for educators to reverse this trend and provide appropriate curriculum implementation based on accurate interpretations of learning differences by valuing diversity. Therefore, in order for RTI curriculum implementation to be effective with diverse learners, it needs to facilitate a context that is relevant both culturally and linguistically. One efficient way to understand diverse needs is to view teaching and learning from an ecological perspective, as described by Bronfenbrenner (1995, 2005). This model is briefly described below, followed by its application to achieve effective RTI curriculum implementation for culturally and linguistically diverse students.

Overview of the Ecological Model

The ecological view within education is grounded in the work of Urie Bronfenbrenner (1958, 1979), who discussed the concept of *social context* as consisting of four distinct yet interrelated levels. A central component in Bronfenbrenner's work is the importance of considering human development within a social context. This is the notion that the impacts of a person's experiences "vary according to their social context and according to their psychological meaning in relation to a person's previous background and experiences, as well as current circumstances" (Rutter, Champion, Quinton, Maughan, & Pickles, 1995, p. 61). According to Bronfenbrenner (1979) and Alwin (1995), *reciprocal influences* exist between an individual and that individual's environment. These reciprocal influences help to shape the individual's development—development that is brought to the teaching and learning environment.

A premise of the ecological model is that to best understand learners' needs (e.g., curricular needs), one must consider the influences of the social environment on the learner's growth and development. In educating diverse learners, an understanding of cultural and linguistic influences on their development may be helpful in distinguishing learning differences from disabilities by alerting educators to possible explanations for educational progress, or lack thereof, by viewing academic and behavioral achievement data within the learner's broader social context. What we believe to be a problem may in fact be highly consistent with the learner's social community context. In addition, a deeper understanding of a learner's social influences on development may provide greater insight into suspected educational needs, which, in turn, may be helpful in making more informed educational decisions. These concepts become important when RTI teams receive data and other information that seemingly point to a learning problem for culturally and linguistically diverse learners. By considering the influences of the four social domains discussed below, RTI team members achieve a more complete understanding of a diverse learner's curricular needs, leading to more accurate multi-tiered RTI curriculum implementation. Discussions of this topic provide an overview of the key concepts of an ecological model, creating a foundation for more informed curricular decisions about culturally and linguistically diverse learners. For a more detailed discussion of this topic, the reader is referred to the literature sources cited in this section, especially Bronfenbrenner (1979) and Moen, Elder, and Luscher (1995).

In an ecological view of education, various environmental factors influence the development of students, which may significantly impact their preparation and preferences concerning academic, social, and behavioral development (Bronfenbrenner, 1995). Four environmental "systems" capture the many environmental factors (Bronfenbrenner, 1979, 1995, 2005) that ultimately influence child development:

MICROSYSTEM ■ This foundational system includes the various relationships, roles, and activity patterns that a learner experiences within specific individual settings (e.g., home).

MESOSYSTEM ■ This second-level system reflects the collective integration of learning and development experienced within individual microsystems (i.e., interrelationships among individual home, community, and school settings).

EXOSYSTEM ■ This third-level system includes different settings associated with various individuals who are significant in the student's life that do not directly involve the learner as an active participant (e.g., a sibling's friend's school, a parent's place of work).

MACROSYSTEM ■ Collectively, the micro-, meso-, and exosystems operate in integrated ways that reflect specific cultures or subcultures, constituting the macrosystem that ultimately solidifies one's cultural values, norms, and expectations.

Curriculum developers, knowingly or unknowingly, reflect values, customs, and backgrounds consistent with their macrosystem and incorporate these into the curricula. For example, a particular reading program may assume that students have prior experience with reading in the home or were provided preschool prereading experiences and activities. A mathematics curriculum that relies heavily on teacher-directed learning assumes that students best acquire knowledge and skills through this methodology. A curriculum that presents content in systematic, discrete steps assumes that students learn best in this manner rather than through a more holistic approach. Many more such examples could be generated. Assumptions associated with developed curricula are rooted in the four ecological systems; an understanding of these systems is helpful in the interpretation of learners' response to instruction.

To sum up, any curriculum is based on assumptions, and if learners do not have the experiences or prior knowledge associated with these assumptions, they may be at a disadvantage in school. In particular, many K–12 culturally and linguistically diverse learners may have different cultural experiences and backgrounds than those underlying curriculum-development assumptions. Table 7.2 provides a summary of the significance of these four ecological factors in the implementation of a multi-tiered RTI curriculum, emphasizing the importance of considering an ecological perspective within RTI models. This is followed by a discussion of the relevance of these ecological factors to culturally/linguistically diverse students.

Table 7.2 relates experience to underlying curricular assumptions. It provides examples of settings in which ecological development occurs and discusses the significance of understanding a learner's experiences within each of the four ecological systems. The extent to which the curriculum matches students' values and experiences developed within these four systems determines whether the curriculum is contextually relevant for the students. Reflecting the need for culturally responsive teaching:

A potential curricular mismatch is often seen in the education of culturally and linguistically diverse students where the curriculum, its implementation, and associated progress monitoring reflect values, experiences, and assumptions different from those of diverse learners.

This, in turn, often leads to misidentifying lack of academic or behavioral progress as a disability, often resulting in decisions concerning the unnecessary need for Tier 2 or Tier 3 interventions and/or special education. Applying knowledge of diverse learners' experiences, consistent with an ecological perspective (i.e., Bronfenbrenner's four systems), assists educators to better understand students' needs by providing a more culturally responsive Tier 1 curriculum, reducing unnecessary referral of students for more intensive tiers of instruction.

Application of Ecological Principles in Curriculum Implementation for Diverse Learners

As describe above, the macrosystem provides opportunities for students to integrate their knowledge and experiences in ways that ultimately shape the values, norms, and educational expectations they bring to the classroom. To best understand the needs of culturally and linguistically diverse learners, educators should

TABLE 7.2 Significance of Ecological Systems in Multi-Tiered Response to Intervention Curriculum Implementation

System	Key Curriculum Question	Experiential Settings	Significance to RTI Curriculum
Micro	Does the student possess the necessary prerequisite experiences associated with learning and development found in the *microsystem*?	Any individual setting, such as the home, playground, store, day-care center, church, or similar real-life settings in which the student is directly involved.	The meanings that students attach to their activities, roles, and relationships are very important. They help to put progress-monitoring results into a more relevant context. The microsystem includes both the physical setting and the perceptions of the learner in these settings. **Significance**: *The meaning that the activities, roles, and relationships hold for the individual within microsystems is highly significant in early learner development and will be reflected in progress made within multi-tiered RTI curriculum implementation.*
Meso	Are the student's learning behaviors consistent with the <u>expected</u> experiences associated with learning acquired by connecting various life settings (e.g., home, school, community)?	As learners move in and out across different micro-settings, their experiences become integrated, modifying the meanings initially developed in the individual *microsystem*.	Knowing that students' development expands beyond individual settings will help educators understand the values, attitudes, and experiential background that the student brings to the teaching and learning environment. **Significance**: *Relationships among home, school, and community values/norms that the learner brings to the teaching and learning environments determine how the student learns best within multi-tiered RTI curriculum implementation.*
Exo	How have events in real-life settings associated with significant others in the student's life (parents, siblings, friends, etc.), impacted the student's development?	Exosystems are the settings of others in the student's life that indirectly affect the student (e.g., a friend's home, a parent's workplace, a sibling's preschool).	Influences from the settings of significant others in a student's life can often have profound effects directly on the learner (e.g., a friend's family issues; a parent's demanding boss; a sibling's teacher's expectations that unrealistically carry over to the student). **Significance:** *The development of any student reflects influences from settings indirectly related to the student, and these influences may significantly promote or inhibit progress in multi-tiered RTI curriculum implementation.*
Macro	What are the student's community life experiences, and how have these shaped values, attitudes, and preferences concerning teaching and learning?	The macrosystem consists of the integration of the previous three systems, and ultimately reflects the values and attitudes students bring from their communities to the classroom.	Cultural values and norms are solidified through macrosystem experiences; these need to be reflected in curricula to provide a relevant context in teaching and learning. **Significance:** *Knowledge of the values, norms, preferences, and heritages that students bring to the teaching and learning environment is critical for providing appropriate education and sufficient opportunity to learn within multi-tiered RTI curriculum implementation.*

be familiar with key aspects of learner development that contribute to growth within the various ecological systems. To put these systems into a practical curriculum context, they are classified within three ecological areas directly related to the school and classroom setting: student, classroom, and home/community factors.

STUDENT FACTORS ■ Several student-related factors associated with cultural and linguistic diversity directly affect learners' progress within the curriculum (Hoover et al., 2008):

Language Competence—the student's native language and English language proficiency

Acculturation—the student's ability to adjust to and succeed in new cultural/linguistic environments

Experiential Background—previous formal school experiences and/or prior experiences with curricular prerequisite skills

Cultural Values/Norms—the values and norms taught to the student that reflect home and community preferences

Higher Order Thinking Abilities—the student's ability to use and apply higher level thinking (i.e., Bloom's taxonomy levels) in the classroom in both native and English languages

Teaching/Learning Preferences—the learning preferences that reflect the student's cultural or linguistic background compared to the teaching preferences often seen in today's classrooms.

▶ **Relevance to RTI Models:** Knowledge, understanding, and accommodations of these six student ecological factors contribute significantly to the implementation of a research-based curriculum within a culturally responsive context, thereby increasing success for diverse learners, especially within the Tier 1 core curriculum.

CLASSROOM FACTORS ■ Through research conducted by Tharp (1997), five ecological classroom factors were generated that reflect several standards for effective instruction for culturally and linguistically diverse learners:

Linguistic Competence—classroom instruction that reflects functional language usage by connecting students' prior and current experiences

Contextualized Learning—accommodations made within the curriculum to reflect home and community values and customs taught to the student

Joint Productivity—classroom activities that facilitate teacher–student interactions

Instructional Conversation—ongoing teacher–student dialogue in the teaching and learning environment in which students are encouraged to interact verbally on a regular basis with the teacher and with other students

Challenging Curriculum—giving all students, including those from diverse backgrounds, a cognitively challenging curriculum that is provided, when necessary, in both native and English languages

▶ **Relevance to RTI Models:** These five classroom factors reflect diversity within teaching and learning. When they are applied in the classroom, properly selected and implemented curricula become more meaningful and contextually relevant to diverse students.

HOME/COMMUNITY FACTORS ■ Four key factors associated with the home and community environment have specific relevance to effective teaching and learning for culturally and linguistically diverse learners (Baca & Cervantes, 2004):

Primary Home Language—the language most often used by the student and family members in the home

Adjustment to the New Community—how well the students are adjusting to the new community and/or culture in which they currently reside

Educational History—the type of formal education to which the student was previously exposed and how that education is similar to or different from the student's current classroom environment and curriculum

Family Structure and Heritage—the diverse cultural values and norms taught to the child by parents, other family members, and community members reflecting family traditions

▶ **Relevance to RTI Models:** Knowledge and understanding of these home/community characteristics, along with appropriate accommodations in curriculum development and implementation, provides a contextually relevant education for diverse learners. In this regard, RTI models are frameworks for valuing culturally and linguistically diverse norms, preferences, and traditions.

Table 7.3, developed from information in Hoover et al. (2008) and Tharp (1997), presents additional examples representing the three ecological factors: student, classroom, and home-community. Their significance to multi-tiered RTI curriculum implementation is highlighted through various questions to guide classroom instruction for diverse learners.

As Table 7.3 shows, each of the identified student, classroom, and home-community factors has a potentially significant impact on progress within the multi-tiered curriculum for culturally and linguistically diverse learners. As discussed, a goal in the education of all students, including diverse learners, is to provide sufficient opportunities to learn. RTI teams should make every effort to generate responses to these and similar questions to make informed curriculum decisions and decisions about the need for appropriate instructional adjustments.

TABLE 7.3 Ecological Factors and Their Significance to Curriculum Implementation for Diverse Learners

Ecological Factor	Significant Questions in RTI Curriculum Implementation
Student Factors	
Language Competence	Has the learner's most proficient language been identified to best meet the learner's academic needs?
Acculturation	Has the learner experienced unusual stress associated with adjusting to a new environment such as a community or school? Have we made certain to avoid misinterpreting this stress as emotional/behavioral disorders?
Experiential Background	Does the learner possess sufficient prerequisite skills, abilities, and experiences to meet academic or behavioral expectations?
Cultural Values/Norms	Have diverse cultural values/norms been accommodated in classroom instruction and expectations?
Higher Order Thinking Abilities	Are higher level thinking abilities emphasized in the curriculum? Are these presented in culturally responsive ways?
Teaching/Learning Preferences	Has the compatibility, or lack thereof, between teaching style and the student's cultural and linguistic background, values, and norms been determined?
Classroom Factors	
Linguistic Competence	Does the classroom contain functional use of language? Is language competence, in both native and English languages, determined and accounted for in the curriculum implementation?
Contextualized Learning	Is the implementation of curriculum put into a relevant cultural and linguistic context for the learner?
Joint Productivity	Does the curriculum engage students and teachers in cooperative classroom activities by facilitating ongoing and joint productive classroom work?
Instructional Conversation	Does the instruction facilitate ongoing verbal interactions between teachers and students, and among students, to facilitate conversation through functional use of language?
Challenging Curriculum	Does the curriculum promote use of higher order thinking skills in both the native language and English if the student is bilingual?
Home-Community Factors	
Primary Home Language(s)	Has the primary language(s) spoken in the student's home and community been determined?
Adjustment to New Community	How effective is the learner in making new friends and adjusting to the new community and school environments?
Educational History	What are the previous school and community experiences and successes of the learner?
Family Structure/ Heritage	Are the home, family, and community values and norms reflected in teaching and learning activities and expectations?

Accommodating the cultural and linguistic values and norms that diverse students bring to the classroom is essential to providing sufficient opportunities in the classroom (Klingner et al., 2008; Tharp, 1997). Valuing diversity in multi-tiered RTI curriculum implementation enriches the education of all students by modeling the significance of all cultures and the contributions they make to a global society. The next section provides a more detailed discussion of practices that teachers may use to become more culturally competent, which in turn leads to RTI curriculum implementation in culturally responsive ways.

Qualities of Culturally Proficient Teaching

Directly related to culturally responsive teaching is the process of becoming a culturally proficient educator. Table 7.4 summarizes the stages in this process (Cross, Bazron, Dennis, & Isaacs,1989; Gay, 2000; Hoover et al., 2008; Mason, 1993).

As Table 7.4 shows, stages 1–3 are highly inconsistent with cultural proficiency, whereas stages 4–6 reflect genuine efforts, necessary practices, and important attitudes in developing and implementing a multi-tiered RTI curriculum for diverse learners. Because stages 4–6 reflect the positive aspects of cultural competence, these stages will be the focus of our discussions.

Cultural Precompetence: Educators in this stage see the value of cultural diversity in the curriculum and actively pursue training and related professional development to become more culturally proficient (Patton & Day-Vines, 2002). This includes efforts to incorporate cultural and linguistic values and norms into the daily curriculum; however, at this stage, this inclusion is sporadic and irregular, such as periodic coverage of specific individuals or events from different cultures. Cultural Precompetence is the all-important first step undertaken by educators to increase their cultural sensitivity and awareness by valuing diverse contributions in teaching and learning.

TABLE 7.4 Stages of Cultural Proficiency

Stage	Evidence within RTI Curriculum
1. Cultural Destructiveness	Cultural diversity is viewed as highly negative and is excluded totally from the multi-tiered RTI curriculum
2. Cultural Incapacity	Cultural diversity is viewed indifferently, yet ignored and given little if any credibility in the implementation of the multi-tiered RTI curriculum
3. Cultural Blindness	Existence of cultural diversity is acknowledged but is viewed as having little significance in the implementation of the multi-tiered RTI curriculum
4. Cultural Precompetence	Cultural diversity is valued, as demonstrated by greater personal awareness and sensitivity, with limited applications in the multi-tiered RTI curriculum
5. Cultural Competence	Perceptions about cultural diversity move from awareness and sensitivity to application and incorporation in the multi-tiered RTI curriculum
6. Cultural Proficiency	Cultural diversity is significantly embedded in both the development and implementation of the multi-tiered RTI curriculum at the school/district level

Cultural Competence: During this stage, educators have acquired the minimum training and experiences necessary to incorporate diversity in curriculum implementation on a regular and consistent basis that goes beyond cultural sensitivity and awareness. This includes personal development and understanding of their own values, norms, and language while respecting those of others (Cross et al., 1989; Mason, 1993). Evidence of cultural competence within the curriculum is seen in daily references and/or instructional tasks that recognize and value examples, items, lifestyles, or heritages of diverse cultures, whether or not these cultures are specifically represented by the students in the classroom. Critical to development within the stage of Cultural Competence is the understanding that learning and behaviors associated with cultural and linguistic diversity are *differences*, not deviant behaviors or disabilities. Recognizing the importance of cultural and linguistic diversity, educators with cultural competence actively pursue positive change that results in corresponding behaviors in the implementation of the curriculum (Hanley, 1999). At this stage, educators also recognize the ecological systems and the role of social context in learners' development.

Cultural Proficiency: The application of cultural competence (i.e., Stage 5) in a systemic manner reflects the Cultural Proficiency stage of development. For most educators, the achievement of this stage is a lifelong process in which greater expertise and additional experiences in teaching and learning are acquired. Curricular examples of the implementation of this stage involve the application of all the elements in the previous Cultural Competence stage, where educators and schools hold "all cultures in high esteem and persistently act to incorporate cultural knowledge to their individual and organization knowledge base" (Hoover et al., 2008, p. 46). Cultural diversity is included systematically in daily curriculum implementation and within the curriculum development process. Therefore, this stage reflects the three aspects of awareness, knowledge, and skills associated with the valuing of cultural diversity within the curriculum for all learners (Patton & Day-Vines, 2002).

Significance of Cultural Proficiency in RTI Curriculum Implementation

The increased diversity in today's classrooms highlights the fact that no one approach, intervention, or assessment device will meet all needs within multi-tiered instruction. Abilities that reflect cultural competence and proficiency are central to providing a classroom context for relevant curriculum implementation within multi-tiered RTI for all learners, especially culturally and linguistically diverse students. The use of curricula, interventions, and methodologies that fail to accommodate diversity often leads to insufficient student progress. Developing the qualities of culturally proficient teaching provides the best opportunities for diverse students to learn and to demonstrate progress toward benchmarks. Form 7.1 (*Checklist of Culturally Responsive Teaching*), previously presented, addresses instruction that facilitates culturally responsive teaching. A more detailed discussion of a culturally responsive multi-tiered RTI curriculum is presented in the following section.

Culturally/Linguistically Responsive Multi-tiered Curriculum Implementation

One major source of controversy within RTI is whether bilingual or English as a second language (ESL) instruction belongs in Tier 1 or Tier 2 (Hoover, 2009b). That issue is the focus of this section. The most appropriate instructional tier for culturally and linguistically diverse learners is determined by the RTI team. Form 7.3 (*Culturally Responsive Curricular Decision-Making Factors*) provides a checklist for guiding such RTI decisions. Next, I provide further discussion and examples expanding on the topical areas addressed in Form 7.3 to assist in clarifying the most appropriate tier of instruction for diverse learners.

Initially, for a class of 20–25 English language learners (ELLs), ESL and/or bilingual instruction become Tier 1 instruction because at least 80% of the students must be progressing successfully with the Tier 1 core curriculum. If a majority of ELL classrooms have most students who are struggling, the first action is to adjust the Tier 1 core curriculum to provide sufficient opportunities to learn so that approximately 80% of students make adequate progress. Adequate progress for these learners depends on their English language and/or native language proficiency levels to maintain an expected rate of progress. Therefore, the expected rate of progress for ELLs needs to be commensurate with their identified language proficiency level (e.g., limited English-proficient learners would be expected to progress in line with their language skills, which may result in a different rate of progress for a bilingual student who is more fluent in English).

Once the appropriate curricular adjustments (i.e., general and targeted differentiations in the Tier 1 curriculum) have been made and realistic rates of progress for ELLs have been identified, the screening and progress monitoring of these students will identify those who are (1) at the bottom 15–20% of the class or grade and (2) making inadequate progress toward benchmarks. These students would then be considered for Tier 2 supplemental supports, which would be designed to support the Tier 1 core instruction. Given the small-group, more intensive structure of Tier 2 supports, it is improper to give all 20–25 ELLs Tier 2 instruction. Below are examples of suggested structures and expectations for (1) a class of 20–25 ELLs who are educated in the Tier 1 curriculum and (2) Tier 2 supplemental supports provided to a small group of students who do not make adequate progress with Tier 1 instruction. For the purposes of this illustration, all the students are ELLs who possess sufficient English abilities to be educated using ESL methodology, including strategic uses of the learner's native language.

Example 1: Tier 1 Core Instruction for ELLs*

Tier 1 core instruction for ELLs includes three interrelated curricular aspects:

1. Effective teaching and learning appropriate for all learners
2. Accommodations for varying English language proficiency levels
3. Considerations of diverse cultural values and norms

Tier 1 core instruction for ELLs includes research-based curricula and evidence-based interventions that address these three elements simultaneously. In addition, sufficient opportunities to learn require educators to generate a realistic and appropriate expected rate of progress for ELLs based on English language proficiency levels and associated cultural diversity, even if this rate of progress temporarily reflects expectations that vary from those concerning nonminority learners. At minimum, educators must allocate time and resources to implement the strongest Tier 1 ESL learning environment possible, rather than attempting to educate significant numbers of ELLs through Tiers 2 or 3 instruction. Therefore, the structure of Tier 1 core instruction for classrooms that include ELLs and emphasizes ESL instruction should be structured within the following general parameters:

CURRICULAR COMPONENT 1—EFFECTIVE TEACHING AND LEARNING APPROPRIATE FOR ALL LEARNERS ■ Subject-specific instruction must be academically and cognitively challenging for all learners, and it must be designed and delivered with differentiations that ensure that all students comprehend both the academic content and the scholastic expectations. Tier 1 core instruction for ELLs includes the following practices found to be effective for use with all learners:

1. Connect new content/skills to those already known by:

   Linking new learning to past experiences

   Assisting learners to activate prior knowledge
2. Develop and utilize physical and visual aids to assist learners to:

   Present and categorize material

   Build shared understanding

   Explain abstract concepts

   Identify and apply patterns across content areas

   Represent key vocabulary or concepts

   Provide multiple points of access to meaning and comprehension by capitalizing on effective body language, altering voice tone, modeling and demonstrating expectations, and hand-on activities

*Contribution by Sue Hopewell.

3. Provide access to a variety of multi-leveled source materials, such as:

   Dictionaries, thesauri, the Internet, informational posters, and pamphlets or textbooks

CURRICULAR COMPONENT 2—ACCOMMODATIONS FOR VARYING ENGLISH LANGUAGE PROFICIENCY LEVELS ■ For classes with students who are acquiring English as a second language, Tier 1 core instruction must be differentiated to accommodate varying levels of English language proficiency. This includes:

- Analyzing linguistic similarities and differences among the languages known (e.g., Spanish, Hmong) and the language being acquired (i.e., English as a second language)
- Utilizing native language, along with English, as needed to help learners acquire necessary concepts and skills
- Using evidence-based interventions to differentiate instruction that have demonstrated effectiveness in educating ELLs who are acquiring English as a second language

CURRICULAR COMPONENT 3—CONSIDERATIONS OF DIVERSE CULTURAL VALUES AND NORMS ■ As discussed, the influences of cultural and linguistic diversity shape a variety of learning characteristics and preferences. These influences must be considered in instructional and classroom management, including:

- Using cooperative small-group learning along with direct instruction
- Valuing associations between home culture(s) and school culture(s)
- Using evidence-based interventions to differentiate instruction that have been shown to be consistent with, and not in conflict with, the learners' cultural values and norms

Tier 1 core instruction that includes evidence of elements in the three areas described above reflects a research-based approach to teaching ELLs. Below are several other specific interventions that should be included to ensure effective Tier 1 core instruction for ELLs:

- Using scaffolded instruction
- Using explicit instruction
- Using targeted language structures to support language development
- Posting sentence stems and language frames in the classroom to scaffold oral and written participation
- Requiring students to incorporate new oral and written language structures into their productive work

- Linking oral and written products to artistic, symbolic, or graphic representations
- Grouping students to support interactive learning, such as using dyads, think-pair-share, or cooperative learning
- Nurturing a safe environment that encourages students to take risks in their learning
- Including sufficient wait time for students to formulate ideas and articulate thoughts
- Initially accepting and validating approximations to correct responses, especially for students acquiring English as a second language
- Providing repeated and varied opportunities to demonstrate proficiency and progress toward curricular benchmarks (i.e., progress monitoring procedures)
- Encouraging students to make multiple attempts to succeed if their initial efforts are less than satisfactory

In summary, Tier 1 core instruction for ELLs must reflect a well-implemented ESL learning environment that clearly balances and pairs comprehensible input with sufficient opportunity for output. The instructional context should be structured and predictable, permitting ESL learners to access resources and materials quickly and efficiently in order to progress toward curricular benchmarks. Effective Tier 1 core instruction should include key concepts and vocabulary posted in predictable locations throughout the classroom to reinforce learning expectations and to scaffold students' ability to demonstrate understanding. The appropriateness of Tier 1 core instruction for ELLs should be corroborated through observation of the classroom instruction, in which anchor posters, language frames, and visual and textual vocabulary definitions coalesce to shape a broad understanding of educational priorities and goals being achieved in the teaching and learning environment.

Therefore, there must be evidence that the above factors exist in the classroom for ELLs and that approximately 80% of the students are making satisfactory progress toward realistic curricular benchmarks commensurate with English language proficiency levels prior to considering ELLs for Tier 2 supplemental supports. As previously discussed, if less than 80% of the class or grade fails to make adequate progress, then the first course of action is to modify and adjust the Tier 1 core instruction. The educator should do one or more of the following:

1. Adjust the expected rate of progress to more realistically reflect English language proficiency levels
2. Adjust the Tier 1 core instruction to more adequately accommodate language needs
3. Increase the emphasis within the curriculum on culturally diverse values/norms

4. Ensure that both the curriculum and assessment of progress are research-based, reflecting the needs of ELLs as well as those of non-ELLs

Once these adjustments to Tier 1 core instruction are made, students who continue to struggle should be provided Tier 2 supplemental supports.

Example 2: Tier 2 Supplemental Supports for ELLs*

As discussed, Tier 2 instruction is designed to supplement, not replace, Tier 1 instruction. It should be given only to the lowest 15–20% of a class or grade, provided that approximately 80% of the remaining students make adequate progress toward curricular benchmarks. For ELLs, this includes all of the previously mentioned Tier 1 curricular structures in addition to supplemental supports that value-add, double-dose, or otherwise increase selected curricular aspects that are already part of Tier 1 core instruction. Therefore, Tier 2 supplemental supports for ELLs are designed to assist the 15–20% of learners in a class or grade who, after receiving high-quality, research-based Tier 1 instruction do not make sufficient progress toward curricular benchmarks commensurate with their English language proficiency levels. Although Tier 2 supports for ELLs, emphasizing ESL instruction, may vary, several elements should be included:

- Use of evidence-based ESL interventions that have been shown to be effective with or grounded in pedagogy consistent with effective education for ELLs
- Small-group instruction
- Supplemental instruction that occurs *in addition to* all Tier 1 core instruction
- Targeted instruction for a defined period of time, such as daily for 30 minutes for 8 weeks
- A direct connection between Tier 2 supplements and Tier 1 core instruction
- Additional sheltered instruction, scaffolding, and accommodations for language proficiency in Tier 2 instruction
- More frequent monitoring of progress (e.g., monthly, biweekly)
- Push-in support to the extent possible rather than pull-out services
- Determining the rate of progress relative to norms established for ELLs with similar English language proficiency levels

As illustrated, Tier 1 core instruction and Tier 2 supplemental supports are to be grounded in effective education for ELLs. This may require modifications or differentiations to the curricula and a rate of progress different from those for

*Contribution by Sue Hopewell.

non-ELLs. The progress of ELLs is often significantly misrepresented when ELLs and non-ELLs are compared. Such comparisons should be avoided to provide accurate multi-tiered RTI curriculum implementation for all learners, especially ELLs. This chapter's *RTI Curriculum in Practice* segment, presented in a later section, describes one example of how to create and implement Tier 1 core instruction that emphasizes ESL methodology for ELLs in elementary school. First, however, Table 7.5 provides examples of diversity considerations in RTI curriculum implementation for culturally and linguistically diverse learners.

As shown, there are specific ways to accommodate cultural and linguistic diversity in each of the five curricular components. Incorporating these and similar suggestions provides diverse students increased opportunities to learn and to demonstrate progress.

TABLE 7.5   Addressing Cultural/Linguistic Factors in Response to Intervention Curriculum Implementation

Component	Cultural/Linguistic Significance	RTI Decision-Making Factors
Content/Skills (Research-Based Curriculum)	Experiential background in mainstream culture needed to develop prerequisite skills may be different from that of other learners due to diverse cultures' views of education	Perceived lack of knowledge may be due to a learning difference rather than a disability and should be addressed within RTI accordingly
Evidence-Based Interventions	Cultural values and norms may provide a basis for selecting culturally appropriate interventions	The extent to which the selected evidence-based intervention(s) within the research-based curriculum provide diverse learners sufficient opportunities to learn is determined prior to adjusting the instruction
Instructional Arrangements	Some cultures prefer and stress cooperative versus competitive learning, leading to the use of small groups rather than independent learning	The type of instructional setting may affect learning due to cultural heritage or preferences and should be consistent with the values and norms of the student to avoid misperceiving lack of involvement in a particular setting as a disability
Class/Instructional Management Procedures	Classroom and instructional management strategies most relevant to classroom diversity have a greater impact on teaching and learning for culturally and linguistically diverse students	One of the most significant aspects in teaching and learning of diverse students is compatibility between the educator's expectations and those of the diverse learner; any incompatibility should be viewed as a learning difference rather than a disability, and RTI instruction and classroom management should be adjusted accordingly
Progress Evaluation	The role of assessment in education may vary across cultures, and knowledge of particular preferences assists educators in implementing a more culturally responsive progress monitoring program for diverse learners	RTI teams must make certain that learners' progress is measured against what is taught; knowledge that diverse students have been provided an appropriate research-based Tier 1 curriculum is essential to making informed progress monitoring decisions

An Example of How to Meet Tier 1 Curricular Demands of English Language Learners in Elementary School

Like any good teacher, I've always assumed that when a significant number of my students make inadequate academic progress, it was probably due to classroom or curricula occurrences, rather than something intrinsic to the learners. One teaching example that challenged me to evaluate issues within my fourth-grade classroom occurred when over half of my students began the fourth grade a minimum of 2 years below grade level in reading. Rather than looking for problems within the learners, I initially considered the effectiveness of the classroom curriculum in reading for students in the process of acquiring English as second language. Significantly, all of the students making inadequate progress in reading were English language learners (ELLs). The primary core Tier 1 reading curriculum employed with these learners was a balanced literacy approach, which included a guided reading component where students were instructed in the use of comprehension strategies and decoding behaviors in small groups organized around instructional levels. While these groupings were meant to be dynamic, the reality for ELLs was that they remained together for significant periods of time in small groups with minimal progress in reading. In addition, students were expected to achieve 95% accuracy in one level prior to moving to the next reading level material. Both of these classroom components provided a less than adequate rate of progress in reading for ELLs, and adjustment to their reading instruction was warranted. To address these Tier 1 core curricular reading needs, I placed greater emphasis on a thematic reading instructional approach. In addition, I deviated from requiring the 95% accuracy parameter prior to moving to the next level by choosing a range of levels related to a theme. Both of these instructional adjustments assisted my ELLs to achieve greater success with reading instruction.

My thematic instructional reading approach included spending more time on each book by incorporating several teaching practices into the curriculum: (a) more direct attention to the language of the text, (b) additional opportunities to make connections between text material and the students' first language, (c) placing less emphasis on the number of miscues when determining readiness to attempt a new level, and (d) purposeful structure of reading lessons to include more oral rehearsal. In considering my instructional arrangements (i.e., groupings), I thought in terms of what I wanted my ELLs to accomplish over the course of a week rather than just focusing on what would happen daily. This resulted in structuring my curriculum so that I could spend more time on each book, regularly introducing only one or two new books per week. The freedom to spend more time on each book created the opportunity to delve more deeply and thoroughly into language analysis.

For example, a typical first day at the start of a thematically based group of texts often was a hands-on, language-laden activity to prelearn the upcoming vocabulary or to practice language structures. If the reading material was about seasons, I would drag in a bag of clothing appropriate for different times of the year, and we would engage in a fun activity where we took turns donning or removing the appropriate items based on the suggested season. Or picture images would be introduced, labeled, discussed, and sorted by season. Students demonstrated their understanding through verbal interactions as well as by appropriately placing each picture in the correct category. Another strategy I used to implement thematic reading instruction was to post sentence stems in the classroom to aid student responses and to call attention to structures we would use during oral rehearsal. All of this occurred prior to looking at the specific book, and by the time we began to read the text, students had sufficient vocabulary control to engage in the reading material.

By choosing a range of levels related to a theme, I created a learning context in which students were likely to see and experience similar vocabulary in multiple contexts across a variety of texts. Each time students read a new text, they extended their language related to

(Continued)

the theme and were able to make connections to previously learned concepts and vocabulary. Finally, my "word work" often used the students' first language as a starting point. Together we created charts to compare explicitly how the students' first language (Spanish) was similar to or different from English. Morphological comparisons were especially powerful. The result of these curricular adjustments was that on average my ELLs made reading gains in English of two grade levels, with some advancing up to four grade levels, while two ELLs did not make satisfactory progress. Through this thematic-based instruction, most ELLs in my classroom were able to make adequate reading progress within the Tier 1 core reading instruction, with only two students requiring more intensive Tier 2 supplemental supports. These curricular adjustments showed that by using appropriate differentiated instruction to meet the needs of ELLs within the Tier 1 core curriculum, the need for Tier 2 instruction is reduced and only provided to those who really require these supports.

—**Sue H. (Bilingual/ESL Educator)**

RTI APPLICATIONS OF KEY CHAPTER CONCEPTS

The success of education for all learners within multi-tiered RTI models is based on the fact that the curriculum is research-based, with demonstrated effectiveness in addressing and accommodating learners' needs. In order for this to occur for culturally and linguistically diverse students, the multi-tiered curriculum must be culturally and linguistically responsive. Ecological principles that help shape a student's values and perceptions about teaching and learning translate into suggested ways to adjust the curriculum to make it more culturally responsive. All educators should value the process and the suggested activities for improving cultural proficiency in implementing the curriculum to best meet diverse learning and behavior needs in the classroom. Adhering to culturally responsive teaching principles and guidelines facilitates effective implementation of each tier of instruction within RTI models.

The application of these curricular principles within multi-tiered RTI provides the foundation for successfully meeting the needs of all learners in today's classrooms. To facilitate this process, educators should do the following:

- Lead a discussion with colleagues on the critical curricular issues to consider in multi-tiered RTI for culturally and linguistically diverse learners

- Identify the manner in which the ecological principles and practices discussed in this chapter are emphasized to meet diverse needs within multi-tiered instruction

- Assess their own cultural competence in teaching and develop a personal professional development plan to continue their growth toward cultural proficiency

- Prepare a PowerPoint presentation on the practices necessary to implement culturally responsive multi-tiered curriculum and deliver it to the school staff

FORM 7.1 Checklist of Culturally Responsive Teaching

Teacher: _____   Date: _____

Instructions: Check each item to reflect its application in the teaching and learning environment for culturally and linguistically diverse learners. Provide relevant descriptive comments to clarify emphasis in the classroom.

Responsive Item	**Descriptive Comments**
___ Instruction is accommodated to meet diverse needs	_____
___ Instruction is provided in student's most proficient language and/or in English if the student is bilingual	_____
___ Students' experiential background is incorporated into class tasks	_____
___ Teacher activates students' prior knowledge through questioning and interactive strategies	_____
___ Active participation occurs throughout the school day	_____
___ The curriculum is cognitively challenging for diverse students	_____
___ Verbal interaction between teacher and students is encouraged and facilitated in the implementation of the curriculum	_____
___ The Tier 1 core curriculum is research-based for the diverse population being served	_____
___ Rate of progress and proficiency levels are considered relative to students' English language proficiency levels	_____
___ Student preferred styles for learning are compatible with preferred and employed teaching styles	_____
___ Cultural values and norms are incorporated into daily curriculum implementation to ensure contextual relevance	_____

Source: Used by permission of John J. Hoover.

FORM 7.2 Checklist of Curriculum Instructional Compatibility for Diverse Learners

Teacher: _____   Date: _____

Instructions: Rate each item to reflect compatibility between student preferences about learning and actual delivery of curriculum in the classroom using the following scale:

1 = No Compatibility   2 = Little Compatibility
3 = Some Compatibility   4 = High Compatibility

To what extent are the following compatible with a culturally/linguistically diverse learner's preferences about teaching and learning?

____ Large-group lecture/discussion format

____ Small-group settings

____ Cooperative learning

____ Paired learning

____ Independent learning

____ Paper/pencil tasks

____ Examples/topics found within reading program/materials

____ Hands-on application of content and skills

____ Assessment process adhered to in universal screening/progress monitoring

____ Assessment devices used for universal screening/progress monitoring

____ Direct instruction

____ Constructivist learning

____ Classroom opportunities to demonstrate knowledge and progress

Summary of compatibility between learner preferences and delivery of curriculum:

Source: Used by permission of John J. Hoover.

FORM 7.3 Culturally Responsive Curricular Decision-Making Factors

Student: _____   Teacher: _____   Date: _____

Instructions: Check each item to reflect its consideration in the curricular decision-making process for the culturally and linguistically diverse student. Provide relevant comments.

Curriculum decision making for diverse learner includes consideration of the following:

___ Cross-cultural values and norms
   Comments:

___ Appropriateness of the Tier 1 core curriculum for use with diverse learners
   Comments:

___ Influences of acculturation on academic and behavioral needs
   Comments:

___ Most appropriate language of instruction
   Comments:

___ Home and community values in education
   Comments:

___ Connection between what is taught and what is assessed
   Comments:

___ If used, translators are properly trained adults proficient in the language
   Comments:

___ Rate of progress is calculated based on English language proficiency level rather than on comparison with highly proficient English speakers only

Comments:

___ The Tier 1 core curriculum is successful in assisting at least 80% of students in the classroom to make satisfactory progress toward curricular benchmarks

Comments:

___ Differentiated Tier 1 core instruction reflecting culture/language diversity is provided PRIOR to considering Tier 2 supplemental supports

Comments:

Summary of Culturally Responsive Curricular Decision-Making Based on the information recorded above, summarize the key aspects that (1) currently exist in the teaching and learning environment that contribute to effective decision making and (2) do not exist that need attention prior to making an informed curricular decision.

1. *Elements that currently exist in the teaching and learning environment that contribute to effective decision making:*

2. *Elements that do NOT currently exist in the teaching and learning environment that require attention prior to effective decision making:*

Source: Used by permission of John J. Hoover.

CHAPTER 8

Strategies to Support Multi-Tiered Curriculum Implementation

▶ Overview

STUDENTS WHO ARE SUCCESSFUL in school possess various study skills and learning strategies that are applied in the teaching and learning environment to help them complete tasks and develop effective ways of learning. One of the more unfortunate situations in any classroom is a learner's failure to demonstrate knowledge and skills because of the inability to select and apply these skills and strategies. An important part of multi-tiered RTI is the measurement of progress and proficiency levels associated with movement toward curricular benchmarks. As a result, accurate and valid measurement data are essential to effective decision making in multi-tiered instruction. Students' use of study skills and learning strategies is important in ensuring that accurate RTI assessment data are gathered. Conversely, ineffective use of study skills or learning strategies may yield progress results indicating lack of knowledge, when in reality these results refer to the student's lack of study skills and learning strategies. The role of these skills and strategies in accurately monitoring progress

toward curricular benchmarks (as well as the response to specific instruction) must be considered in making informed instructional decisions in multi-tiered RTI models.

▶ Key Topics

- ▶ Study skills
- ▶ Learning strategies
- ▶ Significance of study and learning strategies in curriculum implementation
- ▶ Role of study/learning strategies in multi-tiered instruction
- ▶ Importance of study/learning strategies in RTI decision making

▶ Learner Outcomes

After reading this chapter, you should:

1. Be knowledgeable about a variety of study skills and learning strategies
2. Know the significance of study/learning strategy use in the implementation of a multi-tiered instructional curriculum
3. Be able to incorporate study/learning strategy needs into RTI decisions
4. Be able to evaluate student use of study/learning strategies in the classroom and adjust instruction accordingly

SIGNIFICANCE TO CONTEMPORARY CLASSROOM INSTRUCTION

Many students possess the intellectual and academic capacities to acquire higher level content and skills, yet fail to learn or fail to demonstrate their learning because of their ineffective use of study and learning strategies. For effective implementation of the curriculum, students must know how to learn and must apply learning tools to help them acquire knowledge and skills. This is important for the education of all learners because multi-tiered RTI requires adjustments to implementation of the curriculum if screening or monitoring results suggest inadequate progress. One significant adjustment for many learners may be the development and application of appropriate study and learning strategies in curriculum implementation and monitoring. This, in turn, produces more accurate screening, progress monitoring, and diagnostic results gathered within the multi-tiered RTI assessment process.

Study Skills and Learning Strategies in Response to Intervention Models

The manner in which students acquire, maintain, and generalize knowledge and skills in their teaching and learning environment reflects, to a great extent, their success in making adequate progress in school. Although teachers provide the instructional expertise and classroom structures for effective learning, each student must regularly apply a variety of abilities to succeed in the classroom. These abilities refer to two types of skills that interact to assist students in school: study skills and learning strategies. Both are essential for academic and behavioral success, and each is designed to help all learners. Additionally, teaching students how to use study skills and learning strategies promotes effective and efficient implementation of the multi-tiered RTI curriculum in grades K–12. *Study skills* are tools that help students complete individual learning tasks effectively, manage time, organize assignments, and meet daily instructional and classroom management demands more easily (Hoover & Patton, 2007). *Learning strategies* are abilities that help students perform specific types of tasks through instruction that "focuses on making the students more active learners by teaching them how to learn and how to use what they have learned to solve problems and be successful" (KU-CRL, n.d.).

Although study skills and learning strategies are discussed and presented individually, in practice they work together in the teaching and learning environment. However, knowing when each is best used is important to effective curriculum implementation. Study skills are employed when the learner wishes to apply useful hints, tips, or tools to complete specific or assigned tasks more effectively (e.g., taking notes, completing a multiple-choice test, making an oral presentation). Once they are used in a specific situation, they are generally not used again until a similar task is completed (e.g., the next time note taking is necessary).

Learning strategies are more complex than study skills. They challenge learners to alter their ways of thinking rather than providing simple techniques for use in the short term. Unlike study skills, which are primarily used for a defined situation only, learning strategies may be generalized beyond their initial use because of their emphasis on helping students learn how to learn. Similar to implementation of the curriculum, some of the same tasks can be approached in different, yet compatible, ways. The choice between using a study skill or a learning strategy depends on its purpose.

For example, when taking tests, a test-taking study skill should be applied if a superficial technique is needed to help the learner complete individual test items. However, a learning strategy should be applied if a more complex and in-depth way of thinking about tests and test taking is desired. Therefore, if one desires a quick, efficient means for completing a task, a study skill should be used; if one wants to change one's way of thinking about and learning how to perform tasks, a learning strategy should be applied. When used together, study skills and learning strategies help students complete individual daily tasks and assist them in learning how to learn effectively in more generalized ways.

In RTI curriculum implementation, both study skills and learning strategies are necessary for achieving adequate rates of progress, maintaining acceptable levels of proficiency, and building the foundation for meeting increased academic and behavioral demands in elementary and secondary school. Study skills and learning strategies that should be considered in multi-tiered RTI models include those used to:

- Complete assigned tasks effectively and efficiently
- Alter the way in which tasks are viewed
- Use time most effectively in school
- Finish and submit work in a timely manner
- Successfully complete tasks requiring independent work
- Assume greater responsibility for own learning
- Change approaches to learning and studying new material
- Generate more complete and properly edited written assignments
- Develop and implement an organized schedule for task completion
- Break down complex tasks into more manageable components
- Complete homework assignments efficiently and effectively
- Work cooperatively with classmates
- Generalize learning to new and different situations

In implementation of the multi-tiered RTI curriculum, the effective use of study skills and learning strategies facilitates timely completion of tasks and strengthens the ability to learn how to learn. These skills and strategies are discussed below, including their significance in helping all learners succeed within a multi-tiered RTI curriculum framework. The following discussions provide specific details about study skills and learning strategies relative to RTI. For more detailed coverage of these important topics, the reader is referred to the literature sources cited in this chapter and specifically Bender (2008), Hoover and Patton (2007), and the Center for Research on Learning at the Kansas University Web site.

Study Skills

Numerous tools exist to help learners deal with daily tasks, assignments, and expectations. Hoover and Patton (2007) discuss 12 skills that students typically are required to employ to successfully complete most classroom tasks and

TABLE 8.1 Study Skills Used to Complete Instructional and Classroom Tasks

Study Skill	Significance to Completing Educational Tasks
Reading Rate	Different assignments require varying reading rates
Listening	Effective application of listening abilities is central to success in school
Note Taking/ Outlining	Taking effective classroom notes and outlining topics or concepts are essential academic skills
Report Writing	The ability to express oneself in writing becomes increasingly important as learners progress through the grades
Oral Presentations	Making an oral presentation to demonstrate knowledge and skills supplements many assignments and required tasks
Graphic Aids	Visual depictions of content help learners to more effectively understand and/or share complex educational material
Test Taking	Adequate test-taking abilities ensure more accurate universal screening and progress monitoring results
Library Usage	Efficient and effective use of a library is essential to master much core content knowledge and skills
Reference Material Usage	Effective use of reference materials, both hard copy and electronic, improves students' ability to become independent learners
Time Management	Managing time effectively and efficiently becomes increasingly important as requirements in school are increased
Self-Management	Assuming responsibility for one's own learning and behavior facilitates the effective implementation of a research-based curriculum and evidence-based interventions
Organizational Skills	The ability to organize multiple assignments, class schedules, and personal time effectively contributes greatly to efficient and effective learning

assignments. These skills are summarized in Table 8.1, followed by a more detailed discussion of each.

As Table 8.1 shows, each study skill is essential as teachers and students face increased pressure in the areas of achievement, RTI, and accountability. Additionally, Strichart and Mangrum (2002) found that study skills instruction helps learners improve their performance on tasks related to the skills acquired (e.g., taking tests, recording notes, using the library).

Reading Rate

KEY POINTS ■ Various silent reading rates are necessary to deal with the different types of reading material in core content areas (Harris & Sipay, 1990). Two general types of reading rates exist: (1) fast-paced rates (skimming, scanning, rapid reading) and (2) careful rates (normal, study-type rates). *Fast-paced* rates make it easier to find general answers or ideas quickly, *careful* rates are used to identify specific details, master concepts, or deal with more complex material.

CURRICULAR APPLICATIONS ■ *Skimming* is used to grasp general ideas by quickly reviewing the entire passage or material (e.g., skimming to review main headings and general ideas to determine if material should be read in greater detail to complete an assignment or task). *Scanning* is used to quickly locate a specific item (e.g., date, color, telephone number), and *rapid reading* is used to grasp main ideas, reread material, or determine the general plot or theme of a passage. A *normal* reading rate is used for understanding primary and secondary ideas and for comprehension typically emphasized in school curricula; a *study-type* reading rate is reserved for mastery of specific details, for solving complex problems, or when reading unfamiliar material or vocabulary (Harris & Sipay, 1990; Hoover & Patton, 2007).

SIGNIFICANCE IN RTI MODELS ■ When implementing curriculum within the tiers of instruction, a learner's ability to use different reading rates should be incorporated into screening and progress monitoring. Additionally, improper uses of reading rates may help to explain lack of progress in different core content areas rather than lack of knowledge of the material (i.e., a more appropriate reading rate may be required to better understand the content-area knowledge and skills). Educators who consider the appropriate reading rates when implementing the multi-tiered RTI curriculum will be able to make more informed decisions concerning the level and duration of instructional supports required to meet the needs of all learners.

Listening

KEY POINTS ■ Listening is a complex skill with three main elements: (1) information is received; (2) the information is interpreted to determine its meaning; and (3) evidence confirms that the information is understood (Hoover & Patton, 2007). These three aspects of listening emphasize the importance of hearing the message as well as comprehending it.

CURRICULAR APPLICATIONS ■ Educators rely heavily on students' listening in the teaching and learning environment. As a result, curriculum implementation should help them determine the extent to which the learner hears the information and find evidence that the learner understands the information or applies the appropriate meaning. *Hearing* refers to the learner's receiving the information; *comprehending* demonstrates understanding of the information by applying it in an observable manner, such as following directions, summarizing material, or generalizing the information to a new or different situation.

SIGNIFICANCE IN RTI MODELS ■ The implementation of a multi-tiered curriculum requires successful use of listening abilities. Some students, including those who struggle with learning, often experience problems with listening

(Meese, 2001). Often learners experience difficulty when required to attend to listening activities for extended periods of time, and RTI screening and progress monitoring should assess for this possibility. Students who experience difficulty with listening activities should be provided a greater balance between active (doing) and passive (listening) curricular activities. For students who cannot make adequate progress because of problems with listening activities, the multi-tiered RTI curriculum can easily be adjusted by differentiating instruction to include more active, hands-on learning.

Note Taking/Outlining

KEY POINTS ■ The ability to take notes and outline material effectively is essential in curriculum implementation. These interrelated study skills include several subskills:

1. Ability to take clear, brief notes from lectures or reading material
2. Effective use of headings and subheadings
3. Use of various abbreviations to easily and quickly record notes or outline material for reference at a later time
4. Ability to summarize
5. Use of short phrases rather than long, detailed sentences to record information
6. Ability to identify and use key clue words or phrases
7. Ability to develop and personalize a systematic process for taking notes and outlining material

CURRICULAR APPLICATIONS ■ Note taking is one of the most frequently used study skills (Sabornie & deBettencourt, 2009). The ability to record notes and outline curricular material efficiently and effectively is a continuous process, becoming more sophisticated as the learner progresses through the grades. Helping students develop a process for note taking/outlining is essential and should be integral to implementing the curriculum; these two study skills are required for good progress in both academic and behavioral development.

SIGNIFICANCE IN RTI MODELS ■ A multi-tiered RTI curriculum that facilitates continuous development through structured use of note taking and outlining provides educators with increased knowledge and understanding of the potential needs of all learners. Students who cannot take notes or outline material may simply require more direct instruction and guided practice of these skills within the Tier 1 core curriculum rather than Tier 2 instruction. However, the ability to take notes and outline should be central to multi-tiered instruction no matter which tier(s) of intervention a learner receives.

Report Writing

KEY POINTS ■ Report writing provides learners with a performance-based means of demonstrating knowledge and skills. The subskills often associated with this study skill include the ability to select and narrow down a topic, generate an outline of key points to address, create an initial draft, refine the draft, and generate and submit a polished, edited final report. Report writing includes the application of integrated writing skills (e.g., six traits) and, as with the other study skills, requires ongoing instruction and support. "Writing is a complex process" (Sabornie & deBettencourt, 2009, p. 228) and is best addressed through structured approaches that teach students the different stages to follow to complete written assignments.

CURRICULAR APPLICATIONS ■ Research indicates that educators should assist learners to plan and organize their writing assignments (Meese, 2001). The development of report-writing skills is essential to most multi-tiered curricula due to the strong emphasis on writing. Generating and editing written reports requires guided practice, teacher support, and sufficient opportunities in the classroom, along with positive and constructive help when errors occur.

SIGNIFICANCE IN RTI MODELS ■ Educators should consider learners' ability to generate written reports when issues with written expression surface. Some students possess sufficient written language skills yet lack skills in generating a written report that must conform to specified guidelines and expectations. Differentiated instruction should allow flexibility in the way learners present and share their knowledge and skills. Allowing acceptable variations in the Tier 1 core curriculum may help reduce the perceived need for Tier 2 instruction. Students will then have greater opportunity to generate written products in a context with which they more readily identify.

Oral Presentations

KEY POINTS ■ Oral presentations occur periodically in school, either as a required or an optional task. For many students, this is a difficult or stressful situation if not approached properly by the teacher (Hoover & Patton, 2007). Oral presentations are often associated with a written element (e.g., PowerPoint slides, written handouts) and require sufficient attention, beyond the written element, to be most successful. Sufficient time and opportunity should be devoted to preparing for and delivering the oral presentation in addition to the written element. Too often, the oral presentation is so closely connected to the written element that insufficient preparation occurs. Preparation for an oral presentation of any length and in any content area includes sufficient (1) knowledge about the topic, (2) practice of the presentation, and (3) development and use of support materials such as visuals or hands-on aids.

CURRICULAR APPLICATIONS ■ Curriculum implementation often includes various forms of oral presentation. These may be brief, informal presentations completed while seated at a desk or table or longer, formal presentations while standing in front of the whole class or a group of students. Effective curriculum implementation facilitates the ongoing development and use of oral presentations by assisting students to acquire abilities in several areas:

1. Understanding of the main ideas to be presented
2. Inclusion of relevant supporting ideas to strengthen the main ideas
3. Transition statements and clauses to bridge ideas in the presentation
4. Development of a targeted and creative introduction and conclusion

Teacher assistance and guided practice in developing these four abilities, along with practice, facilitates the effective use of oral presentations in any tier of instruction.

SIGNIFICANCE IN RTI MODELS ■ Multi-tiered curriculum implementation that accommodates different types of oral presentations, levels of preparation, and anxiety assists learners with this task. Careful consideration of this study skill relative to other suspected problems may help educators explain certain behaviors, such as acting out, withdrawal, or failure to complete assignments. RTI universal screening and progress monitoring reflecting lack of progress in a content area (that is associated with oral presentations) should consider the learner's previous experience with this task when interpreting assessment results (i.e., would less emphasis on oral presentation increase the learner's progress?).

Graphic Aids

KEY POINTS ■ Graphic aids are an integral part of education, and skills in using and interpreting visual material are key to effective teaching and learning. Visual material is found in all content areas in the form of graphs, charts, units of measure, pictures, or other similar material designed to add value to both written and oral text. Graphic organizers may also be used in structuring learning to depict content visually (Meese, 2001).

CURRICULAR APPLICATIONS ■ Most curricula use graphic material to facilitate learning. Many students require guidance in understanding the relevance of visual material within the overall context of its use in the curriculum. This includes the ability to read and understand captions connected to visual material, understand why the visual or graphic aid is included with the text, and determine how to draw meaning from the visual material. These and related skills are important in curriculum implementation because students must often use them to support their learning and presentation of acquired knowledge and skills.

SIGNIFICANCE IN RTI MODELS ■ In RTI curriculum implementation, graphic aids often assist learners to grasp the main ideas of text, anticipate upcoming ideas, and deal with more complex information. Universal screening and progress monitoring should consider the students' ability to interpret, create, and apply graphic aids in order to help educators make more informed decisions when addressing academic problems (i.e., the extent to which the learner uses this study skill in attempting to understand or present content).

Test Taking

KEY POINTS ■ Perhaps the most critical study skill today is that of taking tests to demonstrate proficiency levels and rate of progress toward curricular benchmarks. Test taking includes three interrelated elements: (1) preparing for the test, (2) taking the test, and (3) reviewing the completed and graded test. Although considered important, most learners do not possess sufficient test-taking skills (Good & Brophy, 1990). Each of these three elements requires specific knowledge about the test along with its content, structure, and intended purpose(s). In addition to these three test-taking elements, learners must familiarize themselves with the items in five different types of tests: (1) essay, (2) sentence completion, (3) multiple choice, (4) true-false, and, (5) matching. The three test-taking elements and the five types of test items requires targeted and specific knowledge for students to succeed in most of the testing situations found in today's classrooms.

CURRICULAR APPLICATIONS ■ Kiewra and DuBois (1998) stressed the importance of test-taking skills, including the test location, test-taking strategies, and test terms. Today's schools are characterized by the increased use of curriculum-based measurement for screening and progress monitoring purposes. Although diagnostic testing is still used in RTI models, the emphasis is on assessing what is taught and monitoring progress toward curricular benchmarks. Effective curriculum implementation involves periodic screening, more frequent progress monitoring, and, under certain conditions, diagnostic assessment. Today's teaching and learning environment must reflect the interrelationship between instruction and monitoring of progress resulting from that instruction.

Therefore, implementation of any curriculum involves the development and application of skills for all types of testing formats. Curriculum-based measurement results are best interpreted by initially ensuring that the learners are familiar and confident with the measurement device and process. Too often over the past several decades, educators have mistakenly perceived a problem as academic in nature, when in reality the issue was the improper application of the test-taking study skill rather than lack of content or skills knowledge.

SIGNIFICANCE IN RTI MODELS ■ Given the strong emphasis within RTI on data-driven decision making derived from universal screening, progress monitoring, and/or diagnostic assessment results, ensuring that all students possess a minimum level of test-taking abilities is essential to making informed curricular decisions and adjustments. Poor test-taking abilities often lead to poor test-taking performance, which, in turn, often leads to the erroneous conclusion that the student does not possess the assessed knowledge and skills. RTI curriculum implementation in all grade levels and within all tiers of instruction should include the development of test-taking abilities to avoid providing a more intensive tier of intervention than is necessary. Implementation of the curriculum can only be effective if different tiers of instruction are provided for the proper reasons. The application of test-taking skills is central to making effective decisions about screening, monitoring, and diagnostic assessment results.

Library Usage

KEY POINTS ■ Use of library facilities is often viewed as an important study skill in learning to read and in completing various classroom assignments, including familiarity with the layout and location of materials (Wesson & Keefe, 1989). This study skill includes knowledge of four key elements:

1. The services and purposes of a library
2. The types of information that students may access through a library
3. Computerized procedures for accessing library material online
4. Where to go in the library and who to consult for answers to questions or for assistance

Although these elements may seem obvious, many students require instruction and guidance to ensure proper use of a school's or community's library facilities.

CURRICULAR APPLICATIONS ■ Effective teaching and learning requires regular use of library resources, either through work completed at the library or through online access. As with some other study skills, successful use of a library is often expected of learners with little or no formal guidance and training, or teachers may mistakenly believe that training occurred in previous grades. Many students require some guidance and/or review of the purposes of a library, including when and why its use facilitates both academic learning and leisure activities.

SIGNIFICANCE IN RTI MODELS ■ Library usage tasks may often lead to incomplete assignments when students do not understand how the library facilitates completion of the task and/or do not know how to locate needed information in the library. Multi-tiered RTI curriculum implementation should ensure that this study skill is emphasized in grades K–12 and that the inability to use a library effectively does not mean that the student does not know the content. Screening and progress monitoring may help clarify the learner's ability to use this study skill and should be part of the assessment process in RTI models.

Reference Material Usage

KEY POINTS ■ The use of reference materials includes four subskills: (1) identifying the resources needed; (2) scanning the reference material to determine its appropriateness for the task or assignment; (3) using the reference material efficiently to obtain needed information; and (4) recording and documenting the information from the material to complete the task. The proper selection and use of a variety of reference materials facilitates efficient completion of classroom tasks when new or unfamiliar information must be gathered.

CURRICULAR APPLICATIONS ■ Many assignments require students to generate written reports, projects, oral reports, or similar products utilizing information that is best gathered from reference materials. Curriculum implementation should facilitate learners' development of this study skill from the the early elementary grades through secondary school (Hoover & Patton, 2007). The use of current periodicals and newspapers, along with a dictionary and a thesaurus, provide students many opportunities to develop, master, and generalize this study skill.

SIGNIFICANCE IN RTI MODELS ■ The ability to use reference materials effectively greatly facilitates progress within each tier of instruction. A multi-tiered RTI curriculum that emphasizes ongoing development and use of this study skill throughout schooling provides all students increased opportunities to learn. Screening and monitoring of academic progress should include assessment of students' ability to use reference materials appropriately because the inability to do so often leads to perceived problems with content. Educators must ensure that lack of ability to use reference materials does not mistakenly lead to decisions about lack of content knowledge, which, in turn, may result in unnecessary Tier 2 supplemental instruction.

Time Management

KEY POINTS ■ Time management is a study skill that greatly affects many different areas in teaching and learning. The subskills within this skill include the ability to:

1. Identify tasks that must be completed
2. Evaluate the importance of the various tasks and prioritize their completion

3. Establish a realistic timeline or schedule for completing the tasks within the necessary time frame

4. Adjust the time management plan for completing the tasks, if necessary, once the plan is implemented

5. Review the effectiveness of the time management procedures for future reference

CURRICULAR APPLICATIONS ■ Increased demands are being made on students to complete more tasks in less time due to increased accountability for achievement of curricular benchmarks. Therefore, it is extremely important to manage time effectively in the teaching and learning environment, particularly for secondary learners (Sabornie & deBettencourt, 2009). As teachers attempt to cover more content in less time, helping students become more proficient in time management also becomes imperative and should be integral to curriculum implementation in all content areas.

SIGNIFICANCE IN RTI MODELS ■ The ability to manage time effectively in order to complete everyday tasks is reflected in the progress observed in screening or progress monitoring. Learners who manage time more efficiently are often more productive in the classroom. RTI curriculum implementation in each tier of instruction needs to emphasize effective time management by providing teacher support and guidance in the development of this study skill. This is important in interpreting the academic and social-emotional needs of all students, especially struggling learners.

Self-Management

KEY POINTS ■ Like time management, self-management promotes effective teaching and learning. Self-management involves students' ability to (1) assess and evaluate their own behaviors; (2) assist in the development and implementation of a personalized program to help manage their own behaviors; and (3) record behavioral occurrences and self-reinforce appropriate behaviors.

CURRICULAR APPLICATIONS ■ Self-management in curricular implementation supports effective teaching and learning in several ways. It:

1. Increases students' responsibility for their own learning and behavior

2. Increases teachers' ability to address other classroom needs and spend less time on management issues

3. Facilitates more production from students due to their efforts to manage themselves

4. Gives teachers time to implement other procedures in the classroom that stretch the effective use of classroom time (e.g., conducting regular progress monitoring probes to assess ongoing progress toward curricular benchmarks).

Moore et al. (2008) wrote that students may be taught self-management and that this skill improves their academic and behavior performance.

SIGNIFICANCE IN RTI MODELS ■ Self-management reinforces positive learning and behavior at all levels of the multi-tiered RTI curriculum in elementary and secondary grades. The more learners are able to do for themselves with teacher guidance, the more students the teacher is able to reach and work with on a daily basis. Therefore, RTI curriculum implementation should include provisions for developing self-management. Also, once developed, this skill should be integrated into the teaching and learning environment for maximum use of both student and teacher time and resources.

Organizational Skills

KEY POINTS ■ As a result of accountability efforts in the nation's schools, students are expected to complete more classwork with greater proficiency. Therefore, the ability to organize required tasks is something all students must learn and apply daily (Bender, 2008). This study skill includes identification of the following elements to be applied within a specified bloc of time (e.g., reading or mathematics instruction time; homework due the next day for four classes): (1) the extent and number of all required tasks; (2) a timeline for completing all tasks and submitting finished assignments; (3) any prerequisites necessary for completing assigned task(s); (4) format, length, and other requirements for completion of tasks; and (5) the level of proficiency of mastery of the material needed to successfully complete task(s).

CURRICULAR APPLICATIONS ■ Curriculum implementation in any classroom requires students to organize their completion of tasks, whether through task analysis of one assignment or completion of three assignments within a specified time frame. Like time management, curriculum implementation that allows students to organize their completion of selected tasks frees up the teacher's time to address multiple needs simultaneously. For example, as previously discussed, in the differentiated classroom, the simultaneous implementation of direct instruction to some learners, independent seatwork for others, and cooperative small-group work for still others in learning centers allows the teacher to meet multiple student needs at the same time. This requires students to use the organizational study skill. It also allows the teacher to provide needed direct instruction to those who require this type of support. Curriculum implementation that teaches organizational skills is more successful in reaching all students by allowing them to assist in organizing their tasks and assignments.

SIGNIFICANCE IN RTI MODELS ■ Multi-tiered RTI curriculum implementation requires learners to organize their work. Lack of such skills may reduce academic or behavioral progress, often leading to the perception of a suspected disability that may not actually exist (i.e., lack of organization is the issue, not content learning needs). Therefore, RTI curriculum implementation should emphasize the development, practice, and generalization of this study skill. It gives learners the best opportunities to acquire knowledge and skills, as well as demonstrate progress through screening or progress monitoring procedures.

Study Skills and Response to Intervention Assessment

As illustrated in the above section, many study skills are integral to effective teaching and learning. Lack of proficiency in these skills reduces progress toward academic or behavioral benchmarks. As a result, another area of learning that requires screening and monitoring is the effective and efficient use of study skills. When progress monitoring results indicate lack of progress, the struggling learner's ability (or inability) to use study skills should be considered and may lead to more appropriate adjustments to instruction. Forms 8.1 (*Study Skills Inventory*) and 8.2 (*Study Skills Usage Rubric*) provide checklists to assist educators in screening for and/or monitoring students' use of the 12 study skills discussed in the previous section. Form 8.1 should be used as a screening device in each grade level and as a teacher rating scale to document the teacher's views of student use of study skills as observed regularly in the implementation of the multi-tiered RTI curriculum.

In addition, Form 8.2 allows teachers to document students' use of each study skill, ranging from minimal to daily use. Together, these two forms provide RTI teams with valuable teacher documentation of a student's use of each study skill, allowing the team to make more informed tiered instruction and management decisions.

This section about study skills concludes with Table 8.2, which provides ways to differentiate the RTI curriculum in order to adjust instruction to best accommodate the development and use of each study skill.

As Table 8.2 shows, there are many ways to incorporate the development and use of each study skill into authentic classroom assignments, provided that flexibility is used in the differentiated classroom. Activities such as those described in Table 8.2 devote small amounts of time to the development of study skills directly related to different assignments; this is time well spent, as it will facilitate more effective teaching and learning.

TABLE 8.2 Differentiating Multi-Tiered Instruction to Support Study Skills Development

Study Skill	Differentiated Instructional Considerations
Reading Rate	Provide opportunities for learners to practice using the various reading rates to best accommodate their needs given the length and type of reading required
Listening	Periodically review effective listening strategies to remind students of instructional expectations related to listening tasks; provide learners with a brief list of listening strategies to include in their class notebooks or binders
Note Taking/Outlining	Provide manageable note-taking and outlining tasks and gradually work up to more complex uses; give learners sufficient time and opportunity to successfully complete tasks involving note taking or outlining by providing periodic review of content covered and additional direct guided practice
Report Writing	Differentiate the development and use of this study skill by breaking writing tasks into their main elements (e.g., introduction, thesis statement, body, conclusion, abstract) and guide students in writing each one
Oral Presentations	Initially, allow flexibility in students' oral presentations, such as seated at a desk, in a small group, or using graphic aids, to create a nonthreatening environment
Graphic Aids	Structure select assignments in which the use of student-generated graphic aids is part of the task; allow flexibility in the types of graphic aids learners wish to develop and make sure that they are challenged to show how the aid fits into the overall assignment
Test Taking	Give students time within the implementation of the curriculum to develop and practice using test-taking abilities; this should occur outside of the actual test situation to reduce anxiety and provide a safe, structured environment for practicing needed test-taking skills
Library Use	Block out sufficient time for library usage that is connected to curricular tasks while also providing guided practice to increase library use abilities
Reference Materials	Structure small assignments that require targeted use of one or two reference materials; increase the scope of the assignments as students master the use of a variety of reference materials
Time Management	Provide a couple of minutes each day to allow students to structure their use of the day's time; periodically review their time management plans to ensure proper development of this study skill
Self-Management	Guide learners to develop and use simple self-monitoring strategies for more efficient self-management in the classroom; review the effectiveness of these strategies periodically, linking them to screening or progress monitoring results
Organization	Give learners an opportunity to establish their own approach to organizing select tasks that must be completed during the day or prior to the end of the week; review the organizational plans to help learners determine their effectiveness in completing several tasks

Learning Strategies

As discussed above, learning strategies are designed to help students become more efficient and effective learners (Bender, 2008; KU-CRL, n.d.). In particular, "a learning strategy may be thought of as a method of cognitively planning the performance of a learning task" (Bender, 2008, p. 92). In addition, Hoover and Patton (2007) wrote that a key goal of using learning strategies is to acquire

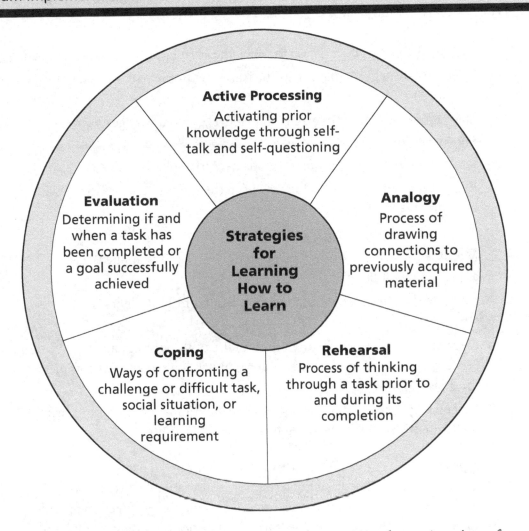

greater control over learning by increasing one's capacity to learn. A variety of learning strategies exist (Deshler, 2006; Lenz, 2006; Mastropieri & Scruggs, 1998); some are targeted to specific learning tasks, whereas others are applicable to many different types of assignments within various content areas. This section presents five learning strategies that, once mastered, may be applied across content areas, in various types of tasks, and within different grade levels. These strategies were selected because of their appropriateness for use within varying levels or tiers of RTI instruction in any content area. Each learning strategy is briefly introduced in Figure 8.1 and is discussed in detail below.

As Figure 8.1 shows, each of these strategies emphasizes a different aspect of learning that facilitates a process for cognitively addressing, completing, and revising the approach to task completion or goal achievement in any content area. Steps to assist learners in developing these learning strategies are presented below, followed by specific examples of their use in RTI curriculum implementation.

Although each learning strategy has its own set of steps to follow for effective use in the classroom, some general guidelines also exist. The following steps were generated from discussions in several sources, including Bender (2008), Day and Elksnin (1994), and Hoover and Patton (2005):

- Identify the task or type of task to which the learning strategy will be applied.
- Select the strategy(s) that assists the learner with the particular task or type of task.
- Determine the learner's current ability level and knowledge about the selected strategy.
- Present the steps, process, or methods used to apply the strategy.
- Provide guided practice and review until the learner acquires the process for using the strategy.
- Apply the learning strategy to an assigned task or assignment.
- Monitor student use of the strategy, ensuring that it is applied appropriately following the correct process.
- Evaluate the effectiveness on task completion of the student's use of the strategy.
- Debrief the student, gathering input on use of the strategy and perceptions concerning its effectiveness in helping the student complete the assigned task.
- If necessary, reteach the strategy, provide additional guidance, and reapply the strategy to another learning task.

A process such as this one for teaching students how to use any learning strategy provides a framework for determining its use and effectiveness when it is actually applied to the teaching and learning situation. The next section provides more detailed coverage of each of the learning strategies, including examples of their direct use with students in the classroom (**T** = teacher; **S** = student in each example). The statements provided for the teacher are examples of what to say to the students; those provided for the student are examples of what to say to the teacher, quietly to oneself, and/or in thinking to oneself. The language and terminology used by the teacher and/or the student may be modified to meet the age, grade, and academic needs of individual students. The description of each learning strategy was developed from discussions found in several sources, including Bender (2008), Hoover and Patton (2005), Hoover and Collier (2003), Marks, Laeys, Bender, and Scott (1996), and Mastropieri and Scruggs (1998).

Active Processing

OVERVIEW ■ Questions generated by the student are related to a specific content area in an effort to activate prior knowledge about the topic of study and to structure a plan for completing a task or achieving a goal.

KEY ELEMENTS ■ Self-talk, self-questioning, and self-reinforcement skills are developed as the learner scans, skims, summarizes, generates questions, predicts, and elaborates on the information to be studied.

RTI CURRICULAR CONSIDERATIONS ■ Students educated within each tier of instruction should be made aware that self-talk, self-questioning, and self-reinforcement are acceptable, encouraged, and appropriate in the classroom. Teachers should demonstrate how and in what manner these three key elements are used through guided practice to help students define, specify, evaluate, monitor, and complete the assignment or task.

RTI Guided Practice: The following steps demonstrate use of Active Processing:

Step 1: Definition

T: To begin, you should think about what you wish to accomplish by completing the task. What do you plan to do, and what might be your reason for completing this task or goal? What do you already know about this topic or subject?

S: First, I ask myself, what am I going to do and what is the purpose for completing the task or goal? What do I already know about this topic or subject?

Step 2: Specification

T: Second, clarify how you will go about completing the task or goal. What is your plan? Begin implementing your plan.

S: Next, I must specify what I will do to complete the task or achieve my goal. What will I do? What is my plan for completing the task or achieving my goal? I will now implement my plan.

Step 3: Evaluation

T: As you implement your plan, you should check to make certain that all is going as planned. Are things going as you put in your plan? Has your plan helped you complete the task or achieve your goal? Did what you already know about the topic help you to complete the task or goal?

S: I need to check to see that I am implementing my plan as designed. Am I following my plan? Did I check my work to complete my task or the steps followed to achieve my goal? Does my answer appear correct? Did I achieve my goal? How did what I already know help me?

Step 4: Monitoring

T: Often you can use several methods to accomplish a task or achieve a goal. Sometimes things do not go as planned, and mistakes are made. This is okay and very natural, and we can learn from our mistakes. Try another approach if the first one you attempt does not lead to completion of your task or achievement of your goal.

S: I am aware that often more than one method can be used to complete a task or achieve a goal. What might be an alternative approach if my first attempt does not work? Did my first approach work or do I need to try another? If I make a mistake, I will learn from it and not worry about needing to make a change. Do I need to make a change? What did I learn from any mistake(s) I made?

Step 5: Completion

T: It is very important to know when you have completed your task or achieved your goal. How will you know that you have completed what you set out to do? Congratulate yourself for a job well done once you have completed your task or achieved your goal.

S: How will I know that I have completed my task or achieved my goal? Did I complete the task or achieve my goal? When I complete it, I will congratulate myself and be proud of my accomplishment.

Analogy

OVERVIEW ■ This process allows students to recall previous learning experiences or patterns of learning that are similar to new items or tasks being studied.

KEY ELEMENTS ■ Analogy emphasizes the use of rhyme, schema, metaphor, and cloze procedures to facilitate the acquisition and retention of new content and skills.

RTI CURRICULAR CONSIDERATIONS ■ Multi-tiered instruction in RTI may be significantly enhanced by teacher and student use of analogies. To facilitate development and use, this learning strategy is mastered by guiding students through procedures that help them to recall prior knowledge and then compare, substitute, and elaborate on that knowledge relative to the new material or skill being studied.

RTI Guided Practice: The following steps demonstrate use of Analogy:

Step 1: Prior Knowledge

T: Recall something that you already know or have previously experienced that is similar to this new content or task. What do you remember about your previous experiences?

S: What do I already know that is similar to this new content or skill? When did I previously need to use this knowledge or skill?

Step 2: Comparison

T: Examine how your previous knowledge/experience is similar to the study of this new content or skill. How do these compare? How are they similar and different? Do they have a similar use or application?

S: How does this new content or skill compare to what I already know? Does it seem to have similar applications or uses? How is it different from what I currently know?

Step 3: Substitution

T: Now identify aspects of what you already know and see if any of these can be substituted for or replace aspects of what you are currently learning. Why might a substitution work in this situation? What aspects will you be unable to substitute and why?

S: Am I able to use some of what I already know about a similar topic or skill in the new content or skill I am studying? In what ways will a substitution of items for what I am studying probably not work and why?

Step 4: Elaboration

T: Now think about other types of experiences in your past where you were able to apply what you previously learned to help you better understand and learn something new. How did your previous experiences help you learn the new material or skill?

S: When I encounter something new or different, I will think about what I already know about the topic or skill. When asked about my prior experiences, I can give examples that are similar to those experiences in the new material or skill.

Rehearsal

OVERVIEW ■ Rehearsal emphasizes the practice of helping students to think about what they are doing prior to and during a task to increase their comprehension.

KEY ELEMENTS ■ The elements of review, recite, and recall are applied to a learning task or situation to help students think through what they are doing for optimum results in teaching and learning. This is accomplished through both questioning and visualization skills.

RTI CURRICULAR CONSIDERATIONS ■ The ability to reflect upon a task or topic prior to and during implementation facilitates effective learning in RTI models. Students may initially require guided practice to acquire this strategy, which requires both teacher and students to take a little time to reflect on the task prior to its implementation. This may be difficult for some due to a perceived need to do things quickly in order to move on to the next task. However, decisions for placement in the correct tier of instruction are improved if learners are given time to think about and briefly plan what they are about to do as an assignment or task is completed.

RTI Guided Practice: The following steps demonstrate use of Rehearsal:

Step 1: Pause

T: Stop for a minute and think about what you are going to do prior to beginning the task. After each new idea or step is completed, pause for a minute and try to visualize what you have just done. This will help you remember what you have learned.

S: I need to pause for a minute and think about what I am going to do. After I begin, I need to periodically pause and think about what I have just done or learned. How can I mentally visualize what I have just learned or done?

Step 2: Question

T: After you complete a task or read the material, ask yourself one or two questions that help you to remember what you have just learned. Your questions should be created by you and stated in your own words.

S: After I complete the task or reading material, I will ask myself two questions about what I just learned or read. Have I generated two questions in my own words? Did these questions help me remember what I learned or completed?

Step 3: Visualize

T: Each time you stop to review what you have just learned or completed, make a mental picture of the idea or material learned.

S: I will make a mental picture to visualize what I have just completed or learned. What is in my mental picture that will help me recall what I have learned?

Step 4: Summarize

T: When you have completed your task (e.g., reading, listening, small-group work), summarize to yourself in your own words what you have learned. In the future, recall this summary each time this topic is needed for additional learning.

S: After I complete my task, I will organize in my mind my questions, mental pictures, and responses. I will then create a brief summary mental picture of what I have learned. I will draw upon my summary to help me in the future to remember this information or skill.

Coping

OVERVIEW ■ This problem-solving strategy assists students in confronting issues and challenges and solving problems in an organized and structured manner.

KEY ELEMENTS ■ The coping strategy includes several skills: recognizing the problem, developing solutions, obtaining needed assistance, attempting solutions, and persisting until a solution is obtained.

RTI CURRICULAR CONSIDERATIONS ■ The coping strategy is useful for successful teaching and learning in each tier of the RTI curriculum for most learners. Developing coping skills in the classroom helps students deal with both academic and social situations in more proactive and constructive ways, leading to improved academic and behavioral performance.

RTI Guided Practice: The following steps demonstrate use of Coping:

Step 1: Recognition

T: Identify the problem you are experiencing. What are the key elements of the problem? How have you tried to control your feelings or address the problem?

S: What can I say about the problem that I am experiencing? How long have I experienced this problem? What have I done to try to control my feelings? How can the problem be broken down into a few main parts or issues?

Step 2: Plan Strategy

T: After you break the problem down into its key parts, prioritize the order to address each component. Develop a plan for confronting the problem in a sequential step process. Visualize one or two solutions or answers to the problem. How will you know that you have successfully resolved the problem or issue? Be realistic in deciding what an acceptable resolution may be; that is, do not expect everything to go exactly the way you would like it to go.

S: What priority should I place on addressing each part of the problem? What step-by-step process will help me resolve the problem? What does a successful solution to the problem look like? How will I know that I have found a solution? Am I realistic in my expectation of an acceptable solution?

Step 3: Assistance

T: Study what you need to do to implement your step-by-step plan. What assistance might you need? What aspects of the plan can you do on your own? It is important to recognize that we all need help from time to time. Knowing when to ask for assistance and where to go for help is often key to resolving problems.

S: What aspects of my plan am I able to do on my own? In what areas do I need assistance, and where can I get the needed help? Who do I know who can help me? How do I know that I may need to ask for assistance?

Step 4: Implementation

T: Once you have analyzed the problem, generated your step-by-step plan, determined the areas in which you need assistance, and prioritized completion of specific aspects of the plan, it is time to take action. You have developed your plan, and now you are ready to initiate it; you should feel confident about the ability of your plan to solve the problem, task, or issue because you have thought through what you will do and sought needed help. How will you know or what will you do that signals that you have begun to implement your plan?

S: When I begin to implement my plan I will take some small action, (such as nod my head, tap my foot, or record a self-monitoring check) to signal that my plan has been set in motion. I will follow my plan as designed, including asking for identified assistance, especially if at first the plan does not appear to be going as well as I would like. I know that resolution may take time.

Step 5: Persistence

T: There are usually several different ways to go about solving a problem or achieving a goal. For different individuals, some ways may work better than others. An approach that works for one student may not work for you, so if your first solution does not work after a couple of attempts, it is important to try other solutions until you come to some resolution of the problem or issue.

S: If my first attempts to resolve the problem or issue do not work, I will not give up. What did I learn from my first attempt that did not work? I will try another solution until the issue or problem is resolved.

Step 6: Resolution

T: A key aspect of coping is to know when the problem or issue is satisfactorily resolved. Stay focused on what you visualized as a realistic and acceptable solution (Step 2). Congratulate yourself once you achieve resolution of the problem, task, or issue.

S: I will persist in finding an acceptable resolution and pay attention to when that resolution is evident. How will I know that I have resolved the problem, task, or issue? What did I learn from the process I followed to resolve the problem? I will congratulate myself once I have resolved the problem, task, or issue.

Evaluation

OVERVIEW ■ The evaluation learning strategy helps students to develop greater awareness of what must be done to complete tasks, monitor behavior, contribute to group work, or resolve similar educational situations.

KEY ELEMENTS ■ The ability to evaluate and study a learning situation or task includes the use of self-monitoring, reflection, prediction, and transfer abilities.

RTI CURRICULAR CONSIDERATIONS ■ RTI instructional and classroom management improves significantly as learners improve their independent and group work abilities. The evaluation strategy helps learners gain greater control over their own learning by increasing their ability to evaluate their work and behavior in more independent ways. Demonstration of the proper ways to check work, monitor behavior, reflect upon learning and task completion, and transfer these skills to new situations are examples of ways to employ evaluation within multi-tiered instruction.

RTI Guided Practice: The following steps demonstrate use of Evaluation:

Step 1: Analysis

T: First, analyze the task or goal to determine what it entails, such as approximate amount of time, materials, space, and other elements. Identify the expected outcome and what steps you need to take to achieve that outcome. Review some of your recently completed assignments to see how you addressed those tasks or achieved your goal, and decide how effective you were.

S: What steps do I need to follow to complete my task? Do I have all the necessary materials, and how much time do I need to complete the task? What have I recently done to succeed in completing a task? Can I use some of that here to complete my task?

Step 2: Strategy Identification

T: Once you have analyzed your task, you need to select one or more strategies that could be used to help you complete your work. What strategies have you used in the past that helped you accomplish a similar task or goal? Think about how one or more strategies you have used in the past could help you address this task or goal.

S: What strategies might I use to help me accomplish my task or achieve my goal? Why do I think these might be good strategies to use in this situation? I will prioritize the selection and use of my selected strategies, beginning with the one I think will be most effective.

Step 3: Strategy Implementation

T: Prior to implementing the first strategy you selected, review its purpose and procedures to clarify its process. Keep in mind that the same strategy may be used in several different situations and that different issues may require one or more strategies to achieve a solution.

S: I need to review the procedures and purpose of my selected strategy. Do I understand how to use the strategy? Do I understand why I am using the strategy for this situation or task? I also need to remember that the same strategy may be used in different situations and that more than one strategy may be necessary to complete the task or achieve my goal.

Step 4: Feedback/Reflection

T: Periodically check to make sure that you are using the strategy the way it is supposed to be used. Also, use ongoing evaluation of what you are doing by asking yourself if the strategy is working and if you are making progress toward accomplishing your goal or completing your task.

S: I will periodically check to make certain that the strategy I have selected is being implemented correctly and that it is helping me accomplish my task or meet my goal. Is the selected strategy working? Am I making steady progress towards my goal or task? Do I think I may need to use an alternative strategy? I will use another strategy and evaluate my progress if the first strategy does not help me to achieve my desired outcome. I will continue using different strategies until I achieve my expected goal or accomplish my task (Step 1).

Step 5: Elaboration/Generalization

T: Here you evaluate how well you accomplished your task or goal. Keep in mind that your expected outcome (Step 1) may be achieved along a continuum ranging from "just met" to "highly met" and that it is okay if you planned to meet your goal in greater detail than you achieved; things happen along the way, and adjusting expectations is often necessary provided that you achieve your goal at a minimum standard. Also, think about the strategies that worked best to help you accomplish your goal or task, and think about other situations in which similar strategies would be of benefit in accomplishing other goals or tasks. Evaluating why you think a particular strategy worked to meet a specific need is helpful in knowing when to use that same strategy in the future.

S: I will ask myself how I know that I have accomplished my task or achieved my goal. Did I achieve my goal at the level I originally hope for? I will not be upset if my goal achievement fell a little short of my initial expectations. I know that sometimes things may not work out exactly as planned. Why do I think the strategies that I used helped me to meet my goal or task? Did I evaluate the implementation of my plan sufficiently to know how well I was progressing towards my goal or task in order to make needed adjustments? In what other situations might I be able to use the same strategies?

As illustrated above for each of the five learning strategies, educators may follow an easy process to help students learn to use the strategy in any tier of the multi-tiered RTI curriculum. Time spent teaching students these learning strategies is time well spent, as they provide a solid foundation for independent and responsible ownership of learning, which in turn increases the teacher's time to address all needs in the teaching and learning environment. Forms 8.3 to 8.7, located at the end of the chapter, provide guides for students to document and structure their use of the five learning strategies.

This section concludes with Table 8.3, which provides an overview of numerous study strategies that may be used in RTI curriculum implementation.

TABLE 8.3 Study Strategies

Strategy	Task Area	Process	Description
CALL-UP	Notetaking	**C**opy ideas accurately **A**dd necessary details **L**isten and write the question **L**isten and write the answer **U**se text to support notes **P**ut response in own words	Helps students to remain focused on what is happening in class during a notetaking task or assignment; helps learners respond more accurately to questions using notes and text to support written responses (Czarnecki, Rosko, & Pine, 1998)
CAN-DO	Acquiring content	**C**reate list of items to learn **A**sk self if list is complete **N**ote details and main ideas **D**escribe components and their relationships **O**verlearn main items, followed by learning details	Assists with memorization of lists of items through rehearsal techniques
COPS	Written reports	**C**apitalization correct **O**verall appearance **P**unctuation correct **S**pelling correct	Provides a structure for proofreading written work prior to submitting it to the teacher
DEFENDS	Written expression	**D**ecide on a specific position **E**xamine own reasons for this position **F**orm a list of points explaining each reason **E**xpose position in first sentence of written task **N**ote each reason and associated points **D**rive home position in last sentence **S**earch for and correct any errors	Helps learners defend a particular position in a written assignment
EASY	Studying content	**E**licit questions (*who, what, when, where, why*) **A**sk self which information is least difficult **S**tudy easy content initially, followed by difficult content **Y**es—provide self-reinforcement	Helps learners organize and prioritize information by responding to questions designed to identify important content to be learned
FIST	Reading comprehension	**F**irst sentence is read **I**ndicate a question based on material in first sentence **S**earch for answer to question **T**ie question and answer together through paraphrasing	Helps students actively pursue responses to questions related directly to material being read
GLP	Notetaking	**G**uided **L**ecture **P**rocedure	Provides students with a structure for taking notes during lectures; uses group activity to facilitate effective notetaking
KWL	Reading comprehension	**K**now—document what you know **W**ant to know—document what you want to know **L**earn—list what you have learned	Helps students with reading comprehension and organization of their thoughts, ideas, and acquired knowledge by relating previous knowledge with desired learning (Ogle, 1986)

(Continued)

TABLE 8.3 (Continued)

Strategy	Task Area	Process	Description
MARKER	Time management Organization	**M**ake a list of goals, set the order, set the date **A**rrange a plan for each goal and predict your success **R**un your plans for each goal and adjust if necessary **K**eep records of your progress **E**valuate your progress toward each goal **R**eward yourself when you reach a goal and set a new goal	Helps students effectively use their time by staying focused on their goals and to reward themselves when goal has been reached (Bos & Vaughn, 2006)
NEAT	Writing	**N**ever hand in messy work **E**very paper should be readable **A**lways keep your paper clean **T**ry to remember to put your name and the date on every paper	Assists students to double-check their written work for neatness prior to submission
Panorama	Reading	**P**reparatory stage—identify purpose **I**ntermediate stage—survey and read **C**oncluding stage—memorize material	Includes a three-stage process to assist with reading comprehension
PARS	Reading	**P**review **A**sk questions **R**ead **S**ummarize	Is used with younger students and with those who have limited experiences with study strategies
PENS	Sentence writing	**P**ick a formula **E**xplore different words to fit into the formula **N**ote the words selected **S**ubject and verb selections follow	Is appropriate for developing basic sentence structure and helps students write different types of sentences by following formulas for sentence construction
PIRATES	Test taking	**P**repare to succeed **I**nspect instructions carefully **R**ead entire question, remember memory strategies, and reduce choices **A**nswer question or leave until later **T**urn back to the abandoned items **E**stimate unknown answers by avoiding absolutes and eliminating similar choices **S**urvey to ensure that all items have a response	Helps learners to complete tests more carefully and successfully
PQ4R	Reading	**P**review **Q**uestion **R**ead **R**eflect **R**ecite **R**eview	Helps students to become more discriminating readers

TABLE 8.3 (Continued)

Strategy	Task Area	Process	Description
5Rs	Test taking	**R**ecord—take notes on right side of paper **R**educe—write in key words, phrases, and questions on left side of paper **R**ecite—talk aloud **R**eflect—question how this relates to what you know **R**eview—read over notes and summarize at bottom of page	Helps students to prepare to take tests; helps students clarify and reflect on what they know and how knowledge relates to potential test items
RAP	Reading comprehension	**R**ead paragraph **A**sk self to identify the main idea and two supporting details **P**ut main idea and details into own words	Helps students to learn information through paraphrasing
RARE	Reading	**R**eview selection questions **A**nswer all questions known **R**ead the selection **E**xpress answers to remaining questions	Emphasizes reading for a specific purpose while focusing on acquiring answers to selection questions initially not known
RDPE	Underlining	**R**eview entire passage **D**ecide which ideas are important **P**lan the underlining to include only main points **E**valuate results of the underlining by reading only the underlined words	Helps learners organize and remember main points and ideas in a reading selection through appropriate underlining of key words
REAP	Reading Writing Thinking	**R**ead **E**ncode **A**nnotate **P**onder	Helps students combine several skills to facilitate discussion about reading material
ReQuest	Reading Questioning	**R**eciprocal **Quest**ioning	Helps students to model teacher questions and receive feedback while exploring the meaning of the reading material
RIDER	Reading comprehension	**R**ead sentence **I**mage (form mental picture) **D**escribe how new image differs from previous sentence **E**valuate image to ensure that it contains all necessary elements **R**epeat process with subsequent sentences	Cues the learner to form a mental image of what was previously learned from a sentence just read
SCORER	Test taking	**S**chedule time effectively **C**lue words identified **O**mit difficult items until end **R**ead carefully **E**stimate answers requiring calculations **R**eview work and responses	Provides a structure for completing various tests by helping students carefully and systematically complete test items

(Continued)

TABLE 8.3 (Continued)

Strategy	Task Area	Process	Description
SOLVE IT	Math word problems	**S**ay the problem to yourself **O**mit any unnecessary information in problem **L**isten for key vocabulary terms or indicators **V**ocabulary—change to fit math concepts **E**quation—translate problem into a math equation **I**ndicate the answer **T**ranslate answer back into context of word problem	Assists students to systematically solve math word problems by focusing on key vocabulary in the problem and relating the terms to math concepts and solutions
SQRQCQ	Math word problems	**S**urvey word problem **Q**uestion asked is identified **R**ead more carefully **Q**uestion process required to solve problem **C**ompute the answer **Q**uestion self to ensure that the answer solves the problem	Provides a systematic structure for identifying the question being asked in a math word problem, computing the response, and ensuring that the question in the problem was answered
SQ3R	Reading	**S**urvey **Q**uestion **R**ead **R**ecite **R**eview	Provides a systematic approach to improve reading comprehension
SSCD	Vocabulary development	**S**ound clues used **S**tructure clues used **C**ontext clues used **D**ictionary used	Encourages students to remember to use sound, structure, and context clues, as well as a dictionary if needed, to address unfamiliar vocabulary
STOP	Writing	**S**uspend judgment (brainstorm) **T**ell thesis **O**rganize ideas **P**lan moves for effective writing	Helps students remember to brainstorm to document potential ideas, generate a thesis statement, document main and subordinate ideas in outline form, and plan for effective writing (de la Paz, 1997)
TOWER	Written reports Organization	**T**hink **O**rder ideas **W**rite **E**dit **R**ewrite	Provides a structure for completing initial and final drafts of written reports; may be used effectively with COPS
TQLR	Listening	**T**uning in **Q**uestioning **L**istening **R**eviewing	Assists with listening comprehension by reminding students to generate questions and listen for specific statements related to those questions

Source: From *Teaching Study Skills to Students with Learning Problems: A Teacher's Guide for Meeting Diverse Needs,* 2nd ed. (pp. 132–136), by J. J. Hoover and J. R. Patton, 2007, Austin, TX: PRO-ED. Copyright 2007 by PRO-ED, Inc. Reprinted with permission.

As Table 8.3 shows, numerous study strategies exist to facilitate both student-directed and independent learning. In implementing the multi-tiered RTI curriculum, these study strategies assist students in meeting their many academic and behavioral needs within each tier of instruction.

Study Strategies Integrated Within Curricular Components

The previous section emphasized the significance and value of using study skills and learning strategies in curriculum implementation. Although these skills and strategies may require greater use at the secondary level, their initial development, practice, and application should take place in early elementary school with simple variations used early on, followed by more in-depth application as the learner matures and grows both academically and socially. As with the other major topics explored in this book, the use of study skills and learning strategies should be integral to the implementation of the five curriculum components to best meet multi-tiered instructional needs. Table 8.4 provides examples of the connections between the five curricular components and study strategies.

TABLE 8.4   Significance of Study Strategies in Response to Intervention Curriculum Implementation

Curriculum Component	Study Strategies and Curriculum	Significance to Progress in RTI Models
Content/Skills (Research-Based Curriculum)	Study strategies facilitate more in-depth acquisition and generalization of new knowledge and skills	Learners who possess multiple learning tools and strategies achieve greater progress toward curricular benchmarks
Evidence-Based Interventions	Evidence-based interventions include or are grounded in various research-based study skills and learning strategies	RTI curricular progress is directly related to effective uses of evidence-based interventions, which reflect use of study/learning strategies that students possess
Instructional Arrangements	Increased study strategy use by students increases their ability to learn in differentiated classroom arrangements (i.e., small or large group, independent work, paired or cooperative learning)	Academic and behavioral progress in an RTI framework is enhanced if learners possess and use a variety of study skills and learning strategies to meet daily curricular demands through education provided in various instructional settings
Class/Instructional Management Procedures	Student use of selected study strategies facilitates increased self-management in the teaching and learning environment	Students' use of study strategies that contribute to self-management increases quality time on tasks, resulting in more efficient classroom management and leading to increased progress toward curricular benchmarks
Progress Evaluation	Curriculum-based or other types of progress monitoring require the effective use of various study skills and learning strategies	The most accurate progress monitoring results are achieved when students employ relevant study skills and learning strategies (e.g., test taking, active processing, time management, reading rates)

As Table 8.4 shows, learning strategies and study skills are interconnected with teaching and learning success. They help provide more accurate universal screening and progress monitoring results, which in turn leads to more informed decisions concerning the level and duration of multi-tiered instruction. The chapter concludes with its example of *RTI Curriculum in Practice* as related to study skill/learning strategy use.

RTI CURRICULUM IN PRACTICE

An Example of a Study Skills Emphasis in Tier 1 Assisting a Learner to Make Adequate Progress

Overview

As a high school special education teacher, I work with many students who possess a variety of different learning styles and associated needs. I have also found that some secondary teachers often assume that their students know how to study and prepare for tests. This assumption may lead to lack of awareness on the part of some teachers of the importance of directly incorporating the use of study skills in the implementation of Tier 1 core curriculum. Below is an example of my efforts in my role as a special education teacher consulting with a general class teacher in my secondary school. I provided consulting assistance to a general education teacher in a state-accredited alternative high school for a student who was struggling in her English class by emphasizing greater use of study skills.

Study Skill Needs

In the Tier 1 core curriculum English instruction, there was one student who came to class every day, listened, participated, and took notes. Yet, this same student was failing on almost every test, which was lowering her grade, indicating lack of adequate progress in the content area of English. In addition to issues with the course grade, the teacher began to notice that the student was making disparaging comments about herself as a learner. The teacher believed that this meant that the student should be considered for more intensive Tier 2 supplemental instruction. However, when I observed the student, I saw her answering questions in class but only after consulting her notes. It seemed that the student understood the material but had difficulty remembering it without directly and frequently referring to her notes. When asked how she studied for a test, the student said she just reread her notes, but it would often take her so long that she would give up studying. She admitted, "I really don't know how to study."

Study Skills Emphasis

The English teacher, the student, and I met to discuss the situation and identify possible solutions to assist the learner make adequate progress within Tier 1 English class instruction. Together we determined that the learner needed more assistance in the classroom, particularly greater opportunities to improve test-studying skills. The English teacher agreed to create a study guide for the student identifying the basics of what would be on the test to assist the student with test studying. I also assisted the student to create flash cards with the same information to help her better organize the material (i.e., organization study skill). This reduced the amount of material the student had to memorize and also gave the student a chance to improve her test-studying skills. As a result of these efforts, the student's test scores climbed and the student expressed renewed confidence in her ability to explain what she was learning. These small, yet significant, study skill differentiations allowed the student to maintain her progress within the Tier 1 core English instruction as well as improve her self-esteem as a learner.

—**Subini A. (Special Educator)**

Study skills are tools used to complete a variety of classroom tasks, and learning strategies are abilities used to help students learn how to learn. Proper use of these skills and strategies in the teaching and learning environment is necessary for students to make adequate progress within the multi-tiered curriculum. Opportunities to learn and demonstrate progress are grounded in effective instruction provided by the teacher as well as effective study and learning skills applied by the students. Although RTI focuses on implementation of the curriculum with fidelity, it also ensures that students possess sufficient study skills and learning strategies to acquire, maintain, generalize, and demonstrate what is taught through the curriculum (i.e., progress toward curricular benchmarks). Readers who wish more information on learning strategies should go to http://www.kucrl.org/sim/strategies.shtml, a link on the main KU-CRL Web site.

The application of these curricular topics within multi-tiered RTI provides the foundation for meeting the needs of all learners in today's classrooms. Educators should do the following:

- Identify the various study skills and learning strategies that students use in your classroom over a 5-day period of a selected class session (e.g., reading, social studies).

- Develop a PowerPoint presentation describing the importance of study skill/learning strategy use in the implementation of the multi-tiered instructional curriculum and present it to your school staff.

- Select two learning strategies used least often in your classroom and develop a process for teaching them to students and incorporating them in your instruction.

- Evaluate students' use of the various study skills and learning strategies to determine their effectiveness in learning the content and skills being taught.

- Record and evaluate students' use of various study skills and learning strategies as applied in screening, monitoring, or diagnostic assessment; consider these relative to the results obtained.

Student Name: _____   Grade: _____

Completed by: _____   Date: _____

Directions: Rate each item using the scale provided. Base the rating on the individual's present level of performance.

Study Skill	Rating			
	Not Proficient	Partially Proficient	Proficient	Highly Proficient
Reading Rate				
Skims	0	1	2	3
Scans	0	1	2	3
Reads at rapid rate	0	1	2	3
Reads at normal rate	0	1	2	3
Reads at study or careful rate	0	1	2	3
Understands the importance of reading	0	1	2	3
Listening				
Attends to listening activities	0	1	2	3
Applies meaning to verbal messages	0	1	2	3
Filters out auditory distractions	0	1	2	3
Comprehends verbal messages	0	1	2	3
Understands importance of listening skills	0	1	2	3
Graphic Aids				
Attends to relevant elements in visual material	0	1	2	3
Uses visuals appropriately in presentations	0	1	2	3
Develops own graphic material	0	1	2	3
Is not confused or distracted by visual material in presentations	0	1	2	3
Understands importance of visual material	0	1	2	3
Library Usage				
Uses cataloging system (card or computerized) effectively	0	1	2	3
Can locate library materials	0	1	2	3
Understands organizational layout of library	0	1	2	3
Understands and uses services of media specialist	0	1	2	3
Understands overall functions and purposes of a library	0	1	2	3
Understands importance of library usage skills	0	1	2	3
Reference Materials				
Can identify components of different reference materials	0	1	2	3
Uses guide words appropriately	0	1	2	3

Study Skill	Rating			
	Not Proficient	Partially Proficient	Proficient	Highly Proficient
Consults reference materials when necessary	0	1	2	3
Uses materials appropriately to complete assignments	0	1	2	3
Can identify different types of reference materials and sources	0	1	2	3
Understands importance of reference materials	0	1	2	3
Test Taking				
Studies for tests in an organized way	0	1	2	3
Spends appropriate amount of time studying different topics covered on a test	0	1	2	3
Avoids cramming for tests	0	1	2	3
Organizes narrative responses appropriately	0	1	2	3
Reads and understands directions before answering questions	0	1	2	3
Proofreads responses and checks for errors	0	1	2	3
Identifies and uses clue words in questions	0	1	2	3
Properly records answers	0	1	2	3
Saves difficult items until last	0	1	2	3
Eliminates obvious wrong answers	0	1	2	3
Systematically reviews completed tests to determine test-taking or test-studying errors	0	1	2	3
Corrects previous test-taking errors	0	1	2	3
Understands importance of test-taking skills	0	1	2	3
Notetaking and Outlining				
Uses headings (and subheadings) appropriately	0	1	2	3
Takes brief and clear notes	0	1	2	3
Records essential information	0	1	2	3
Applies skill during writing activities	0	1	2	3
Uses skill during lectures	0	1	2	3
Develops organized outlines	0	1	2	3
Follows consistent notetaking format	0	1	2	3
Understands importance of notetaking	0	1	2	3
Understands importance of outlining	0	1	2	3
Report Writing				
Organizes thoughts in writing	0	1	2	3
Completes written reports from outline	0	1	2	3
Includes only necessary information	0	1	2	3
Uses proper sentence structure	0	1	2	3
Uses proper punctuation	0	1	2	3
Uses proper grammar and spelling	0	1	2	3
Proofreads written assignments	0	1	2	3

Study Skill	Rating			
	Not Proficient	Partially Proficient	Proficient	Highly Proficient
Report Writing (*continued*)				
Provides clear introductory statement	0	1	2	3
Includes clear concluding statements	0	1	2	3
Understands importance of writing reports	0	1	2	3
Oral Presentations				
Freely participates in oral presentations	0	1	2	3
Organizes presentations well	0	1	2	3
Uses gestures appropriately	0	1	2	3
Speaks clearly	0	1	2	3
Uses proper language when reporting orally	0	1	2	3
Understands importance of oral reporting	0	1	2	3
Time Management				
Completes tasks on time	0	1	2	3
Plans and organizes daily activities and responsibilities effectively	0	1	2	3
Plans and organizes weekly and monthly schedules	0	1	2	3
Reorganizes priorities when necessary	0	1	2	3
Meets scheduled deadlines	0	1	2	3
Accurately perceives the amount of time required to complete tasks	0	1	2	3
Adjusts time allotment to complete tasks	0	1	2	3
Accepts responsibility for managing own time	0	1	2	3
Understands importance of effective time management	0	1	2	3
Self-Management				
Monitors own behavior	0	1	2	3
Changes own behavior as necessary	0	1	2	3
Thinks before acting	0	1	2	3
Is responsible for own behavior	0	1	2	3
Identifies behaviors that interfere with own learning	0	1	2	3
Understands importance of self-management	0	1	2	3
Organization				
Uses locker efficiently	0	1	2	3
Transports books and other material to and from school effectively	0	1	2	3
Has books, supplies, equipment, and other materials needed for class	0	1	2	3

Study Skill	Rating			
	Not Proficient	Partially Proficient	Proficient	Highly Proficient
Organization (*continued*)				
Manages multiple tasks or assignments	0	1	2	3
Uses two or more study skills simultaneously when needed	0	1	2	3
Meets individual organizational expectations concerning own learning	0	1	2	3

Summary of Study Skills Performance

Directions: Summarize in the chart below the number of Not Proficient (NP), Partially Proficient (PP), Proficient (P), and Highly Proficient (HP) subskills for each study skill. The number next to the study skill represents the total number of subskills listed for each area.

Study Skill	NP	PP	P	HP
Reading rate (6)				
Listening (5)				
Graphic aids (5)				
Library usage (6)				
Reference materials (6)				
Test taking (13)				

Study Skill	NP	PP	P	HP
Notetaking and outlining (9)				
Report writing (10)				
Oral presentations (6)				
Time management (9)				
Self-management (6)				
Organization (6)				

Summary comments about student study skills:

_____

_____

_____

_____

_____

_____

Source: From *Teaching Study Skills to Students with Learning Problems: A Teacher's Guide for Meeting Diverse Needs*, 2nd ed. (pp. 50–54), by J. J. Hoover and J. R. Patton, 2007, Austin, TX: PRO-ED. Copyright 2007 by PRO-ED, Inc. Reprinted with permission.

Directions: Circle the level of usage for each specific study skill.   Student Name: _____

Study Skill	1 Minimal usage of skill/No impact on learning	2 Some usage/ Irregular impact on learning	3 Consistent usage/ Regular impact on most learning	4 Daily usage/ Noticeable impact on most daily learning
Reading rate	1	2	3	4
Listening	1	2	3	4
Graphic aids	1	2	3	4
Library usage	1	2	3	4
Reference materials	1	2	3	4
Test taking	1	2	3	4
Notetaking and outlining	1	2	3	4
Report writing	1	2	3	4
Oral presentations	1	2	3	4
Time management	1	2	3	4
Self-management	1	2	3	4
Organization	1	2	3	4

Comments: _____

_____

_____

Source: From *Teaching Study Skills to Students with Learning Problems: A Teacher's Guide for Meeting Diverse Needs*, 2nd ed. (p. 55), by J. J. Hoover and J. R. Patton, 2007, Austin, TX: PRO-ED. Copyright 2007 by PRO-ED, Inc. Reprinted with permission.

FORM 8.3 Student Application Guide: Active Processing

Student: _____   Date: _____

Task/Goal to which Active Processing is applied: _____

Instructions: Respond to each step in the application of Active Processing to the identified task/goal. Refer to the completed guide during task completion to ensure effective use of Active Processing.

Step 1: Definition
What is the purpose of completing the task or goal?

What do I already know about this topic or subject?

Step 2: Specification
What steps will I follow to complete the task/achieve the goal?

Step 3: Evaluation
Am I following my steps?

Does my answer/outcome appear correct?

Did I achieve my task/goal?

Step 4: Monitoring
What might be an alternative approach if my first attempt does not work?

Did my first approach work or do I need to try another? Do I need to make a change?

What did I learn from my first attempt(s) or from any mistake(s) I made?

Step 5: Completion
How will I know that I have completed my task or achieved my goal?

Did I complete my task or achieve my goal?

How will I congratulate myself for my accomplishment?

Source: Used by permission of John J. Hoover.

Student: _____   Date: _____

Task/Goal to which Analogy is applied: _____

Instructions: Respond to each step in the application of Analogy to the identified task/goal. Refer to the completed guide during task completion to ensure effective use of Analogy.

_____

Step 1: Prior Knowledge
What do I already know that is similar to this new content or skill?

When did I previously need to use this knowledge or skill?

Step 2: Comparison
How does this new content or skill compare to what I already know?

Does it seem to have similar applications or uses?

How is it different from what I currently know?

Step 3: Substitution
How can I use some of what I already know about a similar topic or skill to help me learn the new task or concept?

Step 4: Elaboration
How might my prior experiences in learning a new task/skill help me to learn this new task, material or skill?

_____

Source: Used by permission of John J. Hoover.

Student Application Guide: Rehearsal

Student: _____   Date: _____

Task/Goal to which Rehearsal is applied: _____

Instructions: Respond to each step in the application of Rehearsal to the identified task/goal. Refer to the completed guide during task completion to ensure effective use of Rehearsal.

Step 1: Pause
What do I need to do to successfully complete my task or achieve my goal?

Step 2: Question
What two questions can I ask myself to help me remember this task/goal?

      Question 1:

      Question 2:

How did these two questions help me remember what I learned or completed?

Step 3: Visualize
What is in my mental picture that will help me recall what I have learned?

Step 4: Summarize
Did I create a brief summary mental picture of what I have learned?

When do I think I will need to draw upon my mental picture summary to help me in the future to remember this information or skill?

Source: Used by permission of John J. Hoover.

Student: _____   Date: _____

Task/Goal to which Coping is applied: _____

Instructions: Respond to each step in the application of Coping to the identified task/goal. Refer to the completed guide during task completion to ensure effective use of Coping.

_____

Step 1: Recognition
What can I say about the problem that I am experiencing?

How long have I experienced this problem?

What have I done to try to control my feelings?

How can the problem be broken down into a few main parts or issues?

Step 2: Plan Strategy
What priority should I place on addressing each part of the problem?

What step-by-step process will help me resolve the problem?

What does a successful resolution to the problem look like?

How will I know that I have resolved the problem?

Is my expectation of an acceptable resolution realistic?

Step 3: Assistance
What aspects of my plan can I do on my own?

With what aspects of my plan do I need assistance, and where can I get the needed help?

Who do I know who can help me?

How do I know that I may need to ask for assistance?

Step 4: Implementation
Did I follow my plan as designed? Did I ask for assistance, especially if at first the plan did not appear to be going as well as I would like?

Step 5: Persistence
What have I learned to do from previous tasks if my first attempt did not work?

What other solutions should I try if the first one did not help to resolve the problem?

Step 6: Resolution
How will I know that I have resolved the problem?

What did I learn from the process I followed to resolve the problem?

How will I congratulate myself once I have resolved the problem?

Source: Used by permission of John J. Hoover.

Student: _____ Date: _____

Task/Goal to which Evaluation is applied: _____

Instructions: Respond to each step in the application of Evaluation to the identified task/goal. Refer to the completed guide during task completion to ensure effective use of Evaluation.

Step 1: Analysis
What steps do I need to follow to complete my task?

Do I have all the necessary materials, and how much time do I need to complete the task?

What task have I recently completed successfully? Can I use some of what I did in that task to help complete this task?

Step 2: Strategy Identification
What strategies might I use to help me complete my task or achieve my goal?

Why do I think these might be good strategies to use in this situation?

How will I prioritize the selection and use of my selected strategies, beginning with the one I think will be most effective?

Step 3: Strategy Implementation
Do I understand how to use the strategy?

Am I using the strategy for the reasons for which I thought it should be used in this situation or task?

Can I use this same strategy in different situations?

Is more than one strategy necessary to complete the task or accomplish my goal?

Step 4: Feedback/Reflection
Is the selected strategy working?

Am I making steady progress towards my goal or task?

Do I think I may need to try to use an alternative strategy?

If so, which other strategy might I try?

Did I continue using this strategy until I achieved my goal or accomplished my task?

Step 5: Elaboration/Generalization
Did I achieve my goal to the level I originally hoped for?

Did I become upset if I achieved my goal but it fell short of my expectations?

Why do I think that the strategy I used helped me to meet my goal or accomplish my task?

Did I evaluate the implementation of my plan sufficiently to know how well I was progressing toward my goal or task completion in order to make needed adjustments?

In what other situations might I be able to use the same strategy?

Source: Used by permission of John J. Hoover.

CHAPTER 9

Response to Intervention and Secondary-Level Curriculum Implementation

▶ Overview

RECENTLY, THE NEED TO ADDRESS multi-tiered RTI beyond the lower grade levels has become much more apparent as students progress from elementary school to middle and high school. Although the curriculum implementation structures vary between elementary and secondary school, many of the same foundational principles for RTI models are equally applicable at the elementary and secondary levels. Unique needs of secondary learners require adjustments to screening and progress monitoring strategies, so these adjustments are most appropriate for students in grades 6–12. This includes consideration of RTI processes compatible with scheduling, multiple teachers, cross-disciplinary needs, and evidence-based interventions, to name a few. However, the effective implementation of secondary curricula is facilitated by the successful incorporation of RTI principles and practices, thereby creating a natural and logical extension of what occurs in the elementary grades.

► Key Topics

> ► Needs of struggling learners at the secondary level

> ► Secondary-level structural demands associated with RTI

> ► Role of secondary RTI in identifying at-risk learners

> ► The potential ability of RTI to identify learners at risk of dropping out of school

> ► RTI curriculum implementation and the secondary content areas

► Learner Outcomes

After reading this chapter, you should:

1. Acquire an understanding of unique areas in the development and implementation of RTI at the secondary level

2. Acquire an understanding of specific knowledge and skill areas to be screened for the purpose of identifying at-risk secondary learners

3. Be able to initiate the process of developing and implementing RTI at the secondary level, including ensuring consistency across core content instruction

4. Be able to use screening and progress monitoring data to make informed Tier 1, 2, or 3 instructional decisions for secondary learners

SIGNIFICANCE TO CONTEMPORARY CLASSROOM INSTRUCTION

Although RTI originally targeted the needs of elementary students (grades K–5), its principles and practices are also appropriate for those in secondary school. Many students continue to enter the secondary grades (i.e., middle and high school) lacking the skills and abilities needed to deal successfully with the demands of the secondary school curriculum. Although the implementation of RTI will vary from that at the elementary level, it contains many fundamental concepts that assist secondary students to make adequate progress toward curricular benchmarks. This is significant because (as with elementary students) screening and progress monitoring can provide valuable curriculum-based information to design and implement high-quality Tier 1, 2, and 3 multi-tiered instruction for secondary learners. The extension of RTI principles and practices gives secondary learners the best opportunities to progress within various content areas, building on their learning in the elementary grades.

Note: The term *secondary* may include a variety of grade levels, depending on the structure and size of the school or district. In these discussions, *secondary* refers to both middle and high school (i.e., grades 6–8 for middle school and 9–12 for high school); however, the same ideas, concepts, and suggested practices presented for students in grades 6–8 and 9–12 are applicable if a different structure for secondary school exists (e.g., junior high grades 7–9, high school grades 10–12).

Overview of Response to Intervention in Secondary Schools

According to Duffy (2007), secondary students who demonstrate significant lags in academic or behavioral progress are often referred to and placed in special education even though many do not have a disability. Additionally, although RTI models have existed for several years, their application has seen the greatest emphasis in research and implementation at the elementary level, particularly in the content area of early reading abilities. RTI at the secondary level has only recently begun to receive the necessary attention to assist students in middle and high school. Few research-based models exist to guide the development and implementation of RTI in secondary grades (Mastropieri & Scruggs, 2005). However, some efforts in this area have been documented, drawing upon key elements in the overall RTI framework, with specific applications to the secondary level. Following is a summary of some of the main RTI elements that pertain to any level of education.

Multi-tiered RTI at the secondary level initially includes those elements that reflect high-quality teaching and learning, regardless of grade level. Bradley, Danielson, and Doolittle (2007) identified several of these common elements. All learners:

- Are screened periodically throughout the school year to identify potentially struggling or at-risk learners in the areas of academics and behavior development
- Receive instruction that increases in intensity and duration based on progress (i.e., the three-tier model)
- Are educated using research-based curricula and evidence-based interventions with fidelity
- Are monitored on a regular, continuous basis to determine their progress toward curricular benchmarks
- Receive assessments that directly reflect what has been taught within the curriculum
- Can be referred, if necessary, for comprehensive evaluation for a disability within the RTI framework.

Many of the fundamentals of multi-tiered RTI pertain to any level of education, and RTI at the secondary level should initially ensure that all of the above conditions are in place to form a solid base for secondary students. Beyond these similar foundational elements, secondary RTI differs from that seen at the elementary levels in several significant ways (CCSRI, 2008):

- The primary focus is on content area instruction using higher order thinking abilities.

- Students attend multiple classes daily, generally taught by different teachers.
- Interaction among secondary teachers may be less frequent than typically seen at the elementary level.
- Coteaching at the secondary level requires unique scheduling and planning to achieve optimum results.
- Consistent use of evidence-based interventions across different content areas is more difficult due to the number of classes and teachers each student encounters on a daily basis.

Therefore, unique multi-tiered RTI curricular challenges confront educators at the secondary level; however, these challenges are not insurmountable and, if appropriately addressed, provide a solid foundation for meeting learners' needs in the secondary grades. According to Arnberger and Shoop (2008), capacity building and collaboration are central to the successful development and implementation of multi-tiered RTI models at the secondary level. Both of these aspects of RTI are discussed below.

Capacity Building

Secondary school staff should consider the school's existing capacity when implementing a different structure for educating students, no matter which new structure is involved. To begin this process, staff should assess current practices that are consistent with multi-tiered RTI, including several discussed by CCSRI (2008):

1. Screening procedures and devices in each content area for all secondary learners
2. Specific evidence-based interventions used within each content-area instruction
3. Determination that all curricula are research-based
4. Existing procedures and processes used by the school's problem-solving team
5. Extent to which secondary classrooms are differentiated to meet learners' needs in a variety of content areas

The foundation for these and similar practices may already exist in the school structure and should be built upon during the transition to an RTI model. By initially identifying these key capacity-building aspects, secondary school staff continues the transition to an RTI framework. An RTI model may take 3–5 years to develop; during this time, instruction must continue without interruption. Therefore, the extent to which the above five practices exist forms the basis for additional multi-tiered RTI curricular decisions. Thus, capacity building is key to the successful transition to and implementation of a multi-tiered RTI curriculum at the secondary level (Fuchs & Deshler, 2007).

Collaboration

As previously emphasized, effective and efficient collaboration among all educators involved in the transition to RTI is critical for obvious reasons: greater involvement and support generate more effective and long-lasting solutions. Given the individual dynamics often associated with secondary education (e.g., individual content-area foci, students taught by several different teachers daily, much movement throughout the school day), collaboration becomes particularly significant if a multi-tiered instructional model is to be developed. RTI requires professional collaboration to be successful for all learners (Duffy, 2007). The RTI framework at the secondary level must facilitate communication and the sharing of ideas and information.

Therefore, the current status of RTI at the secondary level reflects a continuous and evolving process emphasizing several key areas:

1. It must be recognized that the fundamentals of a multi-tiered RTI curriculum are the same no matter which level of education is involved, elementary or secondary.

2. It must be understood that although many similarities exist, RTI at the secondary level presents unique challenges to learners and teachers, and associated curricular adjustments are required.

3. Initial efforts to begin the transition to RTI should include assessment of several key curricular aspects of the current secondary school structure.

4. Capacity building and collaboration are central to the successful transition to a more diverse, multi-tiered instructional model.

Building on these RTI principles, the next section discusses specific issues related to RTI Tiers 1–3 at the secondary level. This is followed by a discussion of some specific needs of secondary learners—needs that are addressed through a multi-tiered instructional model.

Curricular Issues at the Secondary Level

Research over the past several decades has identified some of the areas that usually require emphasis at the secondary level (Hoover & Patton, 2007; Lyon et al., 2001; Sabornie & deBettencourt, 2009). Four of these areas are presented because of their significance in meeting the curricular needs of learners within an RTI model. Each of these areas encompasses a wide range of abilities in secondary education.

Literacy Issues

Perhaps the most prevalent academic issue confronting secondary learners is in the area of reading and writing. Secondary learners who lack prerequisite reading and writing skills experience problems with most content areas. Haager and Klingner (2005) wrote that "reading and writing difficulties have a pervasive effect on how students fare in their classes" (p. 395).

RTI CONSIDERATIONS ■ The RTI curriculum at the secondary level must specifically address students' literacy needs.

Social Issues

Adolescence brings with it a variety of social issues and demands, which become confounded if the learner also struggles in school. Peer influences become a driving force in students' lives, often creating conflict in social settings both within and outside of school. For example, learners may become self-conscious and withdrawn, and may be afraid to take chances for fear of lack of acceptance. Additionally, some learners may lack the social perception skills necessary to read appropriate behavior to model, such as voice level in conversations, empathy toward others, or uncertainty about what to say or how to say it without damaging peer relationships (Sabornie & deBettencourt, 2009).

RTI CONSIDERATIONS ■ The multi-tiered RTI curriculum should address these social issues by embedding positive social supports in teaching content to all learners.

Study Skill Issues

Secondary education requires a strong sense of responsibility and accountability on the part of learners due to the numerous classes, teachers, and expectations they encounter in school. Unfortunately, many secondary students are not equipped to use the study skills needed to meet the various academic and social-emotional challenges (Hoover & Patton, 2007). This includes the ability to manage time, organize tasks, prioritize assignments, take tests, write reports, and other related skills needed to succeed at the secondary level.

RTI CONSIDERATIONS ■ The RTI curriculum at the secondary level should recognize the study skill needs of all learners, particularly the skills that must be improved for learners to meet the various content and social demands of secondary education.

Structural Issues

The structure of secondary education is very different from that at the elementary level. This includes factors such as increased movement to and from classes, the increased number of core content-area teachers, expectations that place more demands on reading and writing activities completed outside of class, and variations in discipline and classroom expected behaviors. Secondary students who experience problems in these areas may find that these issues have negative effects on their academic performance and behavior.

RTI CONSIDERATIONS ■ RTI curriculum implementation should take into account learners' varying abilities to meet the challenges of secondary education; some students require more consistency, support, or time to make the necessary transition, and these needs should be accommodated. RTI at the secondary level builds on existing structures that ultimately rely on effective core instruction to improve learners' outcomes (Canter, Klotz, & Cowan, 2008).

These and other related issues (e.g., motivation, locus of control) challenge many learners at the secondary level. Addressing these four general areas in a proactive and positive manner within the multi-tiered RTI curriculum will provide a solid foundation that allows learners to meet their needs.

Structure of Response to Intervention at the Secondary Level

The three-tiered model serves as the foundation for RTI at the secondary level. This framework was presented in detail in Chapter 2, and the reader is referred to that chapter for review. Our discussions here will focus on specific issues related to the secondary level within each tier of instruction. This includes both instructional and assessment elements associated with each tier.

Tier 1 Secondary RTI Curriculum

When students enter secondary school, they should be screened for progress toward grade-level curricular benchmarks, particularly in the content areas of language arts/English and mathematics. They should also be screened for potential dropout behaviors or characteristics (Kennelly & Monrad, 2007). Within the RTI framework, approximately 80% of learners should be making adequate progress toward benchmarks. If this is not the case, then initial curricular adjustments should focus on the Tier 1 core curriculum to create a better fit for all learners. Those students who demonstrate low levels of proficiency and/or do not make adequate progress should be considered for Tier 2 supplemental supports. The Tier 1 core curriculum in each content area must be research-based, with instructional and classroom arrangements differentiated as discussed in Chapter 6. Secondary teachers should use screening data to identify learners at risk academically or potential dropouts. They should then implement appropriate differentiated instruction in the general education class and/or provide supplemental value-added supports to the teaching in the Tier 1 core curriculum to address learners' needs. Efforts within the Tier 1 core curriculum should initially concentrate on the screening of all incoming students in both sixth and ninth grades to identify early those who have learning or behavior problems, rather than waiting until midyear or later to discover the need for possible Tier 2 curricular supports. Additional screening should be done as necessary several times per year to support Tier 1 core instruction and more quickly identify potentially struggling learners.

Tier 2 Secondary RTI Curriculum

Learners who struggle should be identified early and provided necessary supports. Within Tier 2 at the secondary level, there are various types of instruction to support the Tier 1 core curriculum. Some of the forms of Tier 2 support were discussed by Burns and Gibbons (2008), Martin (2007), and Windram, Scierka, and Silberglitt (2007) and include the following:

- A first-year course to help students deal with the expectations of secondary education
- A mathematics or English course for first-year struggling learners that takes place at a time reserved for elective classes so that no core instruction is missed
- Courses for upper-class learners who continue to struggle with core academic subjects
- A remedial English class for incoming students who have lower than expected scores or progress on the English curriculum benchmarks, in which students receive both the Tier 1 core curriculum and supplemental support in targeted areas of need as determined by curriculum-based measurement results
- Use of highly trained paraprofessionals to help implement supplemental supports at selected times during Tier 2 instruction to address potential scheduling and time constraints

As the above examples demonstrate, early screening followed by implementation of Tier 2 supports for struggling learners "demonstrate[s] that delivery of supplemental interventions within an RTI framework can be accomplished at the secondary level" (Winram et al., 2007, p. 5). Scheduling of teachers to provide supports can be addressed though strategic planning, targeted usage of trained paraprofessionals, and creative scheduling in which Tier 2 supports are provided during study hall, elective class time, or other times that do not interfere with Tier 1 core instruction. Although not all struggling students will quickly achieve curricular benchmarks, many will make adequate progress and, with continued Tier 2 support, may reach the minimum benchmark levels required, with little or no interference with their Tier 1 core curriculum learning. These Tier 2 supplemental supports complement, not replace, Tier 1 instruction.

In monitoring progress within Tier 2, curriculum-based measurement (CBM) is one assessment practice that can easily be incorporated into supplemental supports. Other practices, such as performance-based assessment or analytic teaching, may also be used. Several assessment practices were described in Chapter 3. These methods may easily be used to monitor the progress of secondary learners, determining their level of proficiency and rate of progress relative to Tier 2 supplemental supports. For those students who continue to make inadequate progress after at least two attempts with Tier 2 supports, more intensive interventions may be warranted in the form of Tier 3 instruction.

Tier 3 Secondary RTI Curriculum

Based on recent estimates, approximately 1–5% of learners will require Tier 3 intensive interventions (Yell, 2004). Secondary students requiring these interventions may have exhibited significant needs for a long period of time, reflecting important academic and behavioral deficits in cognitive, intellectual, and/or emotional areas. According to Martin (2007), secondary RTI Tier 3 intensive interventions may be delivered via home tutoring, special program placements within the school (e.g., a self-contained classroom), alternative placements such as the Job Corps, or other individualized instructional arrangements such as those reflected in a learner's individualized education plan (IEP). Tier 3 intervention is highly individualized and may consist of an alternative curriculum that varies significantly from the Tier 1 core curriculum and Tier 2 supplemental supports. Form 9.1 (*Evaluating Current Secondary-Level Response to Intervention Structures*) is a guide to assist in identifying important aspects to consider when implementing RTI at the secondary level. This form, developed from the sources cited above, reflects some of the key points discussed in this chapter.

Transitioning to Secondary Curriculum

As discussed above, RTI has focused on the elementary grades, with less research directed at the secondary level (Burns & Gibbons, 2008). However, some schools and researchers have begun to explore options for using RTI in the middle and high school grades. Hoover and Patton (2007) and Hughes and

Deshler (2007) have identified several key teaching and learning aspects that reflect several main differences between elementary and secondary levels of curriculum.

The secondary level of education:

1. Focuses on *reading to learn* rather than *learning to read,* in contrast to the elementary levels

2. Has *fewer research-validated* Tier 1 core curricula in the content areas compared to the elementary level

3. Requires students to be educated by *many core content teachers* (e.g., five to seven) versus one or two core classroom teachers at the elementary level

4. Emphasizes the need for efficient time management and associated organization abilities to a greater extent than is typically required at the elementary level

5. Has fewer research-based universal screening and progress monitoring measures than the elementary level

These five areas in the development and implementation of multi-tiered instruction provide a foundation for meeting the needs of secondary-level curricula, no matter which content area is studied. These areas are discussed below, with emphasis on the underlying assumptions for successful teaching and learning, along with their RTI implications. These discussions were developed from information in several sources (Burns & Gibbons, 2008; Duffy, 2007; Hughes & Deshler, 2007; Martin, 2007), bringing together critical issues to focus on when implementing multi-tiered RTI models at the secondary level.

RTI Focus Area 1: Reading to Learn

At the secondary education level, reading expectations change from acquiring to applying reading skills. Textbooks become more sophisticated, much of the learning must be acquired through independent reading of the texts either before or after class, and students are expected to respond to critical thinking issues or questions associated with the texts in every content area.

RTI UNDERLYING ASSUMPTIONS ■ Several key learning abilities are assumed to be achieved in Focus Area 1. These include the ability to read, to have a vocabulary level commensurate with that used in the texts, independent study and reading abilities sufficient to read several higher level texts within defined time frames, and the comprehension skills needed to apply and generalize knowledge and skills obtained from interacting with content area reading materials.

► **Implications for Secondary RTI Curriculum Implementation:** These reading expectations lead to three key RTI considerations:

1. Screening of secondary learners should focus on identifying independent and instructional reading levels.

2. Vocabulary levels in each content area should be identified.

3. The ability to use higher level thinking for different levels of comprehension (e.g., knowledge, evaluation, synthesis) within each content area must be determined.

Initially, each of these factors should be determined through Tier 1 screening. The learning needs identified have direct implications for providing Tier 1 differentiated instruction and Tier 2 supplemental supports using various content-area textbooks.

Focus Area 2: Research-Based Core Content Curricula

As previously discussed, a research-based curriculum for all instruction is the foundation of multi-tiered RTI. Also, as noted, much of the research on effective curriculum has focused on the elementary school curriculum, particularly in early reading. Some research has also identified certain core-content programs appropriate for secondary learners. Two Web sites that contain information about secondary curricula are those of the What Works Clearinghouse and the RTI Action Network. Both sites provide descriptions of selected middle and/or high school curricula, including evidence of effectiveness. The reader is referred to these sites as an initial contact point for locating and evaluating secondary curricula. The types of programs described at these Web sites may serve as a foundation for multi-tiered instruction at the secondary level, provided that several key assumptions are considered in their selection and use.

RTI UNDERLYING ASSUMPTIONS ■ Secondary curricula require certain prerequisite skills and abilities for successful use with all learners in Tier 1 core instruction. These include:

1. Sufficient reading level abilities

2. Adequate content-area vocabulary

3. Compatibility between students' learning preferences and the teaching style used in the curriculum

4. Sufficient higher level thinking skills to meet the demands of the curriculum

Although the selected core Tier 1 curriculum must be research based, educators should review the program's development materials to acquire a more detailed understanding of the curriculum in order to ensure its most effective use with all secondary learners. At a minimum, the following should be understood before selecting and using the curriculum:

1. *Underlying Philosophy of the Curriculum*—On which philosophy is the program grounded (e.g., direct instruction, explicit instruction, cooperative learning, independent learning, constructivism)?

2. *Prerequisite Knowledge and Skills*—What prior learning skills and knowledge are required for student success (e.g., in terms of reading levels, experiential background, cultural values, language proficiency)?

3. *Roles of the Teacher and Learner*—What is the primary role of the teacher in the curriculum (e.g., to facilitate, provide direct instruction)? What is the primary role of the learner (e.g., cooperative, constructivist, passive recipient of teacher-directed instruction, independent learner)?

4. *Primary Concepts*—What are the primary concepts taught through the curriculum, and how do these align with state or district content-area benchmarks for all learners?

Therefore, in addition to knowing that the core content-area curriculum is research based, the educators responsible for selecting the curriculum must have a more detailed understanding about which learners will be most successful with the curriculum and under what conditions. Given the above issues, the use of curriculum at the secondary level has direct implications for RTI.

▶ **Implications for Secondary RTI Curriculum Implementation:** Knowing that a program or intervention is research based is only the first step in selecting and using core curricula at the secondary level to develop the many higher level skills required to deal successfully with the more sophisticated content material, skills, and knowledge. Based on the above discussion, several implications for secondary RTI curriculum exist:

1. A Tier 1 core curriculum must be selected carefully, given the need to meet the many learning needs and reading levels of secondary students.

2. Screening should emphasize both general skills considered important for success at the secondary level and specifics reflecting the philosophy, roles, and expectations of the curriculum.

3. Several forms of Tier 1 screening are needed to understand learners' preparation for each core content area (i.e., different targeted screenings should reflect specifics in each core area, such as English, mathematics, or science).

4. Programs to provide Tier 2 supplemental supports must target both general secondary skills (e.g., improve comprehension abilities that may be applied to any content area) and specific content areas (e.g., science vocabulary).

Consideration of these and similar RTI implications will help secondary educators select the most appropriate research-based curricula and implement them with fidelity.

Focus Area 3: Instruction Provided by Several Core Content Teachers

One of the more difficult transitions for many secondary learners is the need to continuously adjust to multiple content areas taught by different teachers, with classes switching within 1- to 2-hour blocks of time, depending on the school structure. This includes making regular adjustments to varying:

1. Classroom management styles
2. Expected workloads
3. Emphasis on independent learning
4. Lengths of reading assignments
5. Time for completion of assignments
6. Expectations associated with self-management of learning responsibilities

Although these and similar needs are not new to educators who have taught at the secondary level, they are presented to highlight the significant differences that may exist for many students compared to what is typically expected at the elementary level (e.g., only one or two core content teachers, resulting in more consistency and predictability concerning class management styles, workloads, or time for completion of assignments). As in the other focus areas, important assumptions are made as students' need to adjust to multiple teachers and content areas is addressed in RTI models.

RTI UNDERLYING ASSUMPTIONS ■ Perhaps the most significant assumption is that students can easily make the numerous transitions required daily. This assumption may not be valid. Although many learners have the academic and behavioral skills necessary to make smooth transitions, many others need additional guidance, experience, and opportunities to adjust to secondary-level demands. Students who were very successful in elementary school, with its more defined and consistent structures and expectations, may struggle in secondary school, where they are expected to assume more individual responsibility.

Another assumption made in RTI concerning multiple structures and teachers relates to educators' ability to adjust instruction based on universal screening and progress monitoring data. As you may recall, RTI curriculum implementation focuses on instructional needs rather than learners' deficits when inadequate progress is evident. Therefore, the key assumption that instruction will be adjusted may present significant challenges to secondary staff, two or more teachers may need to adjust instruction in similar ways (e.g., using direct instruction in situations where the teacher prefers independent or cooperative learning). That is, the adjustments to instruction deemed necessary in one content area (e.g., science) may also be appropriate for another area (e.g., social studies), and both educators would have to make the adjustments if screening or progress monitoring indicates the need for change. Other assumptions may also apply; however, the two discussed here—-concerning students' transitions and teachers' form of instruction—-if thoughtfully addressed, serve as a solid basis for success in secondary school and have implications for RTI curriculum implementation.

▶ **Implications for Secondary RTI Curriculum Implementation:** Instruction at the secondary level within multi-tiered RTI models includes both regular screening and more frequent progress monitoring for students receiving Tier 2 supplemental supports. Decision making concerning instruction and necessary adjustments is grounded in these screening and monitoring results. Therefore, implications for RTI curriculum implementation at the secondary level suggest that:

1. Teachers structure their teaching and learning to implement these assessments
2. A problem-solving team is in place to make multi-tiered instructional decisions
3. Collaboration and communication among different content area teachers exist to ensure consistency in making needed instructional adjustments
4. Time is provided to facilitate the collaboration and communication needed to best assist all learners

Focus Area 4: Time Management and Organizational Abilities

The development and use of several important study skills and learning strategies help students make a smooth transition from elementary to secondary education to address the new demands in acquiring secondary-level content and skills. Two interrelated skills, which were discussed in Chapter 8, are highlighted here because of their significance in making adjustments to the secondary level: time management and organizational abilities. As highlighted above, new and different expectations confront secondary learners—expectations that were either more directly facilitated or less emphasized at the elementary level. The ability to manage one's time efficiently and organize one's tasks contributes to success in the secondary grades. The screening of students as they enter secondary education should include determining their skills in these areas. This is important because both skills contribute to success in all content areas, cutting across most demands as secondary students adjust to multiple teachers, varying assignment expectations, different amounts of daily assignments in each content area, or different behavioral expectations in multiple classrooms.

RTI UNDERLYING ASSUMPTIONS ■ A key assumption made as RTI is implemented at the secondary level is that learners have the abilities to meet increased time and organization demands. The assumption that they acquired these abilities in elementary school may be incorrect for many students. Additionally, although time and organizational management will most likely occur in part at the elementary level, many students may find it difficult to transfer these skills to secondary settings.

▸ **Implications for Secondary RTI Curriculum Implementation:** The need for effective and efficient time and organizational skills has implications in RTI models. First, the screening for Tier 1 academic and behavior progress should include attention to time and organizational skills. Second, although learners may possess acceptable skills, transferring them to the secondary level may be difficult for some learners; in the RTI secondary framework, this should be facilitated for all learners. Third, as students demonstrate problems with time and/or organizational management, efforts to increase these skills within multi-tiered instruction should be as consistent as possible across multiple content areas and teachers, as well as within consistent classroom structures that best work for the learner.

Focus Area 5: Assessing Achievement: Universal Screening and Progress Monitoring

As with curriculum, most assessments of progress toward academic and behavioral benchmarks within multi-tiered RTI models have focused on elementary students. This includes both assessment measures and procedures. As a result, we know less about RTI assessment in middle and high school (Duffy, 2007) than in elementary school. Over the past few decades, a variety of assessments have been initiated for secondary learners (e.g., grades, year-end testing, promotion requirements based on state standards); Dieker (2007) stated that no matter what methods of assessment are used, challenges continue to surface. Although assessment in RTI models at the secondary level is less clearly defined than at the elementary level, many educators favor applying the strengths of RTI seen in the lower grades, to the extent possible, to the secondary level.

RTI UNDERLYING ASSUMPTIONS ■ Several assumptions underlie the effective implementation of RTI assessment at the secondary level: (1) core RTI assessment principles are embedded in secondary curriculum; (2) screening of learners' reading, writing, and social skills occurs as soon as possible when they enter the secondary grades; and (3) classroom teachers support the premise that monitoring of progress toward benchmarks requires a greater curriculum-based focus. Ensuring that these assumptions are embedded in the RTI model provides a solid foundation for assessment that is sufficiently curriculum-based to make informed instructional decisions.

▶ **Implications for Secondary RTI Curriculum Implementation:**　Several challenges confront secondary educators in implementing schoolwide multi-tiered RTI assessments. Staff must become familiar with the principles of assessment in RTI models, and the resources, time, and support must be provided for educators to perform screening and monitoring assessment. Duffy (2007) wrote that secondary "student progress must be carefully monitored over time, using measures that are tied to local curricular and state content and achievement standards" (p. 8). According to Burns and Gibbons (2008), CBM is an effective means of monitoring the progress of secondary learners receiving Tier 2 or 3 instruction. In addition, a comprehensive secondary RTI model should include screening of progress toward both academic and behavioral benchmarks. A recent national study on the implementation of RTI found a significant increase in its implementation at the secondary level between 2008 and 2009 (SpectrumK12, 2009). As more secondary schools begin to use and apply RTI principles, additional research will further illuminate their success, including the processes and measures used to screen and monitor the progress of learners educated within a multi-tiered curriculum.

As secondary educators work in teams to develop and implement RTI in their schools, addressing these focus areas will help learners make an easier transition from the elementary level to a secondary RTI model. Keeping in mind the differences between elementary and secondary RTI also allows educators to design supports for students who experience difficulties in adjusting to secondary educational demands.

Table 9.1 provides suggestions for meeting the needs associated with these and related issues discussed in this chapter, as applied within an RTI framework. The table considers academic and behavior needs in association with the five curricular components.

As Table 9.1 shows, each of the five curricular components has implications for the implementation of multi-tiered RTI. Secondary educators may use these suggestions as a guide for structuring RTI in their schools. By doing so, they will assist secondary learners to proactively meet the challenges often experienced as they transition from elementary to secondary education. Form 9.2 (*Guide for Recording the Current Emphasis in Key Secondary Curricular Issues*) is

Curriculum Element	Multi-Tiered Secondary Curricular Need Areas	RTI Curricular Implementation Implications
Content/Skills (Research-Based Curriculum)	Literacy instruction; study skills/learning strategies; mathematics computation and reasoning; science concepts; reading levels that affect progress in multiple content areas; critical thinking skills; skills to efficiently meet increased out-of-class reading demands	Appropriate screening upon entry into secondary grades in (1) general skills needed to be successful regardless of content and (2) preparation for success in each core content area; Tiers 1 and 2 instruction addresses literacy needs across content areas through consistent differentiated learning appropriate for learners' ability levels; RTI curriculum facilitates ongoing development and use of study skills and learning strategies as well as critical thinking; corroboration of the fidelity of implementation of a research-based curriculum in each tier of instruction
Evidence-Based Interventions	Supports to acquire content and skills through the use of varying styles and interventions by different content area teachers; differentiated instruction consistent with varying preferences about learning; interventions that facilitate active engagement in teaching and learning	Appropriate adjustments across content areas reflecting learners' strengths; tiered instruction includes the use of a variety of evidence-based interventions to meet learners' needs in each content area; selection and use of interventions based on compatibility between teachers' instructional style and students' preferences about learning (e.g., cooperative versus independent learning, direct instruction versus constructivism, active versus passive involvement, facilitating learning versus "imparting" knowledge); corroboration of the fidelity of implementation of evidence-based interventions
Instructional Arrangements	Supports necessary to learn effectively through various class groupings found in different content area instructional settings (i.e., large or small groups, paired learning, cooperative groups, independent activities); supports needed to assist with transitions to different classroom instructional arrangements on an hourly or block schedule daily basis	Tiered instruction should reflect differentiated instructional arrangements to meet the variety of skills, preferences, and experiential backgrounds of many secondary learners; different content class settings contain similar general types of instructional arrangements for learners to ensure needed consistency and structure across instructional environments; corroboration of the fidelity of implementation of evidence-based instructional arrangements
Class/Instructional Management Procedures	Supports necessary to adjust to multiple classroom academic, social, and behavioral expectations associated with different content area teachers; classroom management procedures that facilitate self-management, self-monitoring, and self-adjustment of classroom behaviors based on teachers' expectations, instructional arrangements, content area demands, and social parameters; further development of time and organization skills	RTI curricular parameters should reflect the creativity, flexibility, structure, and consistency needed to meet simultaneously the varying academic, social, behavioral, and study strategy needs of all learners; screening upon entry into secondary school should identify the learners' ability to deal with different types of classroom management procedures; all content area teaching and learning environments should reflect general parameters that build on the learners' time and organizational management abilities to best meet struggling students' needs through tiered instruction; corroboration of the fidelity of implementation of evidence-based classroom and instructional management practices

(Continued)

Curriculum Element	Multi-Tiered Secondary Curricular Need Areas	RTI Curricular Implementation Implications
Progress Evaluation	Supports necessary to demonstrate acquisition and use of knowledge and skills in each core content area; ability to adjust to different progress-monitoring practices and devices based on content area demands	RTI universal screening that identifies the needs of students who are at risk or struggling as soon as they enter the secondary level; regular and standard process for monitoring effects of Tier 2 supplemental supports on achievement of core content benchmarks; corroboration of fidelity of implementation of universal screening and progress monitoring assessment practices

a guide to document important aspects to address when meeting multi-tiered needs at the secondary level of education. The form, developed from the sources cited above, reflects some of the key points discussed in this chapter.

This chapter concludes with its *RTI Curriculum in Practice* segment, in which a secondary educator describes Tier 2 instructional supports provided in the content area of mathematics.

RTI CURRICULUM IN PRACTICE

Meeting the Tier 2 Mathematics Supplemental Support Needs of Secondary-Level Students

As a secondary mathematics teacher, I have spent a lot of time working with students who struggle with content in my classroom. My goal has always been to keep all students in grade/age-level classrooms and to incorporate appropriate interventions that would allow them to find success along with their peers. I feel that this is critical for high school students' social development; that is, they are kept in grade/age-level appropriate classes as often as possible. Multi-tiered implementation of curriculum assists to achieve this goal. From my experience, the key to success of implementing an intervention program has been getting the entire staff and administrators on board at my school and school district. After much thought, as a school staff we decided to start a class titled Applied Math, which was designed to supplement the Tier 1 core mathematics instruction. The course provided students with needed Tier 2 supplemental support for them to find success in their core mathematics class. The students were identified as struggling learners who experienced problems with basic computational fluency. To meet both Tier 1 and Tier 2 instruction needs, these students were enrolled in dual math classes: Tier 2, Applied Math and a Tier 1 core math class such as Algebra 1, Geometry, or Algebra 2. I am fortunate because I work in a small high school with a staff in support of this arrangement. As a result, scheduling is rather flexible, which allows students to take an additional math class without interfering with their Tier 1 core instruction.

My Applied Math class is a small class of approximately eight students, which allows me to give individual instruction based on each student's needs. These students are of mixed ability, meaning that some students are performing at a higher level than others, but they all have shown a need for supplemental mathematics support. I meet with this group of students two times a week for 140 minutes, using an intervention curriculum created by Voyager Expanded Learning called V-math. As I stated, this occurs in addition to the core mathematics instruction. It is a program that contains a variety of assessments used to monitor progress and guide instruction. I have structured my class so that I give mini-lessons to individuals or small groups

(Continued)

of students on different topics based on their individual needs. Throughout the class sessions, students rotate between teacher-directed instruction and individual practice. V-math also contains an Internet-based game, V-math live, for students to practice and monitor their computational fluency during 1-minute time intervals while also competing with other students from around the world. Since initiating this Tier 2 instruction through the Applied Math course, the students' level of engagement, accuracy, and speed have drastically increased.

Overall, I feel that using this model by providing students Tier 2 supplemental supports along with Tier 1 core math curriculum instruction has worked well with our struggling students. The students seem to be benefiting from supplemental small-group instruction, using explicit instruction to meet individual needs. The long-term goal of this Tier 2 Applied Math supports instruction is to assist struggling learners to improve their computational fluency and mathematical ability in order to achieve greater success in their current and future mathematics classes.

—**Cassie H. (Secondary Mathematics Teacher)**

RTI APPLICATIONS OF KEY CHAPTER CONCEPTS

Research and discussions concerning RTI development and implementation at the secondary level have only recently been emphasized. The fundamentals of multi-tiered RTI models prevail in all grade levels where RTI is implemented. However, secondary RTI has unique characteristics, including multiple teachers and classrooms, increased reading expectations, and varying instructional and classroom management procedures, as well as the need for greater time and organizational management abilities. Secondary learners must deal with greater academic, behavioral, and social demands, which provides unique challenges to secondary educators in their development and implementation of RTI. Accommodating these needs is critical to the success of the secondary RTI curriculum model.

The application of these curricular topics within multi-tiered RTI provides the foundation for meeting the needs of all learners. To facilitate this process, educators should do the following:

- Conduct a school RTI readiness assessment (Form 9.1) and prioritize those areas requiring immediate attention to help all learners meet curricular benchmarks.

- Review the work of your school's problem-solving team to determine the procedures followed to interpret screening, monitoring, and diagnostic data within an RTI model.

- Lead or participate in your school's RTI team to initiate the process of developing and implementing RTI at the secondary level.

- Evaluate the Tier 1 curriculum to ensure that it is research-based and implemented with fidelity for all students.

- Develop and implement Tier 2 supplemental instruction for struggling learners in mathematics and literacy, including procedures for curriculum-base measurement of progress.

School: _____   Date: _____

Instructions: Check each item that currently exists in the secondary school. Provide relevant comments as appropriate.

Foundational Elements

___ All students are screened upon entry to secondary education (and periodically throughout the school year) to identify potentially struggling or at-risk learners in the areas of academics or social-emotional development.

Comments:

___ Learners receive instruction that increases in intensity and duration based on progress (i.e., the three-tier model).

Comments:

___ Each content-area classroom uses a research-based curriculum and evidence-based interventions.

Comments:

___ Learners' progress is monitored on a regular, continuous basis to determine their progress toward curricular benchmarks.

Comments:

___ All students complete assessments that directly reflect what has been taught within the curriculum.

Comments:

___ All learners are provided instruction through implementation of a research-based curriculum, evidence-based interventions, and associated assessments with fidelity.

Comments:

___ If necessary, learners are provided a comprehensive evaluation for a suspected disability within the overall RTI framework.

Comments:

Summary of the Foundation for Secondary RTI:

Key Content-Area Elements

___ Content-area learning emphasizes the use of higher order thinking abilities.

Comments:

___ Students are provided supports in adjusting to attending multiple classes on a daily basis.
Comments:

___ Interaction among secondary teachers occurs as necessary.
Comments:

___ Coteaching at the secondary level successfully addresses unique scheduling and planning issues to achieve optimum results.
Comments:

___ Consistent use of evidence-based interventions exists across different content areas.
Comments:

Summary of Key Content-Area Elements:

Overview of Current Capacity for Schoolwide RTI

___ Current screening procedures and devices exist in core content areas for all secondary learners.
Comments:

___ The interventions currently used in each content area are evidence-based and implemented in a consistent manner.
Comments:

___ It has been determined that all secondary curricula are research-based.
Comments:

___ Problem-solving team procedures and processes are understood by all educators and adhered to by the school's RTI team.
Comments:

___ Secondary classrooms are differentiated to meet varying classroom and instructional management needs.
Comments:

Summary of Current Capacity:

Source: Used by permission of John J. Hoover.

School: _____   Teacher: _____   Date: _____

Instructions: Rate each item as it reflects your school's current level of emphasis in the implementation of the following key secondary-level curricular elements using the following scale:

1 = No Emphasis   3 = Some Emphasis
2 = Little Emphasis   4 = High Emphasis

The extent to which each of the following elements is emphasized on a schoolwide curricular basis:

Literacy Issues (Reading/Writing)

___ Remediation to develop requisite knowledge and skills

___ Instruction in students' most proficient language

___ Accommodations for cultural/linguistic diversity

___ Linking reading experiences with students' experiential background

___ Increasing content-area vocabulary development

___ Silent reading abilities

___ Written language skills in content area(s)

___ Other (specify):

Summary of Literacy Development Across Content Areas:

Social Issues (Positive Social Supports)

___ Adjusting to peer influences at the secondary level

___ Transition to increased need for independence

___ Social acceptance skills

___ Social perception abilities

___ Modeling appropriate social behavior

___ Demonstrating empathy toward others

___ Maintaining positive peer relationships

___ Peer acceptance

___ Other (specify):

Summary of Social Development Across Content Areas:

Study Strategy Issues (Assuming Responsibility for Learning)

___ Time management

___ Organizational abilities

___ Ability to prioritize assignments

___ Test-studying and test-taking skills

___ Writing reports

___ Library use

___ Self-monitoring of behavior

___ Working effectively in groups

___ Completing assignments in a timely manner

___ Other (specify):

Summary of Study Strategy Use Across Content Areas:

Structural Issues (Transitioning from Elementary to Secondary Education)

Adjustments necessary to successfully transition to:

___ Increased movement to and from classes

___ Increased number of core content-area teachers

___ Increased reading and writing expectations and demands in core content areas

___ Need for additional reading and writing activities completed outside of class instruction

___ Accepting variations in discipline and classroom expected behaviors

___ Different teaching styles across content-area instruction

___ More efficient management of learning time and time on tasks

___ Creating effective study patterns to meet multiple subject demands

___ Other (specify):

Summary of Structural Issues That Facilitate a Smooth Transition from Elementary to Secondary Education:

Action Plan: Based on the above (and other related information about the secondary learning environment that may have been gathered), briefly describe and prioritize the area(s) in greatest need of immediate attention to assist at-risk and struggling learners to best succeed with RTI at the secondary level:

Source: Used by permission of John J. Hoover.

References

Adelman, H. S., & Taylor, L. (1997). Toward a scale-up model for replicating new approaches to schooling. *Journal of Educational and Psychological Consultation, 8,* 197–230.

Allington, R. L. (2009). *What really matters in response to intervention: Research-based designs.* Boston: Pearson.

Alwin, D. F. (1995). Taking time seriously: Social change, social structure, and human lives. In P. Moen, G. H. Elder, Jr., and K. Luscher (Eds.), *Examining lives in context: Perspectives on the ecology of human development* (pp. 211–262). Washington, DC: American Psychological Association.

Appelbaum, M. (2009). *The one-stop guide to implementing RTI: Academic and behavioral interventions, K–12.* Thousand Oaks, CA: Corwin Press.

Arnberger, K., & Shoop, R. J. (2008). Responding to need. *Principal Leadership, 8*(5), 51–54.

Arreaga-Mayer, C. (1998). Increasing active student responding and improving academic performance through classwide peer tutoring. *Intervention in School and Clinic, 34,* 89–94.

Baca, L., & Cervantes, H. T. (2004). *The bilingual special education interface.* Columbus, OH: Merrill.

Barnett, D. W., Hawkins, R., Prasse, D., Graden, J., Nantais, M., & Pan, W. (2007). Decision-making validity in response to intervention. In S. R. Jimerson, M. K. Burns, & A. M. VanDerHeyden (Eds.), *Handbook of response to intervention: The science and practice of assessment and intervention* (pp. 106–116). New York: Springer.

Batsche, G. M., Curtis, M. J., Dorman, C., Castillo, J. M., & Porter, L. J. (2007). The Florida problem solving/response to intervention model: Implementing a statewide initiative. In S. R. Jimerson, M. K. Burns, & A. M. VanDerHeyden (Eds.), *Handbook of response to intervention: The science and practice of assessment and intervention* (pp. 378–395). New York: Springer.

Bender, W. N. (2008). *Differentiating instruction for students with learning disabilities: Best teaching practices for general and special educators.* Thousand Oaks, CA: Corwin Press.

Bender, W. N., & Shores, C. (2007). *Response to intervention: A practical guide for every teacher.* Thousand Oaks, CA: Corwin Press.

Bloom, B. S., Englehart, M. D., Furst, G. J., Hill, W. H., & Krathwohl, D. R. (1956). *Taxonomy of educational objectives: Handbook 1—The cognitive domain.* New York: McKay.

Bos, C., & Vaughn, S. (2006). *Strategies for teaching students with learning and behavior problems.* Boston: Allyn & Bacon.

Bradley, R., Danielson, L., & Doolittle, J. (2007). Responsiveness to intervention: 1997–2007. *Teaching Exceptional Children, 35*(5), 8–12.

Bronfenbrenner, U. (1958). Socialization and social class through time and space. In E. E. Maccoby, T. M. Newcomb, & E. L. Hartley (Eds.), *Readings in social psychology* (pp. 400–424). New York: Holt.

Bronfenbrenner, U. (1979). *The ecology of human development.* Cambridge, MA: Harvard University Press.

Bronfenbrenner, U. (1995). Developmental ecology through space and time: A future perspective. In P. Moen, G. Elder, & K. Leuscher (eds.) *Examining lives in context: Perspectives on the ecology of human development* (pp. 619–647). Washington, DC: American Psychological Association.

Bronfenbrenner, U. (Ed.). (2005). *Making human beings human: Ecological perspectives on human development.* Thousand Oaks, CA: Sage Publications.

Brown-Chidsey, R., & Steege, M. W. (2005). *Response to intervention: Principles and strategies for effective practice.* New York: Guilford Press.

Bruner, J. (1996). *The culture of education.* Cambridge, MA: Harvard University Press.

Burns, M. K., & Gibbons, K. A. (2008). *Implementing response-to-intervention in elementary and secondary schools: Procedures to assure scientific-based practices.* New York: Taylor & Francis.

Burns, M. K., & VanDerHeyden, A. M. (2006). Using response to intervention to assess learning disabilities: Introduction to the special series. *Assessment for Effective Intervention, 32,* 3–5.

Callender, W. A. (2007). The Idaho results-based model: Implementing response to intervention statewide. In S. R. Jimerson, M. K. Burns, & A. M. VanDerHeyden (Eds.), *Handbook of response to intervention: The science and practice of assessment and intervention* (pp. 331–342). New York: Springer.

Canter, A., Klotz, M. B., & Cowan, K. (2008). Response to intervention: The future of secondary schools. *Principal Leadership, 9*(2), 12–15.

CEC Today. (2008, November). *RTI for emotional/behavior disorders shows promise.* Retrieved August 10, 2009, from http://www.cec.sped.org.

Center for Comprehensive School Reform and Improvement (CCSRI). (2008, June). *Response to intervention: Possibilities for service delivery at the secondary school level.* Retrieved February 22, 2009, from http://www.centerforcsri.org/index.php?option=com_content&task=view&id=559&Itemid=5.

Chapman, C., & King, R. (2008). *Differentiated instructional management: Work smarter, not harder.* Thousand Oaks, CA: Corwin Press.

Cohen, L. G., & Spenciner, L. J. (2010). *Assessment of children and youth with special needs.* Boston: Pearson.

Colorado Department of Education (CDE). (2008). *Response to intervention (RtI): A practitioner's guide to implementation.* Denver: Author.

Colvin, G., Kame'enui, E. J., & Sugai, G. (1993). Reconceptualizing behavior management and school-wide discipline in general education. *Education and Treatment of Children, 16*, 361–381.

Compton, D. L., Fuchs, D., Fuchs, L. S., & Bryant, J. D. (2006). Selecting at-risk readers in first grade for early intervention: A two-year longitudinal study of decision rules and procedures. *Journal of Educational Psychology, 98*, 394–409.

Crone, D. A., & Horner, R. H. (2003). *Building positive behavior support systems in schools: Functional behavioral assessment.* New York: Guilford Press.

Cross, T., Bazron, B., Dennis, K., & Isaacs, M. (1989). *Towards a culturally competent system of care.* Washington, DC: National Technical Assistance Center, Georgetown University Child Development Center.

Czarnecki, E., Rosko, D., & Pine, E. (1998). How to call up note-taking skills. *Teaching Exceptional Children, 30*, 14–19.

Day, V. P., & Elksnin, L. K. (1994). Promoting strategic learning. *Intervention in School and Clinic, 29*(5), 262–270.

de la Paz, S. (1997). Strategy instruction in planning: Teaching students with learning and writing disabilities to compose persuasive and expository essays. *Learning Disability Quarterly, 20*, 227–248.

de Valenzuela, J. S., & Baca, L. M. (2004). Procedures and techniques for assessing the bilingual exceptional child. In L. M. Baca & H. T. Cervantes, *The bilingual special education interface* (pp. 184–203). Columbus, OH: Merrill

Deno, S. L. (1985). Curriculum-based measurement: The emerging alternative. *Exceptional Children, 52*, 219–232.

Deno, S. L. (2005). Problem-solving assessment. In R. Brown-Chidsey (Ed.), *Assessment for intervention: A problem-solving approach* (pp. 10–40). New York: Guilford Press.

Deshler, D. (2006). An interview with Don Deshler: Perspectives on teaching students with learning disabilities (interview conducted by Steve Chamberlain). *Intervention in School and Clinic, 41*(5), 302–306.

Developmental Reading Assessment 2 (DRA). (2007). Boston: Pearson Learning Group.

Dieker, L. (2007). *Demystifying secondary inclusion: Powerful school-wide and classroom strategies.* Port Chester, NY: Dude.

Donovan, M. S., & Cross, C. (Eds.). (2002). *Minority students in special and gifted education.* Washington, DC: National Academy Press.

Duffy, D. (2007). *Meeting the needs of significantly struggling learners in high school: A look at approaches to tiered intervention.* Washington, DC: American Institutes for Research–National High School Center.

Echevarria, J., & Graves, A. (2003). *Sheltered content instruction: Teaching English language learners with diverse abilities.* Needham Heights, MA: Allyn & Bacon.

Eisner, E. W. (2002). *The educational imagination: On design and evaluation of school programs* (3rd ed.). Columbus, OH: Merrill/Prentice Hall.

Ervin, R. A., Schaughency, E., Goodman, S. D., McGlinchey, M. T., & Mathews, A. (2007). Moving from a model demonstration project to a statewide initiative in Michigan: Lessons learned from merging research-practice agendas to address reading and behavior. In S. R. Jimerson, M. K. Burns, & A. M. VanDerHeyden (Eds.), *Handbook of response to intervention: The science and practice of assessment and intervention* (pp. 354–377). New York: Springer.

Fixsen, D., Naoom, S., Blasé, K., & Wallace, F. (2007, Winter/Spring). Implementation: The missing link between research and practice. *The APSAC Advisor*, pp. 4–10.

Friend, M., & Cook, L. (2003). *Interactions: Collaboration skills for school professionals* (4th ed). Boston: Allyn & Bacon.

Fuchs, D., & Deshler, D. D. (2007). What we need to know about responsiveness to intervention (and shouldn't be afraid to ask). *Learning Disabilities Research & Practice, 22*(2), 129–136.

Fuchs, D., & Fuchs, L. S. (1998). Treatment validity: A unifying concept for reconceptualizing the identification of learning disabilities. *Learning Disabilities Research & Practice, 13*, 204–219.

Fuchs, D., & Fuchs, L. S. (2006). Introduction to response to intervention: What, why, and how valid is it? *Reading Research Quarterly, 41*(1), 95–99.

Fuchs, D., & Fuchs, L. S. (2007). The role of assessment in the three-tier approach to reading instruction. In D. Haager, J. Klingner, & S. Vaughn (Eds.), *Evidence-based reading practices for response to intervention* (pp. 29–42). Baltimore: Paul H. Brookes.

Fuchs, D., Stecker, P. M., & Fuchs, L. S. (2008). Tier 3: Why special education must be the most intensive tier in a standards-driven, no child left behind world. In D. Fuchs, L. S. Fuchs, & S. Vaughn (Eds.), *Response to intervention: A framework for reading educators* (pp. 71–104). Newark, DE: International Reading Association.

Fuchs, L. S. (2003). Assessing intervention responsiveness: Conceptual and technical issues. *Learning Disabilities Research and Practice, 18*(3), 172–186.

Gardner, H. (2006). *Multiple intelligences: New horizons.* New York: Basic Books.

Gartin, B. C., Murdick, N. L., Imbeau, M., & Perner, D. E. (2002). *How to use differentiated instruction with students with developmental disabilities in the general education classroom.* Arlington, VA: Council for Exceptional Children.

Gay, G. (2000). *Culturally responsive teaching.* New York: Teachers College Press.

Gersten, R., Compton, D., Connor, C. M., Dimino, J., Santoro, L., Linan-Thompson, S., & Tilly, W. D., (2008). *Assisting students struggling with reading: Response to intervention and multi-tier intervention for reading in the primary grades—A practice guide.* Washington, DC: National Center for Education Evaluation and Regional Assistance, Institute of Education Sciences, U.S. Department of Education. Retrieved February 22, 2009, from http://ies.ed.gov/ncee/wwc/publications/practiceguides/.

Gersten, R. M., & Jimenez, R. T. (1994). A delicate balance: Enhancing literature instruction for students of English as a second language. *The Reading Teacher, 47*, 438–449.

Good, T. L., & Brophy, J. E. (1990). *Educational psychology: A realistic approach.* New York: Longman.

Greenwood, C. R., Arreaga-Mayer, C., Utley, C. A., Gavin, K. M., & Terry, B. J. (2001). Class Wide Peer Tutoring Learning Management system: Applications with elementary-level English language learners. *Remedial and Special Education, 22*, 34–47.

Gregory, G. H., & Chapman, C. (2002). *Differentiated instructional strategies: One size doesn't fit all*. Thousand Oaks, CA: Corwin Press.

Haager, D., & Klingner, J. K. (2005). *Differentiating instruction in inclusive classrooms: The special educator's guide*. Boston: Allyn & Bacon.

Hall, S. L. (2008). *A principal's guide: Implementing response to intervention*. Thousand Oaks, CA: Corwin Press.

Hall, S. L. (n.d.). *Create your implementation blueprint: Introduction*. RTI Action Network Web site. Retrieved January 19, 2009, from http://www.rtinetwork.org/GetStarted/Develop/ar/Create-Your-Implementation-Blueprint.

Hallahan, D. P., & Kauffman, J. M. (2003). *Exceptional learners: Introduction to special education*. Boston: Allyn & Bacon.

Hanley, J. (1999). Beyond the tip of the iceberg: Five stages toward cultural competence. *Today's Youth: The Community Circle of Caring Journal, 3*(2), 9–12.

Harris, A. J., & Sipay, E. R. (1990). *How to increase reading ability*. New York: Longman.

Heller, K. A., Holtzman, W., & Messick, S. (Eds.). (1982). *Placing children in special education: A strategy for equity* (pp. 322–381). Washington, DC: National Academy Press.

Hill, J. D., & Flynn, K. M. (2006). *Classroom instruction that works with English language learners*. Alexandria, VA: Association for Supervision and Curriculum Development.

Hoover, J. J. (1987). Preparing special educators for mainstreaming: An emphasis on curriculum. *Teacher Education and Special Education, 10*, 58–64.

Hoover, J. J. (2001). *Class management* [CD-ROM]. Boulder: University of Colorado, BUENO Center for Multicultural Education.

Hoover, J. J. (2008). *Changing focus: Reducing misidentification of culturally and linguistically diverse learners for special education* (Keynote Presentation and Conference Presenter). NYC Public Schools Special Education Conferences (March 27–28, June 12–13).

Hoover, J. J. (2009a). *RTI assessment essentials for struggling learners*. Thousand Oaks, CA: Corwin Press.

Hoover, J. J. (2009b). *Differentiating learning differences from disabilities: Meeting diverse needs through multi-tiered response to intervention*. Boston: Pearson, Allyn & Bacon.

Hoover, J. J., Baca, L. M., Love, E., & Saenz, L. (2008). *National implementation of response to intervention (RTI): Research summary*. University of Colorado, Boulder, BUENO Center for Multicultural Education. Retrieved February 15, 2009, from the National Association of State Directors of Special Education (NASDSE) Web site: http://www.nasdse.org.

Hoover, J. J., & Collier, C. (2003). *Learning styles* [CD-ROM]. Boulder: University of Colorado, BUENO Center for Multicultural Education.

Hoover, J. J., & Klingner, J. K. (in press). Promoting cultural validity in the assessment of bilingual special education students. In M. R. Basterra, E. Trumbull, & G. Solano-Flores (Eds.), *Cultural validity in assessment: A guide for educators*. Taylor & Francis/Routledge.

Hoover, J. J., Klingner, J., Baca, L. M., & Patton, J. M. (2008). *Methods for teaching culturally and linguistically diverse exceptional learners*. Columbus, OH: Pearson.

Hoover, J. J., & Love, E. (in review). School-based RTI: Implications for practitioners. Article in review. *Teaching Exceptional Children*.

Hoover, J. J., & Patton, J. R. (2005). *Curriculum adaptations for students with learning and behavior problems* (3rd ed.). Austin, TX: PRO-ED.

Hoover, J. J., & Patton, J. R. (2007). *Teaching study skills to students with learning problems: A teacher's guide to meeting diverse needs* (2nd ed.). Austin, TX: PRO-ED.

Hoover, J. J., & Patton, J. R. (2008). Role of special educators in multi-tiered instructional programming. *Intervention in School and Clinic, 43*(4), 195–202.

Hosp, M. K., Hosp, J. L., & Howell, K. W. (2007). *The ABCs of CBM: A practical guide to curriculum-based measurement*. New York: Guilford Press.

Howell, R., Patton, S., & Deiotte, M. (2008). *Understanding response to intervention: A practical guide to systemic implementation*. Bloomington, IN: Solution Tree.

Hughes, C., & Deshler, D. (2007). *RTI in middle and high school: How will the game play out?* Presented at the 2007 CEC Convention. Retrieved January 25, 2009, from http://www.kucrl.org/cec2007.

Hummel, J. H., Venn, M. L., & Gunter, P. L. (2004). Teacher-made scripted lessons. In D. J. Moran & R. W. Malott (Eds.), *Evidence-based educational methods* (pp. 95–108). Amsterdam: Elsevier Academic Press.

IDEA. (2004). *Individuals with Disabilities Education Act Amendments of 2004*. Washington, DC: U.S. Government Printing Office.

Invernizzi, M., Swank, L., Juel, C., & Meier, J. (2003). *Phonological awareness literacy screening–kindergarten*. Charlottesville, VA: University Printing.

IRIS Center for Training Enhancements. (n.d.). *RTI: Assessment*. Retrieved December, 2008, from http://iris.peabody.vanderbilt.edu/gpm/chalcycle.htm.

Jimerson, S. R., Burns, M. K., & VanDerHeyden, A. M. (Eds.). (2007). *Response to intervention: The science and practice of assessment and intervention*. New York: Springer.

Joseph, P. B., Bravmann, S. L., Windschitl, M. A., Mikel, E. R., & Green, N. S. (2000). *Culture of curriculum*. Mahway, NJ: Erlbaum.

Kaminsky, R., & Good, R. (1996). Toward a technology for assessing basic early literacy skills. *School Psychology Review, 25*, 215–227.

Kansas University Center for Research on Learning (KU-CRL). (n.d.). *Strategic instructional model: Learning strategies*. Retrieved February 18, 2009, from http://www.kucrl.org/sim/strategies.shtml.

Kavale, K. A., & Flanagan, D. P. (2007). Ability–achievement discrepancy, response to disability identification: Toward a contemporary operational definition. In S. R. Jimerson, M. K. Burns, & A. M. VanDerHeyden (Eds.), *Handbook of response to intervention: The science and practice of assessment and intervention* (pp. 130–147). New York: Springer.

Kennellly, L., & Monrad. M. (2007). *Approaches to dropout preventions: Heeding early warning signs with appropriate interventions.* Washington, DC: National High School Center. Retrieved February 10, 2009, from http//:www.betterhighschools.org.

Kiewra, K. A., & DuBois, N. E. (1998). *Learning to learn.* Boston: Allyn & Bacon.

Killu, K. (2008). Developing effective behavior intervention plans: Suggestions for school personnel. *Intervention in School and Clinic, 43*(3), 140–149.

Klingner, J. K., & Edwards, P. E. (2006, January–March). Cultural considerations with response to intervention models. *Reading Research Quarterly,* pp. 108–115.

Klingner, J. K., Hoover, J. J., & Baca, L. (Eds.). (2008). *Why do English language learners struggle with reading?: Distinguishing language acquisition from learning disabilities* (pp. 37–56). Thousand Oaks, CA: Corwin Press.

Klingner, J. K., Mendez Barletta, L. M., & Hoover, J. J. (2008). Response to intervention models and English language learners. In J. K. Klingner, J. J. Hoover, & L. M. Baca (Eds.), *Why do English language learners struggle with reading?: Distinguishing language acquisition from learning disabilities* (pp. 37–56). Thousand Oaks, CA: Corwin Press.

Klingner, J. K., Vaughn, S., Dimino, J., Schumm, J. S., & Bryant, D. P. (2001). *From clunk to click: Collaborative strategic reading.* Longmont, CO: Sopris West.

Knotek, S. E. (2007). Consultation within response to intervention models. In S. R. Jimerson, M. K. Burns, & A. M. VanDerHeyden (Eds.), *Handbook of response to intervention: The science and practice of assessment and intervention* (pp. 53–64). New York: Springer.

Kovaleski, J. F. (2003, December). *The three tier model of identifying learning disabilities: Critical program features and system issues.* Paper presented at the National Research Center on Learning Disabilities Responsiveness-to-Intervention Symposium, Kansas City, MO.

Kovaleski, J. F., Roble, M., & Agne, M. (n.d.). *The RTI data analysis teaming process.* Retrieved August 5, 2009, from http://www.rtinetwork.org.

Lenz, B. K. (2006). Creating school-wide conditions for high quality learning strategy classroom instruction. *Intervention in School and Clinic, 41*(5), 261–266.

Lyon, G. R., Fletcher, J. M., Shaywitz, B. A., Torgensen, J. K., Wood, F. B., Schulte, A., & Olson, R. (2001). Rethinking learning disabilities. In C. E. Finn, A. J. Rotherham, & C. R. Hokanson (Eds.), *Rethinking special education for a new century* (pp. 259–287). Washington, DC: Thomas B. Fordham Foundations.

Malecki, C. K., & Demaray, M. K. (2007). Social behavior assessment and response to intervention. In S. R. Jimerson, M. K. Burns, & A. M. VanDerHeyden (Eds.), *Handbook of response to intervention: The science and practice of assessment and intervention* (pp. 161–171). New York: Springer.

Margolin, J., & Buchler, B. (2004). *Critical issue: Using scientifically based research to guide educational decisions.* North Central Regional Educational Laboratory (NCREL). Retrieved July 20, 2009, from http://www.ncrel.org/sdrs/areas/issues/envrnmnt/go/go900.htm.

Marks, J. W., Laeys, J. V., Bender, W. N., & Scott, K. S. (1996). Teachers creating learning strategies: Guidelines for classroom creation. *Teaching Exceptional Children, 28*(4), 34–38.

Marston, D., Lau, M., & Muyskens, P. (2007). Implementation of the problem-solving model in the Minneapolis public schools. In S. R. Jimerson, M. K. Burns, & A. M. VanDerHeyden (Eds.), *Handbook of response to intervention: The science and practice of assessment and intervention* (pp. 279–287). New York: Springer.

Martella, R. C., Nelson, J. R., & Marchand-Martella, N. E. (2003). *Managing disruptive behaviors in the schools: A schoolwide, classroom, and individualized social learning approach.* Boston: Allyn & Bacon.

Martin, J. (2007). *Implementing response to intervention at the high school level: Every student, every day!* Retrieved January 15, 2009, from http://www.nwrel.org.

Mason, J. L. (1993). *Cultural competence self assessment questionnaire.* Portland, OR: Portland State University, Multicultural Initiative Project.

Mastropieri, M. A., & Scruggs, T. E. (1998). Enhancing school success with mnemonic strategies. *Intervention in School and Clinic, 33*(4), 201–208.

Mastropieri, M. A., & Scruggs, T. E. (2005). Feasibility and consequences of response to intervention: Examination of the issues and scientific evidence as a model for the identification of individuals with learning disabilities. *Journal of Learning Disabilities, 38,* 525–532.

Mathes, P. G., Denton, C. A., Fletcher, J. M., Anthony, J. L., Francis, D. J., & Schatschneider, C. (2005). The effects of theoretically different instruction and student characteristics on the skills of struggling readers. *Reading Research Quarterly, 40*(2), 148–182.

McCook, J. E. (2006). *The RTI guidebook: Developing and implementing a model in your schools.* Horsham, PA: LRP Publications.

McKernan, J. (2008). *Curriculum and imagination: Process theory, pedagogy and action research.* New York: Taylor & Francis.

McLaughlin, B. (1992). *Myths and misconceptions about second language learning: What every teacher needs to unlearn.* Santa Cruz, CA: National Center for Research on Cultural Diversity and Second Language.

Meese, R. L. (2001). *Teaching learners with mild disabilities: Integrating research and practice* (2nd ed.). Belmont, CA: Wadsworth/Thompson Learning.

Mellard, D. F., & Johnson, E. (2008). *RTI: A practitioner's guide to implementing response to intervention.* Thousand Oaks, CA: Corwin Press.

Mercer, C. D., & Pullen, P. C. (2009). *Students with learning disabilities.* Columbus, OH: Pearson Merrill.

Moen, P., Elder, G. H., Jr., & Luscher, K. (1995). *Examining lives in context: Perspectives on the ecology of human development.* Washington, DC: American Psychological Association.

Moore, A. L., Armentrout, J. A., & Neal, L. I. (2008). Methods for behavior, classroom, and schoolwide management. In J. J. Hoover, J. K. Klingner, L. M. Baca & J. M. Patton (Eds.), *Methods for teaching culturally and linguistically diverse exceptional learners* (pp. 142–178). Columbus, OH: Pearson Merrill.

Moran, D. J., & Malott, R. W. (2004). *Evidence-based educational methods*. Boston: Elsevier Academic Press.

National Association of State Directors of Special Education, Inc. (NASDSE). (2005). *Response to intervention: Policy considerations and implementation*. Alexandria, VA: Author.

National Center for Learning Disabilities. (2008, September 11). *RTI and universal screening*. New York: Author. Retrieved January 26, 2009, from http://ncldtalks.org/content/interview/detail/2255/.

National Reading Panel Report. (2000). *Teaching children to read: An evidence-based assessment of the scientific research literature on reading and its implications for reading instruction: Summary report*. Washington, DC: National Institute of Child Health and Development.

No Child Left Behind Act. (2001). The Elementary and Secondary Education Act of 2001, P.L. 107–110, 115, *Stat.1425*. Washington, DC: U.S. Government Printing Office.

Ogle, D. (1986). A teaching model that develops active reading of expository text. *The Reading Teacher, 39*, 564–570.

Oliver, R. M., & Reschly, D. J. (2007). *Effective classroom management: Teacher preparation and professional development*. Washington, DC: National Comprehensive Center for Teacher Quality.

O'Malley, J. M., & Pierce, L. V. (1996). *Authentic assessment for English language learners: Practical approaches for teachers*. Boston: Addison-Wesley.

O'Neill, R. E., Horner, R. H., Albin, R. W., Sprague, J. R., Storey, K., & Newton, J. S. (1997). *Functional assessment interview for problem behavior: A practical handbook* (2nd ed.). Pacific Grove, CA: Brooks/Cole.

Orosco, M. J. (2005). Accommodations in assessment and instruction to meet special needs. In J. J. Hoover (Ed.), *Current issues in special education: Meeting diverse needs in the twenty-first century* (pp. 87–94). Boulder, CO: BUENO Center for Multicultural Education.

Ovando, C. J., Collier, V. P., & Combs, M. C. (2003). *Bilingual and ESL classrooms: Teaching in multicultural contexts*. Boston: McGraw-Hill.

Palincsar, A. S., & Brown, A. L. (1984). The reciprocal teaching of comprehension—fostering and comprehension-monitoring activities. *Cognition and Instruction, 1*, 117–175.

Palincsar, A. S., & David, Y. M. (1991). Promoting literacy through classroom dialogue. In E. H. Hiebert (Ed.), *Literacy for a diverse society: Perspectives, practices and policies* (pp. 122–139). New York: Teachers College Press.

Patton, J., & Day-Vines, N. (2002). *A curriculum and pedagogy for cultural competence: Knowledge, skills, and dispositions needed to guide the training of special and general education teachers*. Unpublished manuscript.

Peregoy, S. F., & Boyle, O. F. (2001). *Reading, writing, and learning in ESL* (3rd ed.). White Plains, NY: Longman.

Pierangelo, R., & Giuliani, G. (2006). *The special educator's comprehensive guide to 301 diagnostic tests*. San Francisco: Jossey-Bass.

Polloway, E. A., Patton, J. R., & Serna, L. (2008). *Strategies for teaching learners with special needs*. Columbus, OH: Allyn & Bacon Prentice Hall.

Rutter, M., Champion, L., Quinton, D., Maughan, B., & Pickles, A. (1995). Understanding individual differences in environmental risk exposure. In P. Moen, G. H. Elder, Jr., & K. Luscher (Eds.), *Examining lives in context: Perspectives on the ecology of human development* (pp. 61–93). Washington, DC: American Psychological Association.

Sabatino, D. A. (1987). Preventive discipline as a practice in special education. *Teaching Exceptional Children, 19*(4), 8–11.

Sabornie, D. J., & deBettencourt, L. U. (2009). *Teaching students with mild and high-incidence disabilities at the secondary level*. Columbus, OH: Merrill Pearson.

Schubert, W. H. (1993). Curriculum reform. In G. Cawelti (Ed.), *ASCD 1993 yearbook: Challenges and achievements of American education* (pp. 80–115). Alexandria, VA: Association for Supervision and Curriculum Development.

Shapiro, E. S. (1996). *Academic skills problems: Direct assessment and intervention*. New York: Guilford Press.

Shapiro, E. S. (2008). Best practices in setting progress monitoring goals for academic skill improvement. In A. Thomas & J. Grimes (Eds.), *Best practices in school psychology V* (pp. 141–157). Bethesda, MD: National Association of School Psychologists.

Shinn, M. R. (1989). Identifying and defining academic problems: CBM screening and eligibility procedures. In M. R. Shinn (Ed.), *Curriculum based measurement: Assessing special children* (pp. 90–129). New York: Guilford Press.

Skrtic, T. M., Harris, K. R., & Shriner, J. G. (2005). *Special education policy and practice: Accountability, instruction and social change*. Denver: Love.

Slocum T. A. (2004). Direct instruction: The big ideas. In D. J. Moran & R. W. Malott (Eds.), *Evidence-based educational methods* (pp. 81–91). Boston: Elsevier Academic Press.

Smith, T. E. C., Polloway, E., Patton, J. R., & Dowdy, C. A. (2004). *Teaching students with special needs: Inclusive settings*. Boston: Pearson.

SpectrumK12. (2009). *Response to intervention (RTI) adoption survey 2009*. Towson, MD: Spectrum K12 School Solutions.

Sprague, J., Cook, C. R., Wright, D. B., & Sadler, C. (2008). *RTI and behavior: A guide to integrating behavioral and academic supports*. Horsham, PA: LRP Publications.

Sprenger, M. (2008). *Differentiation through learning styles and memory* (2nd ed.). Thousand Oaks, CA: Corwin Press.

State Education Resource Center (SERC). (n.d.). *Best practices in education*. Retrieved December 20, 2008, from http://www.ctserc.org.

Stecker, P. M., Fuchs, L. S., & Fuchs, D. (2005). Using curriculum-based measurement to improve student achievement: Review of research. *Psychology in the Schools, 42*(8), 795–819.

Strichart, S. S., & Mangrum, C. T., III. (2002). *Teaching learning strategies and study skills to students with learning disabilities, attention deficit disorders, or special needs* (3rd ed.). Boston: Allyn & Bacon.

Sugai, G., Lewis-Palmer, T., & Hagan, S. (1998). Using functional assessments to develop behavior support plans. *Preventing School Failure, 43*(1), 6–13.

Swanson, H. L. (1999). Instructional components that predict treatment outcomes for students with learning disabilities: Support for a combined strategy and direct instruction model. *Learning Disabilities Research and Practice, 14,* 129–140.

Tharp, R. G. (1997). *From at-risk to excellence: Research, theory and principles for practice.* Santa Cruz, CA: Center for Research on Education, Diversity and Excellence (CREDE).

Thompson, S. J. (2004). Choosing and using accommodations on assessments. *CEC Today, 10*(6), 12.

Thousand, J. S., Villa, R. A., & Nevin, A. I. (2007). *Differentiating instruction: Collaboratively planning and teaching for universally designed learning.* Thousand Oaks, CA: Corwin Press.

Tomlinson, C. A. (1999). *The differentiated classroom: Responding to the needs of all learners.* Alexandria, VA: Association for Supervision and Curriculum Development.

Tomlinson, C. A. (2001). *How to differentiate instruction in mixed-ability classrooms* (2nd ed.). Alexandria, VA: Association for Supervision and Curriculum Development.

Torgeson, J. K. (2000). Individual differences in response to early interventions in reading: The lingering problem of treatment resisters. *Learning Disabilities Research and Practice, 15*(1), 55–64.

U.S. Department of Education. (2002). *The facts about investigating in what works.* Washington, DC: Author. Retrieved January 15, 2009, from http://www.ed.gov/nclb/methods/whatworks/whatworks.html.

Vanderwood, M. L., & Nam, J. E. (2007). Response to intervention for English language learners: Current development and future directions. In S. R. Jimerson, M. K. Burns, & A. M. VanDerHeyden (Eds.), *Handbook of response to intervention: The science and practice of assessment and intervention* (pp. 408–417). New York: Springer.

Vaughn, S. (2003, December). *How many tiers are needed for response to intervention to achieve acceptable prevention outcomes?* Paper presented at the National Center on Learning Disabilities Responsiveness-to-Interventions Symposium, Kansas City, MO.

Vaughn, S., & Fuchs, D. (2003). Redefining learning disabilities as inadequate response to instruction: The promise and potential problems. *Learning Disabilities: Research & Practice, 18*(3), 137–146.

Vaughn, S., Wanzek, J., Woodruff, A. L., & Linan-Thompson, S. (2007). Prevention and early identification of students with reading disabilities. In D. Hagger, J. Klingner, & S. Vaughn (Eds.), *Evidence-based reading practices for response to intervention* (pp. 11–27). Baltimore: Paul H. Brookes.

Walker, H. M., & Severson, H. H. (1990). *Systematic screening for behavior disorders (SSBD).* Longmont, CO: Sopris West.

Waller, R. J. (2009). *The teacher's concise guide to functional behavioral assessment.* Thousand Oaks, CA: Corwin Press.

Webber, J., & Plotts, C. A. (2008). *Emotional and behavioral disorders: Theory and practice.* Boston: Allyn & Bacon.

Weiner, H. M. (2003). Effective inclusion: Professional development in the context of the classroom. *Teaching Exceptional Children, 35*(6), 12–18.

Wesson, C. L., & Keefe, M. (1989). Teaching library skills to students with mild and moderate handicaps. *Teaching Exceptional Children, 20,* 29–31.

Wiles, J., & Bondi, J. (2007). *Curriculum development: A guide to practice* (7th ed.) Upper Saddle River, NJ: Prentice Hall.

Windram, H., Scierka, B., & Silberglitt, B. (2007). Response to intervention at the secondary level: Two districts' models of implementation. *NASP Communique, 34*(5), 1–7. Retrieved January 15, 2009, from http://www.nasponline.org.

Wright, J. (2007). *RTI Toolkit: A practical guide for schools.* Port Chester, NY: Dude.

Yell, M. (2004, February). *Understanding the three-tier model.* Presented at the Colorado State Directors of Special Education meeting, Denver.